MUSIC BUSINESS HACKS

The Daily Habits of the Self-Made Musician

SIMON S. TAM

Cover Designed by: Daniel Soucy

Photography by: Igor Bass (front cover) and Tommy Byrd (rear cover)

Copyright © 2014 Simon Tam

All rights reserved.

ISBN: 0615980155
ISBN-13: 978-0615980157

CONTENTS

Appendix of Useful Stuff

Introduction

"I don't know what to do or how to make the most of my time."
"I don't have any extra time to worry about the music business."
"I'm just trying to keep up with what I'm already doing."

Sound familiar?

These are three of the most popular excuses that I hear from artists who express the desire to break into the music industry but for some reason or another, they feel like they can't. In fact, you might have used these same excuses yourself. I know I have. I hear these kinds of things from several hundred artists who email me every week asking for help. That's how the idea for this book came about: I want to help you overcome these excuses by getting you to commit at least 15 minutes a day to your music career.

I believe in the concept of consistency. I believe that when you mentally create space for something that you are passionate about every day, it's easier to make progress than if you simply wallow in excuses that prevent you from doing anything.

Now you might be asking, why 15 minutes? Why not 30 minutes? Or an hour?

Well, you have to start somewhere. And to be frank, some people feel like an hour a day is too much to ask. So I created a book full of exercises that you could spend at least 15 minutes a day on. More than anything else, it's to get you started and spur some ideas when you're not sure what to do with your time. If you can commit 15 minutes per day to building up your music career, that's 91 hours per year. If you can add an extra 5 minutes per day, you'll invest over 121 hours per year. You decide how much time you want to invest: just make sure it is at least 15 minutes and that you do this every day.

The daily mindfulness, consistency, and discipline is ultimately more important than the amount of time. In other words, it's more about quality than quantity. If you use 15 minutes effectively, you'll accomplish more than you would be able to with two hours of unfocused, random actions.

So set a daily appointment with yourself specifically for building your music career. Then, begin working...really working and you'll see payoffs almost immediately.

How to Use this Book

I've separated this book into sections by grouping together relevant topics. Some things will just be a lesson about how to do something with some instructions for you to follow. Others are intended to get you thinking about how to use your time effectively. You can conquer one category at a time or you can chronologically progress through each one (Day 1: first chapter of music business, Day 2: first chapter of marketing, Day 3: first chapter of musicianship, and so on). Or, you can randomly flip through. It's up to you.

When you see an activity, focus on those instructions by dedicating your "15 minutes" to that activity. It's that simple. Some chapters will have more than one activity. Choose one and then work on the complementary activity the next day.

I recommend keeping an online calendar that is synchronized to your smart devices. Set an alarm for yourself and allocate a certain amount of time every day to work on your music. Then, take notes about what you learned or achieved. If you want to know how much you've learned or accomplished, you'll need to measure your progress. So, write down your current statistics. In particular, you'll want to pay attention to:

- **Website traffic**
- **Number of followers on your social media channels**
- **Your "Klout" score**
- **Views on your videos**
- **How much media attention you're getting**
- **Turnout for shows**
- **How many "conversions" you are getting at shows: mailing list sign up, merch sales, new fans, etc.**
- **How many live performances you are making**

These are things that you should be measuring on a weekly or bi-weekly basis anyway. If you want to do music for a living, you'll need to run your career like a business...which means you'll need to hold yourself accountable for the results of the "business."

Alternatively, you can treat this book like a cookbook.

With a cookbook, when you are wanting to get some ideas on what to make for dinner, you can flip around until you find something interesting. It's easy to get an idea of how much time it takes and what the end product will look like. In this way, you can flip around and find something appropriate for your career.

Whatever you choose to do, you should do it with purpose and strategy. It's important to set goals for yourself as well as create measurement systems to track your progress.

When I first started writing this book, I did so by working on it for about 15 minutes per day (trying to keep up with the mindset that I preach – developing consistent, daily habits). I wrote about half of the book in 15 minute bursts. Then, as the book became a bigger priority, I started dedicating larger amounts of time to it. You might find that to be the case with your music career as well. No matter what you do though, you should set aside regular, consistent time. In just a few months, you'll see a difference from when you first started.

Section 1: Becoming Independent in the Music Business

It's the dream of nearly every musician: to quit the day job and make a sustainable living from art. It doesn't have to be much, as long as you can be left to do what you love most. Many artists see this as the measuring stick of success, probably more than hard goals such as selling a certain number of albums or achieving a certain number of followers online. In fact, the dream of being independent has, in most cases, replaced the dream of signing with a record label. However, unlike jumping from job to another, the transition into full time musicianship is often gradual and requires an investment into the music business itself.

Learning more about the music industry and how to run a business is never a waste of time. Even if you pick up a manager or a record label some day, you'll still want to be familiar with concepts that will make you successful. Like it or not, these days, learning the music industry has become just as important the art of music itself.

1. How to Book Better Shows

Whether you are trying to get on the bill with your favorite artist or you are booking in a new town for the first time, there are some things that you ought to know.

What You Should Do:

- **Find the Right Venue:** I can't stress this enough, even for seasoned veterans. Not only should you pick the right venue by scene (appropriate genre of music), but you should find a venue that is just a little bit smaller than what you need so that you can pack it out. A promoter would much rather you bring in 100 people to a place that fits 75 than if you bring 400 people to a place that fits 2,000. Realistically determine what you can do and find out what the venue capacity is before you even bother contacting them.

- **Book at Least 2-4 Months in Advance:** The further in advance you can book a show, the better chance that the date will be available. Many venues require a two month minimum advance but actually prefer at least 4-6 months notice.

- **Read Their Booking Requirements:** This might seem obvious but check out the venue's booking policies page. They'll usually tell you what they need and who to contact. Sometimes they want a phone call or a booking form filled out, usually they just want an email.

- **2 Paragraphs or Less:** In 2 paragraphs or less, explain how you will make them money: basically, how well you can draw and how you'll promote the show. The more you focus on that, the better. If they want to know what you sound like, they'll click on your link. No need to spend 4 sentences describing who you sound like – just use one line. Don't include your band history or bio unless it has something relevant or important.

- **Give Options:** Throw out a few different dates that you're interested in. You might not be able to get a weekend the first time around.

- **Ask For Help:** Contact other bands in the area or people you know in the scene who are actively performing and ask if they can get you on as an opening act for one of their shows. If you can prove that you can bring people out, that venue will be more likely to have you back.

What You Should Not Do:

- **Don't Send Attachments:** Most talent buyers do not want mp3 attachments filling up their inbox. Unless they specifically request them, send a link to someplace they can hear your music instead of the files. Same with photos or anything else (plus you don't want that a spam filter blocking your message).

- **Don't Overbook:** It's tempting to look at the empty dates on your band's calendar but whatever you do, do not saturate a market. Wait at least one month between shows in any 50 mile radius. The only exception is if you have a weekly residency. Promoters hate overbooking, it kills your draw, and it bores your fans.

- **Don't Expect The Promoter to Handle the "Promotion:"** It seems a like a misleading title, doesn't it? The fact is that venues are relying on artists more than ever to do the marketing and to bring the crowd in. They will expect you to contact the local press, to promote online, to create flyers, and to promote on social media. Yes, you should be doing all of those things.

- **Don't Pay to Play:** I do not believe in the "Pay to Play" model where you end up paying some kind of fee to get on a show. Those shows typically either mean the promoter is unsure themselves whether or not a decent crowd will be there and that it probably isn't a good fit.

- **Don't Oversell Yourself:** If you are not ready to play larger sized rooms, don't try to worm your way in. Remember, it's always better to oversell tickets than to oversell your band's ability to sell them.

- **Don't Assume The Show Is On:** Unless you receive a confirmation with load-in times or see the show listed on their website, don't assume that you've got the gig. Sometimes, promoters will just give you a tentative "hold" but still need to confirm the calendar. Make sure that this is absolutely clear first.

Activity 1: Refine Your "Pitch"

One of the most important parts of booking is how you "pitch" your band (more on this in Section 1, Chapter 18). Your booking email should be less than two paragraphs and every line should answer the question: why should *this* venue book you? Take some time to review the email that you send when booking shows. Look at some other examples/templates online. If you'd like to see some examples of actual booking emails I've written and used, check the Appendix. Afterwards, rewrite your booking email a few times. Check all of your links, shorten them using bit.ly if they're taking too much space. Send different versions of it out to friends and get some feedback.

Activity 2: Gather More Contacts

Do you have a database of your booking contacts? Or, do you search for venues to book every time you're about to embark on a tour?

It's important to keep an updated list of appropriate venues for your music. Some places, like Indie Venue Bible and Billboard Music will sell lists of contacts. Others, like Indie on the Move or byofl.org lists promoters and contacts in a searchable format. However you choose to find venues, you'll want to keep them in a format that can be organized and sorted. I recommend keeping them in a spreadsheet that can be sorted by zip code or city and state.

Spent at least 15 minutes creating and filling in contacts for your local city or nearby towns. Specifically, look for the following information:

Venue Name:
Address:
Website:
Booking Contact Name:
Booking Email:
Booking Phone Number:

Venue Capacity:
Genres of Music Booked:
Booking Requirements:

In your spreadsheet, you might also want to keep a column dedicated for any exchanges you have with the promoter so you know when you've heard from last. This is how I like to organize everything:

Your venue database will save you hours of work later when you're trying to book a tour. Doing this will also give you an excuse to look at venues' calendars and see if there are any shows that you'd make a good fit for.

I like using Google Docs or Evernote rather than keeping an Excel file because it allows me to access the information or work on the document from multiple devices, including my cell phone. This comes in handy when you're on the road and a show falls through: you'll have a list of people you can call in a pinch.

2. Make New Contacts

It's no secret that often in the world music, it's more about "who you know" than what you know. The industry generally favors pre-existing relationships, whether you are looking for a venue, a sponsor, a review on your new album, or a slot at SXSW. Like it or not, networking can make or break an act.

Today, focus on taking a few steps closer to your goal by working on your contacts. Here are some of my favorite tips on networking:

- **Start With a Goal in Mind:** Before you haphazardly contact just anyone in the music industry, think about what you want to achieve and who some of the people are that might be able to help you. You might also think about how you can help them in return. Most of the time, you'll make new contacts in social situations but you can also be strategic about who you want to meet and why.

- **Use "Pull" Marketing Strategies:** "Push" marketing is exactly what it sounds like: taking a proactive approach to reach out. However, "pull" marketing is far more effective. That's when you draw people in. You can achieve "pull" marketing when you are charismatic/magnetic, have industry buzz, and/or give an incentive or reason to draw people in.

- **Make Networking a Lifestyle, Not an Activity:** While some people will be more inclined to be the social butterfly, it doesn't mean that you can't make networking a normal part of your career. Don't be the one who is shoving their business cards in everybody's face. Instead, be the one that listens to others' needs and the one who takes the initiative in helping meet those needs.

- **It's Not Who You Know, it's Who Knows You:** Your name is a brand and the more excitement and buzz about you, the more likely you'll attract others. Learn how to market yourself so more people will begin to know you (social media, especially Linkedin, is a great place to start).

- **Give Them a Reason to Call You:** With each exchange (whether online or in person), show the person that you respect their time by giving them something of value. This can be a tip, an interesting story, an incentive, or answer to a lingering question.

You can find more tips on networking with a quick Google search or at the library. I highly recommend books on sales, especially by Jeffrey Gitomer, Jeffrey Fox, and Dale Carnegie.

Activity 1: Create Your Strategy

Create a networking strategy. You can use a spreadsheet, a notebook, email/contact management system, or whatever system you are most comfortable with. Start with:

- **Your Goals:** Who are the people you want to get in touch with and why. What industries are they in? What do you hope to gain out of a relationship with them? Organize these contacts in categories (Managers, record labels, promoters, media, sponsors, etc.).

- **Degrees of Separation:** Who do you know who might have the ability to get you one degree closer to the contact? This is where sites like Linkedin are exceptionally useful. Don't worry if you don't have a line of contact for each person, just start with who you know.

- **Add Contact Information:** Include their basic contact information as well as any public social media accounts that they might use, such as Twitter.

- **Value Proposition:** List what they are interested in, what you can do to bring value to them. Can you help market their product/service? Create a partnership? Expand their roster?

- **Contact Plan:** Keep a track record of when/how you contact them. Treat this like a sales call sheet. There are many templates available online for this.

- **Timeline:** Group together contacts and create a regular schedule on when you'll reach out to new contacts and build up existing relationships. It doesn't take much, consistency goes a long way!

Activity 2: Generate Some Buzz

Build "pull" marketing strategies. Sometimes the best way to make new contacts is to give them a reason to contact you. In other words, find ways to make them take the initiative. There are a couple of ways to do this online:

- **Become a Resource for Them:** Create some "online capital" by writing a regular blog or contributing to content on sites like Quara, HARO, or Linkedin. If you create meaningful content for things that your target contacts are interested in, they'll be more inclined to contact you.

- **Generate Some Buzz:** Hire a publicist, find ways to create some momentum through social media, create some industry buzz. Remember, focus on *their* industry. It doesn't help you to reach #1 on ReverbNation for bands in your area if they have never heard of the website before. The best publicity gained is in areas where they will "stumble" across you and your work.

- **Draw Them In:** Think of other ways that your target contacts will discover you. What interests them? What kind of websites or trade journals do they visit and read? Who do they know that could make that introduction? Some research can save you a lot of time and make your efforts much more effective.

3. Create Something Press Worthy

Perhaps you have a list of accomplishments that you are proud of, but you've struggled with getting the word out about those things. Sometimes, you have the wrong story (it isn't that interesting). Other times, you have the wrong audience (you just need to find the right media source). This is where having a publicist will be great asset to you: they have existing relationships with journalists and have a feeler over what "sells" and what doesn't. Besides, it's always nice having an objective opinion from someone outside of your band helping you create a story that journalists will be interested in writing about.

However, if you don't have a publicist, you can still send out a press release. Some topics that could be considered "press worthy" could be momentous occasions, such as:

- Releasing a new album
- Releasing a new music video
- Embarking on a tour
- A change in your band's line up
- A controversial situation or battle
- Being invited to a prestigious show or music festival
- A fundraiser or major charitable effort

- Winning an award
- A new partnership or sponsorship
- Signing a new agreement with a booking agency or record label
- Receiving press coverage in a major media source
- Anything that could be seen as "major" news

There are many more situations that could spark an interest. To get an idea of what kinds of stories are interesting, look at newspaper and magazine headlines. More than anything else, the headlines or topics deal with some kind underlying story. The press loves controversy and conflict because it makes stories more interesting (which in turn, makes them more likely to be shared). What sounds more interesting, a band releasing a new album and going on tour or a band releasing a new album and going on tour after a 20 year hiatus? They could very well be the same story but the slight change in angle adds depth and interest that can help sell the story.

News should also be current. However, you should also keep a log of notable accomplishments or moments on your music career because they can often resurface or be used as fodder for a press release.

Activity 1: Story Collecting and Sharing

Create a folder to archive your band's stories. Think about the different areas of interest listed above. Having a catalog of press worthy material will always be helpful, especially if you create an online press room on your website.

If you keep a blog for your music, you could always keep track of the larger stories with a certain hashtag or keyword. That way, they're easier to find.

Activity 2: Write a Press Release

When you write about a story or incident for a press release, always keep the following in mind:

- **Audience:** Who would be interested in the story?
- **The Point:** Why would people be interested in hearing about the story?
- **Location:** Where is the story taking place?
- **Timing:** When does the story take place? Is it still relevant?
- **Format:** Look a the standard format of a press release and follow it so that it's familiar to journalists/reporters/bloggers.

These aspects of the story can help you narrow down which media channels to pitch the story to as well as distill it in a way that resonates with them. Even if you don't end up pitching the story to media or bloggers, you can still turn it into good content for a blog, social media posts, or video.

4. Create Partnerships Instead of Sponsorships

When most people who want sponsorships think about their ultimate goal, it involves usually money. They're looking for someone to fund their event, to pay for their tour, to raise money for their charity, and so on. When many business think about sponsoring someone, it ultimately involves money as well: even if it is an incredible cause, at the end of the day, they want to know how sponsoring will help them get more customers. Each party treats the sponsorship as a transaction. However, I believe it is important to shift the definition from "a cash and/or in-kind fee paid to a property (typically sports entertainment, non-profit event, or organization) in return for access to the exploitable, commercial potential associated with that property" (IEG, 2000) to something more equitable: a partnership.

Sponsorship as a Partnership

A sponsorship insinuates something more akin to a one-sided relationship: the sponsor gives money in the hope for more customers or being associated with a positive cause. A partnership denotes an agreement where both parties share the risks, responsibilities, and rewards. By approaching the relationship as a partnership, it also implies a long term agreement.

By examining how we approach sponsorships more closely, we can also identify a few other important factors that should be considered:

- **Who do we want associated with our brand, event, or organization?** You hear about companies dropping their advertising dollars or sponsorships of athletes all the time because they don't want to be affiliated with improper behavior. Recently, talk show host Rush Limbaugh lost multiple major advertisers due to some of his controversial statements. However, sometimes as an artist or non-profit event, we don't think deeply about who we are getting our money from and how our fans' perception of us might change as a result.

- **What kind of people do we want to work with?** If you are planning a cross-promotional marketing campaign where you work closely with a brand, you'll want to know their customers, their work-flow, communication processes, and their approach. Does it make sense for what you are doing?

- **Is everyone getting fair value for their work?** If you are getting a $20,000 sponsorship, are you providing *at least* $20,000 worth of deliverable returns back to the investor? Conversely, is the amount of work you're doing worth the money/partnership or are there other ways you can get the same resources more easily?

- **What are some creative ways that this partnership can be highlighted?** You should be able to do more than simply trade logos on websites and your printed materials. How can you use your respective brands to drive customers towards one another? Is there a way that you can involve the employees of a sponsoring business?

Sales guru Jeffrey Gitomer puts it best: "All things being equal, people want to do business with their friends. All things being not so equal, people still want to do business with their friends." By elevating the value of sponsorship to an established, friendly partnership, you'll instill loyalty, and get more in return than a simple check could ever provide.

Activity 1: Create a Contact Database of Sponsors

Create a contact database by types of outreach based on each of your band's target audiences. For example, if you have fans who like a certain type of product, food or drink, service, etc. each of those could be a set of potential sponsors. Also, create a list of products that you already use (both from music gear to practical things on tour). Once you have your lists, start brainstorming with your band who you all know could help: an employee, mutual friend or contact, client, etc. If you have an insider make the introduction (or if you already know someone there), your chances of success are much greater.

Activity 2: Create a Sponsorship Proposal Packet

Create a sponsorship proposal packet that is dedicated to a specific, target audience. For example, if you want music instrument companies, you should focus your attention on the kinds of audiences that they'd want to reach. Every line in the packet should, in some way, answer the potential sponsor's question: "How will sponsoring this band help sell my products?"

Most sponsorship proposal packets will include the following:
- A one sheet
- Notable press or accomplishments
- Sponsorship levels or offerings at different financial commitment levels
- Testimonials from other sponsors and partners

Think of the sponsorship packet as an EPK but with the primary goal of developing a mutually beneficial partnership in mind instead of a gig or radio play. Remember that goal on every page; don't include excessive information that doesn't speak to that it.

Rather than focusing on the money being exchanged, focus on the value of the partnership. Think of creative ways to leverage the relationship for everyone involved.

Activity 3: Learn Some More

To learn some more information about how to treat sponsorships as partnerships (as well as tips on how to obtain those relationships), use this link to unlock everything I've written about it online: http://bit.ly/IMfjSW (or go to www.laststopbooking.com and click on "How to Get a Sponsor" to access the complete archive).

5. Research Potential Sponsors

It's important to be strategic about the potential sponsors that you reach out to; in many ways, it's a similar process to finding your target audience. You want to focus on finding the right people who will not only understand what you are doing, but enthusiastically support it as well. By being more selective about who you target, you can spend more time crafting a proposal that is effective (rather than sending out generic emails in hopes of getting to the right person).

Start With Who You Know

It's always a good idea to start with your own network before reaching out to others. There are several reasons for this:

1. It's easier to secure a sponsor if there is already an existing relationship or connection.

2. Securing sponsorships early on will add credibility for your proposal to future prospects.

3. Your existing relationships can help guide you through the sponsorship process so that you'll feel more confident (and experienced) about pursuing other contacts.

4. If you have a tough time getting buy-in from your friends and allies, you'll have a much more difficult time winning others over. That's a strong indicator that you need to work on your brand and/or sponsorship proposal before moving onto other contacts.

5. Often times, we rule out contacts who are ready/willing simply because we forget that they are right there!

When you begin sorting your contacts, these are some simple steps that you should take to ensure that the right people are included.

Activity 1: Sponsor Brainstorming Session

Collect your bandmates, manager, close friends, or anyone who wants to seriously work with you on your music and:

- **Have everyone in your band go through their contact lists:** If you have a LinkedIn account, this is even more helpful since it lists your contacts with their organizations and the positions they hold there. Check your email contacts, cell phone, Rolodex, Facebook, and so on.

- **Go through the membership directory of any membership organization that you belong to:** Include chamber of commerce memberships, professional networking organizations, religious groups, clubs, etc.

- **Look for common connections at companies where you don't have a contact:** You can close friends, colleagues, or business contacts to make an introduction if you don't have an established relationship. Social media sites like Facebook and

Linkedin often have a "people you may know" function or ability to search mutual contacts.

This should provide a pretty extensive initial list of those who would most likely support your organization.

Activity 2: Find Additional Potential Sponsors

There's often a number of potential sponsors waiting for you that you don't directly know (or aware of). This could be do to write-up's, media mentions, being involved with the community, or other forms of publicity where your message carries. Businesses and individuals who know of you through reputation make a better fit than those who have no familiarity with you at all.

Here are some ways to find them:

- **Conduct an extensive search engine investigation to see where you've gotten publicity:** Use multiple search engines (Google, Yahoo, DuckDuckGo, etc.) as well as Boolean logic (such as quotation marks or brackets) to aid with your research. Find out who has written about you or where you have coverage and pay attention to the readership or audiences of those sources.

- **Use the power of a survey:** Ask participants on your mailing list if they'd be willing to take a survey (it helps to offer an incentive) and include questions about their businesses or if they'd be willing to help or are interested in partnering with you.

- **Check your neighborhood:** Check with neighboring businesses if you have an office/retail location or organizations of the areas you host events in. You can even begin with a soft ask or make initial contact by asking if they'd be willing to hang a poster of an upcoming event, have a place for brochures, etc.

Once you come up with this second list, find ways to nurture those relationships so that they can become direct contacts. Either way, these individuals/organizations make great potential prospects.

.

6. Learn the Art of RSS

RSS stands for "rich site summary," but is sometimes referred to as "really simple syndication." Neither of those really explain what it is. I like to call it a reader subscription service, since it acts like an aggregator for all of your subscribed content. If you're web savvy, you probably already know because you see its image everywhere:

When you use a RSS reader, you subscribe to published posts of websites, including e-magazines, blogs, news, event pages, and more. A reader acts as a single point of entry for all of those sites so that you don't have to repeatedly visit them. When an update appears, it automatically syncs with your reader so you can see the newest content. It saves time and hassle from repeatedly visiting multiple websites.

You might or might not be using a RSS reader, but there are several takeaways from RSS programs that you can definitely apply to your music career. Here are some ideas:

1. You can use a RSS reader to **subscribe to all of your**

favorite music industry news, career advice, and music blogs so that you can easily keep up with multiple websites. This is what most people who use RSS services do. In fact, if you want to subscribe to my site, you can at www.laststopbooking.com

2. **Follow the tour dates of bands that you want to perform with**. As soon as a tour is announced, you can see where these acts will be performing so that you can request to be on the show before anyone else. Some regional promoters also offer RSS feeds for their calendars. This is a great way to get in the door earlier.

3. **Subscribe to local event pages, conferences, or festivals, especially non-music related ones.** There will often be local events in your city where event planners don't even think about live music immediately. Sometimes, these can be large festivals or events with a built in draw (and they often pay pretty well too). If you find local calendars for your town, you can see upcoming events that you can follow-up on right away.

4. **Offer RSS on Your Band's Website.** Be sure to allow RSS subscriptions for your band's news, blogs, and tour dates so others can easily get your updates.

RSS also teaches a few valuable lessons about how people use the internet:

- Sometimes people just want one, easy site for all of their content (this is probably why some people gravitate towards certain social media sites)

- Internet users want to spend less time searching and more time enjoying the content that they are looking for

- The easier something is, the better

- RSS often provides a short summary with a link to expand if users want more.

These same concepts should be applied to your website and social media content: it should be easy to navigate, easy to share, and require little time to get to the heart of the content.

Activity 1: Find a RSS Reader

Unfortunately, my favorite RSS, Google Reader, was discontinued. But here are some other good alternatives that I recommend:

- **Digg:** Simple, easy to use. It syncs with your computer, tablet, or other mobile devices. Offers a list view or expanded, has a few shortcuts. The downside is that there is no search capability so it's a little tougher to find older content.

- **Feedly:** Has some more features than Digg, very clean looking, and easy to sync across multiple devices. Search feature is available, at a cost.

- **RSS Bot:** Very simple, no sync option. In fact, almost no options at all. It's very straightforward.

Test a few out on whatever devices that you use the most. It's also a great way to kill time while you are waiting somewhere.

Activity 2: Begin Making Your Content RSS Friendly

Let's assume that you already offer RSS for the content on your website. Are you filling it with RSS friendly content? In other words, if you are posting news or a blog, readers should be able to get the "hook" within the first two sentences (since it's likely that's what you'll end up with). Keep things short and sweet. When you post content, it should always be share worthy and compatible on multiple devices. You might also consider creating a RSS feed option on your website that feeds from fans' content.

7. Add to Your Music Business Filing Cabinet

Are you collecting valuable articles and information about the music business? Do you keep a record of every press mention or post about your band? Maybe there are just interesting articles about art, marketing, social media, current events, books, or other content that can help fuel inspiration for a new song or teach you how to do something. When I see this kind of material, I put it in my "music business filing cabinet."

Too often, we see something of interest but then forget about it later. Sometimes, we create a bookmark but the content is no longer available. Don't miss a moment - create an archive!

While I do keep physical files - I print out the most important items because it's easier to read on paper and it's nice to have a collection - I also like to create digital folders that are labeled, organized, and easy to access. It's kind of like my own private Pinterest or bookmark list, except I create a copy and store it into an online folder.

With sites like Google Drive, Dropbox, and Evernote, it's easier than ever. Every time I see something of interest, a press mention, etc. I save it as a .pdf, name the file, and place it into an appropriate folder. Then, it serves as my own music industry library, record of all the press I've received, or idea generator when I'm songwriting. I've also found this to be helpful with legal issues as well - it's always good to have a good track record of organized files.

You might have your own way of organizing content or prefer different labels, but these are the folders that I currently save things to:

- Music industry articles
- Social media tips
- Marketing ideas
- Inspiration:
    - Quotes
    - Song Ideas
    - Album artwork
    - Marketing Ideas
    - Good stories
- Press :
    - Interviews
    - Music Reviews
    - Tour press
    - Features
    - Other
- Booking Agreements and Contracts
- Music Studio Tips:
    - Gear
    - Recording Techniques
- Important Emails
- Stuff the Fans Like
- Contacts

While it's good to save things are you come across them (or when someone sends you something interesting), it's also a good idea to carve out regular sessions where you look for specific things to add to the cabinet.

Activity 1: Setting Up Your Filing Cabinet

If you don't have one, create a series of folders that you can use to capture information. You can use a cloud-based storage system (online), create something on your computer's hard drive, or use a program that syncs the two together. I recommend using either Google Drive, Dropbox, or Evernote. All of them offer free, limited space profiles or professional accounts with expanded capacity for a small monthly fee.

Once you have that setup, I would also recommend setting up tags or folders in your email system that use the same labels. That way, it makes things much easier to find. You might also consider backing up your entire email account if there's a lot of important information there.

It's important to spend some time setting things up right the first time around. It's always easier if you begin with well-organized system in place than if you have to sort through hundreds of files.

Activity 2: Add Content to the Cabinet

Spend some time finding content for your files. If you want to focus more on the music business, you could browse industry blogs or look for helpful files. I also recommend looking for general tips outside of the music industry to get ideas for a more creative approach to managing a music career. For instance, look at articles aimed at small businesses, restaurant owners, event planners, photographers, or college outreach planners.

If you're feeling creative and want to work on song ideas, you can begin searching for content. For example, if you search for photographs or artwork using a keyword (on Google Images or Flickr), that might help provide some context for album artwork later on.

8. Learn the Art of Crowdsourcing

There are numerous detailed guides on how to run a crowdsourcing campaign as well as many different sites that offer the service, such as Kickstarter or Indiegogo. Whether you decide that it is right for you to launch one or not, it's a good idea to know what is involved because there are some great principles that you can apply to raising support for your band.

Here's a quick rundown of the main concepts that you should know:

- **Your fundraising campaign begins long before you even join Kickstarter, Indiegogo, or any other fan funding website.** The most important part of having a successful campaign is having a dedicated audience who is vested in your art. You should be building relationships with your fans long before you make the "ask." Kickstarter is more of a vehicle for you to work with your existing fans, and less of a platform for you to find new ones. This is why an artist like Amanda Palmer was able to meet her goal of a $100,000 within hours of the launch and ended up raising $1.2 million by the end of the campaign. Her campaign wasn't just the 30 days that the project was live. Her campaign began the moment she began playing live shows and making fans one at a time.

- **Build Alliances to Help You.** A large part of success is having an army of fans, sponsors, promoters, people in the media, and other artists who are happy to tweet/share/post the link and encourage people to support your campaign. Before a campaign begins, it's good to have a solid working relationship with other artists (maybe they can collaborate, help offer incentives, etc.).

- **The Goal:** Don't worry about making the goal as high as possible, make it as realistic as possible. What will it take to fully fund your project? Don't try and pad it, thinking you can use the extra money for other things. Many people prefer to support a campaign after a goal has already been met because they want to be a part of the success. However, the goal should be high enough to motivate your supporters as well.

- **Don't Treat Pledges Like Donations.** The emphasis should be on pledges, not donations. Remember, backers are investing into your art and they will expect to get concrete rewards in return. If you treat it more like an album pre-ordering campaign where fans have the chance to be intimately involved with your music rather than a project asking for sympathy, people will be more receptive.

- **Get Creative with the Rewards.** Explore as many other projects as you can. People are willing to give more if they are able to get something exclusive, unique, fun. If you have other skills, bring them into this. Can you cook? Offer a private party where you cook your fans some dinner. Can you paint? Include some rare, personalized canvas pieces for limited contributors. You get the idea.

- **Make Every Feature Count.** There are many features that Kickstarter Offers. Use them all. Spend the extra time preparing your video – make it short and sweet, make it compelling. Post frequent updates to keep fans excited, treat it like a blog. Post photos or videos of your progress.

- **Match Your Brand/Process.** Focus on the tools that you already use instead of forcing things to happen. For example, I use Twitter often so for my crowdsourcing campaign, I created a custom hashtag and would tweet every time someone made a pledge. I looked up Twitter handles of people who pledged and tagged them, began conversations about it. Fans started tweeting celebrities, actors, bands, media contacts, etc. on my behalf, asking them to RT the link to the campaign.

- **Make the most of your campaign by spending as much time to prepare as possible.** I spent more time researching, studying, learning, building a fan base, and preparing for a Kickstarter campaign than I ever spent running it. If you take the time to build your audience, they'll help make the campaign successful for you.

Activity 1: Outline a Potential Campaign

If you are thinking about launching a crowdsourcing campaign to fund a project, begin by creating a budget. How much will it cost for the project to be completed? Whether you are looking to fund a new album or tour, you should include all of the variables possible. Use that as your starting number. Then, factor it costs for rewards, including shipping, packaging for shipments, labor, international fees, etc. Finally, add everything up and add 10%, the average fees assessed by crowdsourcing sites and their payment processing systems.

Once you have a financial goal in mind, think about the steps needed to reach that goal. For example, if your goal is $15,000, you would need to raise $3,750 per week (if your campaign ran for one month). Since the average Kickstarter pledge is about $70, that means you'd need to find 54 people per week to pledge. Also, keep in mind that the most popular gift size though is $25. Between you and your band members, does that sound realistic? If yes, begin thinking about how to reach those 54 every week (personal calls, emails, social media, letters, etc.). If not, begin working on a plan to build those relationships.

Remember, always begin with the financial goal and work backwards. None wants to waste their time on a project that can't be completed, so have a plan and a group of people who are committed to making it happen.

Activity 2: Perfect the Ask

As one of the most virally shared websites on the Internet, Upworthy spends a significant amount of time writing headlines. In fact, every article headline and social media post is written at least 25 different ways. They choose the best headlines and test them before launching them.

Your campaign should adopt a similar strategy. Don't just email your fans or update your Facebook followers with a boring ask: spend some time creating a short, powerful reason why they should click through to your crowdfunding campaign. Need some ideas? Look at posts from Upworthy, Buzzfeed, and Huffington Post - they have some of the most shared content online.

It might be easier to just send something that sounds "pretty good," but if your new album is on the line, why not take those extra steps to make sure you have a compelling ask that gets people there?

9. Create SMART(er) Goals

Author Zig Ziglar was often quoted as saying, "If you aim at nothing, you'll hit it every time."

Your music career is no different. Unless you have a target that you are reaching for, you'll just continue down random pathways hoping to get somewhere better. How will you know what success looks like if you haven't defined success for yourself? You need to begin by creating (or revisiting) your goals.

There's a popular business acronym that says goals should be S.M.A.R.T., or **S**pecific, **M**easurable, **A**ttainable, **R**elevant, and **T**imely. In a band, I think goals should be SMARTER, because they need to include **E**veryone and be **R**evisited often.

There are many good articles on how to be more effective at writing and reaching goals. In fact, there have been many great books about them. It's one of the most important aspects of your career, so it's good to spend time on goals as well as to learn how to be more effective at goal setting.

Here's a quick rundown on how you can make goals S.M.A.R.T.E.R.:

Specific

Ask yourself the big questions: Who, what, when, where, why, and when? A specific goal lets you know *what* you want to achieve, *when* you want to achieve it by, *why* you are doing it, *who* will be involved, and *where* it will happen.

Many artists have a generic goal of "making a living from doing music." But what does that mean to you? Most independent artists who are making a living from music also manage their own careers, book their own shows, solicit sponsors, etc. in addition to creating and performing music. For them, their goal was to be independent of another job or career. For others, they want to concentrate solely on music so a booking agent, a manager, a lawyer, and publicist would be involved as well. How much money do you need to live on? Spell out the goal completely.

For example, a goal I've used before: *Tour the continental U.S in August 2013 with at least 18 shows, playing a mixture of all-ages, 21+, and convention shows making an average of $500 per night. Also, see an increase on social media and web traffic by at least 10% and increase online sales by 20% for the month before, during, and after the tour.*

Measurable

A goal should have specific metrics so you know if you're making progress. If you have one larger goal, you should break it up into smaller parts over the course of time. That way, you and your team can always know where you stand against the overall goal. During this time you should be asking questions with *how*, *when*, and *what*: how much do you have left to go? When will you reach your goal? What do you have to do to stay on track?

Using the example listed above, one could easily measure against the tour goals in a number of ways:

- How many shows have been booked for August 2013?
- What kinds of shows have been booked?
- How much income is being earned per night?
- What is the average monthly online sales? Have they increased - and if so, by how much?
- What do I need to do to help increase merchandise sales, at shows or online?

Attainable

The goals that you develop should be ambitious but realistic. For example, if you don't have the right resources, abilities, finances, or followers, perhaps you should create a smaller goal and adjust it as the situation improves. If you focus on what you can do, it sometimes reveals new opportunities. For example, in Section 1 Chapter 5, I talk about looking for potential sponsors - many are probably in your own backyard but are often overlooked for the larger, sexier opportunities.

Goals should grow with you. As you gain more resources, abilities, finances, and followers, your goals should get respectively larger. Having them just out of reach helps you stretch. However, having them too far away will only cause frustration.

Relevant

The goals that you choose should matter. They should motivate you and drive your career forward. For example, I've talked to many artists who have a goal of playing a large festival like SXSW even though it doesn't relate to the current state of their music career. Things shouldn't be goals just because others are doing them. Ask yourself these questions: Is this the right time? Is this worthwhile? How will this directly help me?

Timely

Your goals should have a time-bound deadline. When would you like to reach your goal by? If your goal is shrouded in the idea of "someday," you'll have a much more difficult time of reaching it. If you want to achieve a goal by the end of the year, you'll work more aggressively for it. For example, if your goal is to sell 5,000 records, you would treat it much differently if that was 5,000 *someday* as opposed to 5,000 *by this December*.

Everyone

This is one that I like to use for musicians. In a band, goals should have everyone involved. If some of your bandmates aren't on board with the goals, then you might consider having someone else replace them - that's how important this is. People should be on the same page, have the right expectations, and the proper work ethic for reaching the goal.

Also, when I say everyone, I mean *everyone*. This includes spouses or other people whom we depend on for support. If your band members would like to tour 8-10 months out of the year but their significant others aren't supportive of that goal, some serious issues could arise - especially when that opportunity presents itself. If you want to focus primarily on licensing for films but your manager wants you to focus on festivals, those incongruent goals would also cause issues. Make sure the key players, as well as the most important people in your life, are in alignment when it comes to your goals.

Revisited

Goals should be revisited often. Not only should you be checking on your progress toward your goal, but you should also see if those goals need to be adjusted. Ask: are these goals still relevant? Is this what I want/need still?

Years ago, most artists had a goal of signing on a major record label (a few still do). However, since the market has completely changed, most have realized that this isn't always the most appropriate opportunity for them. Major things can alter our goals: relationships, the market, our fans, political instability, and so on. Revisit those goals and make sure they meet the criteria above.

Activity 1: Set Some Freakin' Goals

Now that you've reader about S.M.A.R.T.E.R., it's probably time to jot some ideas down about what you want to accomplish and when you want to accomplish those things by. You'll also want to pull in your key people and involved them as well. Try creating some larger, distant goals as well as ones that can be met soon. These are some areas that you might want to consider:

- Income
- New projects (album tour, music videos, etc.)
- Performance schedule (when, where, what)
- Career milestone
- Awards or recognition
- Album or merchandise sales
- Your team (manager, booking agent, lawyer, etc.)
- Creative (songs written, artwork, etc.)

Activity 2: Track Your Goals

In addition to revisiting your goals, you'll want to record your progress along the way. A good comparison is when parents mark their kids' height on a door frame using a pencil and a date. It can be as simple as having a journal or spreadsheet that shows when you checked in on them, what kind of progress has been made, and figuring out what is left to do in order to reach them. Take a few minutes out right now to check on the progress of your goals, measure them, and write down any progress made. In fact, I'd recommend doing this at least twice a week: the more often you check in, the less work that is required each time around. It also keeps them on top of your mind all the time so you can be aware of opportunities that come up.

Activity 3: Share Your Goals

It can be a good idea to share your goals if you do it in a way that encourages others to hold you accountable to them. For example, I once heard of an author who had an ambitious word count goal for his book but kept letting other things get in the way. So, he wrote a series of checks for $100 each to an organization he hated (Westboro Baptist Church) and gave them to a friend. Every time he failed to meet his weekly word count goal, the check would be automatically mailed out. It was definitely a great way to make sure he reached his goals every week!

Derek Sivers has a great article on not sharing goals, unless you use a similar approach. He says, "If you do tell a friend, make sure not to say it as a satisfaction ("I've joined a gym and bought running shoes. I'm going to do it!"), but as dissatisfaction ("I want to lose 20 pounds, so kick my ass if I don't, OK?")." You can read the full article here: http://sivers.org/zipit

So, share your goals in a way where they can help you stay accountable for your work.

10. Find New Music Revenue/Promotion Opportunities

These days, it seems that there are opportunities to promote your music everywhere you look. Some band services sites like Sonicbids and ReverbNation are full of opportunities that you can submit your music to (though often, that submission requires you to pay a fee). However, it doesn't always require a submission service, a paid EPK site, or contests where you try to prod friends and fans into voting for you. Sometimes, it just takes some creativity and a lot of drive.

I'm always look looking for opportunities on the road less traveled. Not only is there simply less competition for attention, but when you find the right opportunity, there's generally a higher payoff as well. Here are some idea generators that you can use to find more ways to get income and/or attention:

- **Bottoms Up!** Do you frequent a local watering hole or know someone who bartends? While the "provide them with free coasters" idea has been done to death, bands seldom ask to be put on the bar jukebox. Even more rare: designing a custom drink for the bar and have it named after you, your single, etc. In return, you put that drink on all of your business cards and flyers, telling people to visit that bar or club. You could even provide free download cards to patrons who order that drink. You could even do the same thing with a dish at a restaurant. It's a win-win.

- **Contact the Chamber.** I've been a part of various local chamber of commerce and business networking groups for 15 years now and I've never seen another artist as a member. Chamber members are often looking for live music for special events and they often rely on their network. The fee to join is nominal; not only can you meet business owners of important resources for your music career (printers, screen printing, graphic designers, auto mechanics, etc.), but if you book a single gig from it, it more than covers the dues. The chamber itself often needs music for each gathering, so offer to come up with a playlist for meetings and include some of your music!

- **At the Car Wash!** When the weather is warm, you can almost always expect to see high school students and local charities washing cars to raise money. Why don't you consider doing the same to raise money for an album or tour? With every car wash, you could even include free samples of your music or sell CD's while there. Plus, it could be a bonding event for you and the hardcore fans that volunteer.

- **Consignment.** You can almost always place your record on consignment at your local record store, but have you considered making it available at other stores as well? For example, if many of your fans love comic books and you have songs about comics, you could put your CD on consignment at that type of shop (same with skateboards, art stores, sports, coffee shops, or whatever the interest might be). In addition, you could ask the store to play the music, offer to do an in-store performance or signing to help promote it as well.

- **Turn it Up in the Library!** Did you know that many libraries allow their members to check out music? In fact, many have a local music section, especially college libraries. Talk to your local library about putting your music in the lending catalog - but don't stop there. Ask to perform at the library, especially if you have songs that are related to books, about reading, inspired by stories or poetry, etc. There is an entire genre of music called "wizard rock" comprised of bands inspired by Harry Potter. The most popular act, Harry and the Potters, has been touring libraries for over ten years now.

This is a simple list to get ideas going. Think about all of the interests that you and your fans share, where you get inspiration from, where you spend your time, where you shop, and how other businesses promote themselves. The list includes some of my favorite ways to find new opportunities to promote my music and make new fans.

I've used every one of the ideas listed above and they've all worked quite well (especially when you can work with a group of volunteers to help promote). It's often just a matter of thinking creatively about your music and finding nontraditional methods for getting the word out. One time, I contacted the small town of Astoria, OR because our band had a song about it. I simply contacted their local paper and called the tourism office, letting them know that we wrote a song about the city and would love to share it. Shortly after that, we got booked to headline the Astoria Crab, Wine, and Food Festival and played for thousands of people. Also, every time we make it into the news, the Astoria paper writes a story on the band!

Activity 1: Interest Brainstorming

Spend 10-15 minutes thinking about all the interests that you and your fans share. Facebook graph search and page insights is great for this because it can group together other pages/interests your fans follow. Then, think about what inspires your music, what themes are present, what kinds of images come up. Write it down or put it in a spreadsheet. From there, think about opportunities that might be related to those interests, hobbies, etc. This may include retail stores, festivals, conventions, charities, local events, faith-based organizations, locations, the list goes on. Then, think about how you can find ways to work with those groups, places, etc. to bring in music, perform, provide art, or do something else of interest to their audiences.

Love pets? Donate proceeds for a song to the humane society or shelter. Hate cancer? Play a Relay for Life Fundraiser. Wrote a book? Do a reading at the library and play a song. It can be as simple as that.

Activity 2: Work the List

Like your booking database or sponsor list, this is a collection of ideas that you should check in with on a regular basis. If you create a database or spreadsheet, you can keep up the document with contact information, ideas, call schedule, reminders, and notes. Consider this a friendly reminder to work that list. I'd recommend making a regular appointment to this, at least once a month. In fact, I do this on the 19th of every month myself.

Activity 3: Word Association

Not all of your ideas have to be based on an actual store. You could use a search engine to help you generate keywords. This will help get you new ideas as well as show you what is most searched for by people who are interested in the topic. Google auto-complete is a great tool for this because as soon as you type a letter, it begins filling it in with suggestions.

You might also use these keywords along with your subject/interest to help get you started:

- event
- convention
- store
- festival
- club
- college
- student group
- message board
- [interest] + city name
- game
- songs

For example, if "pirates" were a theme or interest for you/your fans and you began searching, you'd quickly find pirate conventions throughout the country. Many of these events book live pirate bands, too!

Word association can be a great way to open up new opportunities and get inspiration for new ways of promoting your music.

11. Learn From Someone Else

When I was in my MBA program, I often learned more about business from business owners (and running one myself) than the instructor. Usually, the people out in the field have a different perspective than those who are teaching. With the music industry, you have experts who come at it from many different angles: managers, lawyers, record labels, promoters, booking agents, publicists, journalists, solo artists, bands, studio musicians/session players, academics, consultants, and more. One of my favorite ways of learning is to study how other people are approaching their music career. Another is to look completely outside of the music industry itself.

When I want to improve on something specific, I often see what other successful artists are doing. This can be anything from a website layout, social media posts, biographies, and press kits to music videos, color palettes, song formats, and live performances. I often keep a portfolio of these artists' work to monitor trends, key words, and imagery. It's like having a list of reference songs in the studio when recording and mixing: the collection becomes a good point of reference to compare against.

When I want a different perspective on the music industry, I'll look for articles written by people who are involved from completely different jobs. Then, I'll meet up with someone in the industry, take them out to lunch, and bounce ideas off of them. It's a great way to help keep each other informed and to build those relationships.

When I want to get more creative, I look outside of the music industry itself to either get ideas or find new ways of approaching problems. For example, when I begin designing merchandise for an upcoming tour, I'll often look at Pantone (www.pantone.com) and see what the hot new colors are for the upcoming season. Then I'll incorporate those colors in if possible. Or, when I want to get creative about promoting, I'll look and see what other independent creators are doing: authors, chefs, designers, and so on. In many ways, the book publishing industry has followed the same path of the music industry, so authors and musicians can definitely learn from each other.

Activity 1: Nerdfighters, Assemble!

Brothers John and Hank Green have come up with some of the most brilliant ways to connect with their audience that I've ever seen. Between the two of them, they've built up a loyal army of fans called Nerdfighters. They have helped launch an independent record label with several Billboard charting songs, promoted multiple New York Times bestselling books, supported several extremely successful webseries on YouTube, established a massive annual convention called Vidcon, and raised hundreds of thousands of dollars for various charities. If you want to learn how they did this, take some time out and learn everything that you can about the "vlogbrothers." Or take a crash course here: http://youtu.be/Yk05_6Mf1GU

The vlogbrothers are a great example of how developing a very fine niche and appealing to a core community of followers can explode into a worldwide phenomenon. Every independent artist who is serious about their career should be studying the careers of these two brothers.

Activity 2: Comparison Charts

Create a list of ten artists (any genre, but preferably successful ones in your own genre) that you can follow in almost every way: look at their biographies, their social media feeds, their "brand" or image that they project to the world and look for common language, imagery, or behaviors. See what kinds of posts they make that get the most feedback (likes, comments, shares, retweets, and so on). Keep a list or chart and find ways to gain some ideas so that you can create your own set of best practices.

Activity 3: Follow the Leader

Check out articles and posts from business leaders who are outside of the business industry. Need some ideas of who you should be paying attention to? Try these lists:

https://twitter.com/FastCompany/lists
https://twitter.com/EntMagazine/lists
http://adage.com/power150/

Entrepreneurs, digital and social media marketers, business owners, etc. can all help you refine the business side of your music career by helping you make better managerial decisions, create better goals, learn how to use social media, and offer other tips that you might not get from following the usual suspects in the music industry world (ASCAP Daily, Music Think Tank, and so on). Many of these individuals who tweet will post useful links and articles throughout the day that you should be reading.

So begin following/subscribing to several business leaders. If you tweet, follow their accounts. If you use blogs, use RSS. Many also have

YouTube accounts, Linkedin Influence accounts, etc. It's an endless source of ideas that can help you develop your own artistry and business finesse. In fact, might also find content that is relevant to your audience that you could repurpose or retweet yourself.

12. Use an Email List Effectively

As artists, we're often told to collect fans' contact information for newsletters or letting them know about shows. Despite it being one of the most important components for artist success, it is often one of the most ignored. This could be for a number of reasons: it seems to require more work than a social media update, it doesn't have the instant gratification or feedback that comes with social media, or artists simply don't know how to use this effectively.

Having a large, detailed mailing list actually gives you more leverage when it comes to negotiating deals in the music industry than having many Twitter or Facebook followers. So it's important to learn how to effectively use this, both for your fans, as well as your industry contacts.

In most instances, you'll want to develop a regular communication pattern with whoever is on your list.

Developing a Fan Mailing List

For fans, I would recommend sending a regular update once or twice per month, but not anything less than that. This should be sent on a consistent schedule. For example, I usually send my band's newsletter on the first Monday of every month. Whatever you choose to do, just make sure it is consistent. To make things easier, you can use an email newsletter delivery service and work on the newsletter whenever you have free time. That way, you can pre-schedule the newsletter to be delivered at a consistent time and date.

There are many services that offer email newsletters. Some of the most common include:

- Constant Contact
- MailChimp
- My Emma
- Fanbridge
- iContact

Each company has their own templates and advantages. Most will charge a small monthly fee. I prefer Fanbridge myself: ASCAP members get a discount, it's catered specifically for artists, and they have other widgets that you can use for your social media. You can also collect additional information from fans, such as their zip code, which is especially helpful when you're trying to send email blasts about shows in their specific area.

For your newsletter, I would recommend keeping it to just a few stories, a specific call to action, and a list of some upcoming shows. Spend extra time writing and rewriting headlines that are compelling but don't sound too much like spam (avoid sales language and the overuse of punctuation or capitalization). Some email services even allow you to test multiple subject lines on a small portion of your contact list first, then have the rest delivered based on the subject that had the highest open rate.

The average email open rate is about 20%, so you can use that as a metric to measure against (the average Facebook post only reaches about 12% of your followers).

Try and keep focus to one main item each newsletter: if you want them to watch a video, tweet a specific message, attend a show, etc. then just focus on that one item. If you try to cram too much in, it can be overwhelming or it will only dilute your message.

There are many other best practices, but the most important one is consistency. If you email fans sporadically, they'll lose interest.

Developing an Industry List

Something else that you might consider is developing a regular contact list specifically for industry. This could be media/press, sponsors, promoters, or whoever else you want to have semi-regular business contact with. For example, with my sponsors/endorsements, I provide a quarterly update that's formatted like a business report. I'll focus on web traffic, show attendance, upcoming tours or opportunities for brand partnerships, and any exciting news that could be relevant to their partnership with my band.

While this doesn't have to be sent on a regularly scheduled basis, it's useful to have these contacts in a newsletter database (preferably on their own list, apart from fan mailings), so that you can track open rates, click through rates, and other vital metrics. This is especially important with press contacts, as some email services will show you which contacts actually opened your message. This will help when sending follow-up if you're trying to get media coverage for your story, a new album review, tour press, etc.

Design with a Purpose

No matter who you are sending the email to, be sure to test it in a variety of platforms, especially because more emails are being read on mobile devices than ever. Your email should be optimized for mobile, both in content and in design.

An email that is optimized for mobile means that it automatically adapts to the device your recipients are using. Most email delivery services have templates with the proper code to do this. You just need to ensure that the content is brief and easy to digest with a quick glance.

Activity 1: Design Your Newsletter

If you don't have a regular newsletter that you send out (or if you think it looks a little dated), check out a couple of different email service providers to see if there are some interesting templates that you'd like to work with. You'll also want to test the email designs on a few different devices if possible - iPad, phone, desktop, etc.

While any email delivery company should have a variety of attractive templates, most will offer some kind of customization option so that you can drop in your own header/banner, logo, photo, or other artwork. Try a few different ideas, like designing a custom banner just for an album release, upcoming tour, or something that is appropriate for the season.

The templates should also allow you to provide a Hex color code so that you can match the design exactly to your band's image/branding.

Activity 2: Develop an Editorial Calendar

Consider creating an editorial calendar for your newsletter so you know what stories, message, call to action, etc. will be featured in every issue. This can be based on any major activities or milestones that you have coming up. Here's an example of a monthly newsletter with the next six months planned out:

January: Kickstarter Campaign/Album Pre-Order
February: New Album Release
March: SXSW Tour
April: New Music Video Release
May: Merchandise Sale
June: Summer Tour

While you might not have everything set for the entire year, it does help to plan it out in advance so that each issue helps go towards your overall goal. Also, this will guide your social media posts too, since everything should build on one another. You don't need to have every detail set, but having broad themes will make life easier down the road.

Finally, set due dates on your newsletter so that everything can be prepared in time. For example, try to collect everything for the newsletter at least one week before it is being sent out. That gives you time to check for errors, test out any links or video content, and get feedback from your band.

Activity 3: Newsletter Database Cleanup

Another important part of managing your newsletter is keeping the data up to date. Not only is it important to enter contacts into your fan list on a regular basis, but you should take the time to clean up the existing list so that you can reduce email bounce rates. An email bounce is when the email is returned. Sometimes, it's because the email address is incorrect, other times, because their server rejected your message.

There are a number of ways to keep your email list up to date:

- Use social media or other outreach tools to remind fans to complete their fan/email profile. This is also a good way to capture their physical mailing address as well.

- Look for formatting errors. For example, if the punctuation is wrong, there's a misspelling, etc.

- See which email addresses are bouncing and compare them against what you have: email sign-up lists, previous email conversations, social media, etc. If it's someone that you interact with often, you can probably figure out how to get the right email.

- Include an email subscription management link in each of your newsletter issues. Most companies offer this and it allows users to update their preferences or information.

- When all else fails, remove the continuously bouncing email addresses from your database.

Activity 4: Promote Your Email Newsletter

An email list isn't going to promote itself. How are you promoting your newsletter? Try some of these suggestions to get the job done:

- Offer a fan incentive (free mp3(s), wallpapers and/or artwork, merchandise, exclusive news, or other benefits). Some email programs, such as Fanbridge have built-in programs to issue an incentive for those who sign up.

- Make a contest out of it. For example, I give out seasonal cards or postcards on tour to a few, random fans on our list. Not only do we promote this on social media, but fans are often eager to share photos of their swag, too.

- Place the email signup in a prominent place on your site(s). Make it as easy as possible for fans to join your email list - ask for the bare minimum amount of information (you can always collect more later).

13. Build the Right Team: manager, publicist, and booking agent

It's important to assemble the right group of people when it comes to your band. Like any business, you want to make sure that you have the right employees on hand to take care of the work. Even if you're capable of handling everything on your own, you can be much more effective if you have specialists on board with their own network of contacts who can help you get even further ahead in your career.

Below is a list of different people you can hire to help run your band, suggestions on when you should bring the person in, and what you can typically expect from them.

The Band Manager

The manager probably the most important person on your team - or at least, certainly, most versatile. They're responsible for handling all the business/administration parts of your music career. While they might not specialize in booking, publicity, or legal affairs, they should have a working knowledge of each of these areas and how they affect you. In fact, they should be able to dabble in each of these areas comfortably. They should be able to help you create a long term strategy which should incorporate your music's branding, business plan, and goals. They will be the social butterfly that naturally networks with people and isn't afraid to close the sale. They make you more money, so they can make money themselves.

When to Hire a Manager: If you don't know how your shows or records play into your long term business strategy (or if you don't have a business plan), you either desperately need a manager or you're not ready for one. Managers are generally paid 15-20% of your band's total income, but it is not uncommon these days to find ones working on a fixed monthly stipend, especially for artists who are at an earlier stage of their career. If you are struggling with the business aspects of your career but you're still finding your success growing, it's a good time to start looking. As an alternative, you could find a mentor (such as more experienced band or industry person) who might be willing to help. If you feel pretty capable in managing many aspects of the band yourself, you might consider hiring a consultant that you could talk to occasionally to help address unanswered questions or make sure that you're on the right track. Either way, an independent, objective opinion is always good to have on hand.

The Tour Manager

The main role of a tour manager is to make sure that the tour runs as smoothly as possible. This means that they take care of the band members and crew on the road, deal with the venues and promoters directly for run-of-show and payment, and manage the band's finances during the tour. Sometimes, the band manager and tour manager are one and the same. A tour manager should have excellent skills when it comes to logistics, accounting, and organization. It's also helpful if they have a working knowledge of lights and sound as well. On larger tours, there will usually be a few staff helping with these roles, including a production assistant, a tour accountant, road crew lead, production manager, and so on. Unlike the band manager, a tour manager will get paid a fixed amount for the duration of the tour. At the very least, they'll need their expenses covered (transportation, meals, and lodging).

When to Hire a Tour Manager: Obviously, you won't need a tour manager until you're touring on a regular basis and making enough income or having enough shows to warrant having one. Often, a band can have all of the information about the tour set in advance and take care of themselves, but it is helpful to have someone with experience stepping in when things don't go as planned. Some bands have their manager step into this role, others will appoint someone in the band. You can also ask tour veterans from other bands to help as well. Either way, it's important to consider the impact on the tour: the finances (increased costs), logistics (less space), and return on investment for the additional expertise and help.

The Publicist/PR Firm

The publicist is responsible for getting you media attention. This is the person who will get you features, interviews, and reviews in magazines, radio stations, TV shows, and websites. They find media coverage for you appropriate for your level. Dollar for dollar, this is probably going to be your best investment as an artist. If you want to grow your audience, build a buzz for your music, and have some press to show off to record labels, promoters, or your mom, you need a publicist or PR firm. There is a huge difference between hiring someone who can do "press work" (sending in press releases to magazines or press kits to radio stations) and a publicist who has established relationships with media contacts and who understand your genre of music/your audience. For a good publicist, you're paying for their relationships with the media, their tenacity and follow-up, and their ability to pitch a story.

Most publicists charge per campaign (usually in 3-6 month increments). Prices usually range between $1,000 to $5,000 for a short campaign. Also, note that most publicists/PR firms have a specific specialty or focus based on the type of medium - print, radio, web, etc. Finally, most publicists are objective-based: Do you want a campaign to get press on your new album or do you want tour press? Some publicists will work with you to get press releases and stories out, working as your long term partner. Others will only work on the campaign at hand. Whatever the nature of your relationship, have expectations sorted out ahead of time and get it in writing.

When to hire a publicist: You should have a publicist from the point you decide you want others to take you seriously and when you have something about you that is press-worthy. The optimal time to have people writing about you is when you're about to tour, release a new album, or both. While it is undoubtedly costly to have one, hiring a publicist will impact your career almost immediately and is worth every penny of the investment if you find the right match. Even after the campaign ends, you'll continue to reap the benefits of receiving solid press on your music. It will positively impact nearly every area of your career.

The Booking Agent

Booking agents help get you shows, showcases at festivals, college gigs, and other performance opportunities. They get you more/better shows than you can get on your own, negotiate terms with promoters, and can help you find an opening slot for larger acts. They also juggle the logistics of your tour schedule so that you can spend more time focusing on your music. They have established relationships with promoters and have a broader knowledge of out-of-town markets. A good booking agent will understand your market, get you shows that play into your long term business strategy, and find opportunities that will allow you to make new fans in traditional, as well as new and innovative markets. Booking agents generally charge a percentage of your income from performances (usually, 10-20%), though these days, some charge a flat-rate per show when booking a tour.

When to Hire a Booking Agent: If you're only playing the occasional regional show, chances are that you don't need someone (your manager could probably handle these). But if you find yourself wanting to tour more often, it might be time to look for one. For established agencies who work off of a percentage, they'll want to see you performing at least 100-150 decent paying shows per year, usually in mid-sized venues (approximately 500 capacity). You should also be able to have a solid draw in multiple markets. If you're just starting out and need some help, a flat-rate booking agent might be more appropriate. They can help you determine which venues to approach, guide you on tour routing/logistics, and get you shows that you have a hard time getting on your own. Promoters like working with people that they know and trust, so having an agent can be advantageous. If you want to book a tour, try to approach an agent at least six months in advance.

The Entertainment Lawyer

Whenever you are dealing with contracts or agreements, it is a good idea to consult a lawyer. Nearly every lawyer can take things on specific jobs or projects, so you can just hire them as needed. Your band's lawyer can help you negotiate or understand contracts, resolve claims, help you with copyright or trademark registrations/infringements, or set up your band as a business entity. These days, it's common for the lawyer to also be the one who approaches record labels on your behalf as well.

Lawyers usually cost around $150-$250 per hour or more) but will usually give you an estimate for the job at hand. For example, helping you write a performance agreement or reviewing your interband agreement will usually take one hour. On the other hand, something like a lawsuit for copyright violation will cost several thousand dollars and require a hefty retainer. Some attorneys will work *pro bono* if it is a good cause or if they can earn a percentage of the outcome later.

When to Hire an Entertainment Lawyer: First, determine how much legal work you need done. If you find that you have a lot of legal issues going on (contracts, copyrights, or scandals), you might want to consider hiring an attorney on retainer (a regular monthly rate). If you only have projects once in a while, find one who understands your needs and budget. Lawyers have their specialties and focus areas, so find one appropriate for your situation. Usually, a firm with a focus on entertainment law will have everything that you need.

The Consultant

In the music industry, a consultant is a specialist that you can talk to who will give you specific advice about the music industry, introduce you to valuable contacts or resources, or even fill-in for one of the other music roles listed above (depending on their specialty). Many music consultants have years of experience in the industry and will charge an hourly rate (average of $50-$150 per hour) to provide these services to you. Sometimes, it is less expensive to hire a consultant than a full-time manager, booking agent, or lawyer, especially if you have a pretty good understanding of these concepts on your own. Sometimes, managers or other industry professionals will seek the advice of a consultant with greater experience as well. Finally, there are also songwriting consultants that specialize in music theory, production, lyric-writing, etc. Whatever are of your career that you need help with, you can usually find someone willing to consult.

When to Hire a Consultant: A consultant is often a great person to turn to when you're beginning a new project or when you feel like you are in a rut. A consultant can also be a great person to turn to when you need outside, objective opinions, especially to help answer the tough questions that you might have.

Others

There are many other people that you can consider hiring or asking to help with your band, depending on the need. It might be for a specialized skill or talent (which usually requires more payment or favors), but it could also involve getting some general help as well. Here's a list of some of the people you might consider bringing on board:

- Hired musicians/additional instruments
- Road crew
- Photographer or videographer
- Live sound technician
- Producer
- Audio engineer
- Graphic designer
- Merchandise seller
- Marketer
- Writer
- Web designer
- Driver
- Music instrument technician (guitar, drums, etc.)
- Vocal coach
- Choreographer
- Sponsorship/endorsement procurer

The list can certainly go on.

As you can see, there's a huge variety in the skills needed in a band or touring performing arts organization. As you build your team or recruit people for your band, consider people who have multiple skillsets who might be able to tackle some of the basic needs for the band as a business. Not only does it make the workload easier when it is shared, but it also means less people that you'll have to turn to outside of the band as well. If you're investing into long-term music project or band, you might even consider taking specific classes to improve upon any needed skills for the band. It could be a formal study (for example, through a local community college or technical school), or independent, informal study (books, videos, mentors). Either way, it's important to consider these needs when looking at the band.

When to Hire Other Help for Your Band: With limited resources, it's important to sort out the needs of the band and what kind of skills/talent you have in the group in light of your overall goals. For one-time needs, you might be able to trade a favor in return for the service. Sometimes, you can get someone with a lot of potential who is willing to donate their skills in order to use the project for a future work portfolio. Other times, you just have contacts or friends of the band who are happy to help. But whether the work is for hire or being donated, things should always be done with the expectations spelled out in advance and the quality/delivery should be consistent with your overall band's efforts.

Activity 1: Figure Out the Need

Look at your next big goals, projects, or efforts and begin compiling a list of needs. Start detailing out any expenses that you think you'll run into for the things that you want to accomplish. Then, prioritize that list based on the importance of each phase of your project and see if you have some room in your budget to hire out the work. Some people, such as the band manager or booking agent, will actually help you increase your income. Others, like an entertainment lawyer will help protect your assets. It's much easier to figure out who to hire next once you've had a chance to look at your objectives, budgets, and resources first.

Activity 2: Get Ready to Hire

While some industry contacts are more difficult to get on board than others, it's important to remember: you are hiring them to do the job. Even if they are in high demand for their abilities, you're still the one paying them so it's important set the expectations and keep them accountable for their work. Whether you have someone in mind or not, take a moment to write a job description for the role that you'd like to hire for. What skills or qualifications should they posses? What are they going to be responsible for and how will you measure success? Also, even if you know the person, there should be a written agreement in place so that both parties can refer to it when expectations or roles are unclear.

Activity 3: Search for the Right Talent

In some ways, you'll want to treat the search for hiring a band manager, booking agent, publicist, etc. like you would hiring an employee for any organization. You can post job notices in music industry publications, ask mutual contacts for referrals, and use sites like Linkedin. You can also use search engines to find reputable organizations or people to help. Sometimes, you get what you pay for so don't be afraid to invest in talent with a proven history of success. However, many industry professionals also like to tout their past credentials to get a higher pay rate so don't be afraid to get multiple bids in order to find a competitive price. Finally, you might not be ready to hire for any of these positions yet but it's a good idea to monitor the landscape so that you get to know who the key players are, who is on your "wish list" of people to work with, and to learn who you should avoid.

14. Go Over Your Interband Agreement

An interband agreement is one of the most important documents in your band. However, it is one of the most overlooked or forgotten about. Essentially, it is the contract that binds your band together and addresses things like money, responsibilities, and conflict resolution. It's also something that should be examined on a regular basis. Think of it like your band's constitution: it should be a living document that stresses the main priorities, but it should also be flexible to accommodate for growth or change.

When creating an agreement, it's important to set realistic expectations over each other's duties as well as having a plan on how money, responsibilities, debts, and things will be divided. What if some band members believe that merch should only be sold to bring in income but others believe some things should be given out to promote the band? What if someone has a lot of friends and takes up all of the guest list spots? Who will handle social media and promotion? Some simple communication, especially things in writing, can save a lot of heartache on the road.

Activity 1: Create an Interband Agreement

If you don't have an interband agreement, you should definitely begin working on one immediately. It's also recommended that after you draft one up, that you have an attorney look it over as well. There are many templates available online. If you'd like to see the one I created, use this link: http://bit.ly/1I31Acc or look in the appendix.

A few tips/things to keep in mind:

- Think of this in terms of a best case scenario/worst case scenario. If you make a lot of money, how would you want that distributed? If you lose a lot of money or need to do a lot of work, how will that be divided?

- Who "owns" the band name? If the band members part ways, who gets to keep using the name?

- How will you divide up credit for songs and artwork? What about shared property like a band bus or PA system?

Activity 2: Review the Agreement

If you already have an agreement in place, it might be a good idea to revisit it. Compare it with other templates or versions of the agreement online (or maybe with other bands that you know). Is it addressing your needs? Is everyone in the band being held accountable for things that you all agreed on? Has there been a lineup change?

15. Put Timers on Your Contracts/Agreements

It's easy to fall into the routine of scrolling past terms and conditions agreements without thinking much about them. However, they can often affect the future of your music, where it can be released, who controls it, and how it can be distributed. For example, a licensing agreement can change how future revenues are received (or waive future royalties entirely); a contract with one distributor might limit future opportunities with another; some sponsorship agreements will bind you/your band members to one specific type of product. These are all instances when you are limited by the choices made without full consideration of long-term effects.

Many contracts have expiration dates and/or auto-renewals. While these kinds of terms make the flow of services consistent, they can also be tricky to get out of if you don't contact the party within a certain window of time. Also, keep in mind that these clauses are designed to benefit the service provider so that they can continually receive business. For example, I once signed a digital distribution deal years ago that was a three year contract. In order to cancel the contract, I had to submit a written request 30 days before the expiration - otherwise, it would renew for another three years. That could easily be a six year agreement that would block me from changing distributors or accepting opportunities from a service with a better fit.

There are also a few other reasons to mind the expiration dates of contracts. For example, some contract providers (such as licensing agencies) have non-exclusive agreements. However, if you want to switch to an exclusive service, you'll have to cancel those agreements first.

In general, you should make it a habit to save copies of each agreement so that you can be aware of these restrictions. You might even consider having a lawyer look over the agreement as well. The longer or more complex the agreement, the more likely you should have a lawyer involved.

Activity 1: Create a File for All of Your Contracts and Review Their Dates

You should have written/printed copies of every agreement you make on behalf of your music: licensing deals, distribution, recording contracts, etc. However, you should also have the cancellation clause, auto-renewal terms, and expiration date highlighted in every agreement. If you don't have the contracts in a readily accessible place, take a few minutes out to print out copies of your agreements. I also recommend scanning these and keeping pdf copies in your digital records as well. As you look up the expiration and renewal dates, set a reminder for each one in your calendaring system so you can review agreements and decide if you want to continue them or not.

There's another reason for this as well: sometimes, you want something to be renewed every year but you need to reapply for it (such as a sponsorship or roster position). Setting an annual reminder to review and prepare for the application process will keep you ahead of the game so that you can submit things on a timely basis without being rushed last minute - or worse, miss a deadline entirely.

16. Perfecting Your Band's Pitch

If you were presented with the opportunity to pitch your band directly to the Chief A&R representative for Capitol Records, what would you say? If there was a venture capitalist looking to invest significant money into an artist, how would you convince them to choose you? If your favorite band was in town and looking for an opener, what would you tell the promoter about your act?

Being able to pitch your band is one of the most important skills, if not the most important skill, that you'll need to get anywhere in the music industry. Knowing how to "sell" your band will help you book shows, secure sponsorships, get a booking agent or manager, receive media attention, and snag a record deal. The right pitch can sometimes help you get into an otherwise-closed door, such as catching the attention of someone who is not accepting submissions. The wrong pitch will have someone shut you out before you even have a chance to showcase your music or any of your other selling points.

The pitch is also something that should be honed and refined over time, as you accomplish more or have a better grasp on your niche. I receive at least 100 pitches and EPK's per week (sometimes upwards of 300-400) but sadly, most of them end up sounding the same. Artists almost always describe themselves as "unique," "hardworking," and/or having "great music" but they don't actually say how or why so it comes across as generic and thoughtless.

Here are some tips on how you can pitch your music and stand out from the crowd:

- **Understand Your Niche:** If what your uniqueness sounds like every other band's description of unique, then you've got a problem. What can you brag about that no one else can? If you need some help with the process, try using 15secondpitch.com - it's a free service. Remember, craft a pitch in a way that is easy to remember and for others to connect to. Don't list obscure artist influences, etc.

- **Choose Wisely:** Don't use the same pitch for every person. What appeals to a potential sponsor is going to be different than a booking agent. Think about your objective and shape your pitch around the target. If you are sending the same one page bio to the radio station as a record label, opportunities to really sell your act will be lost. Each person has different motivations and interests - your pitch should appeal to them.

- **Do Your Homework:** Find out as much as you can about the person you are contacting. Address them by name. What kinds of bands do they enjoy working with? What's their past career experience been like? How can you connect to them better?

- **Keep it Short:** We live in a microwave society, everyone wants you to get to the point quickly. If you can't explain why someone should book you, why you are different, or why your music is a good investment in 3 sentences or less, it is unlikely that you'll get any further. Remember, the point of a pitch isn't to get you a show, a label deal, or a sponsor. The point of a pitch is to create enough interest for them to want more

information so you get future, deeper conversations about the
deal you want.

- **How Short?:** If the entire email is less than two paragraphs,
  you'll be fine. Less is better - if you can condense your pitch to
  one sentence, that is ideal. Measure every word and see if it is
  necessary. Does every sentence serve to entice them to want
  more information? Just as pop music has an optimum song
  length of 3:30 for radio, there's an optimum email length too.
  However, those pop songs are filled end-to-end with
  memorable hooks. Do the same. By the end of the email, you
  want that recipient singing your praises too!

- **Spit It Out:** Be sure to include your objective - in fact, start
  with it. Many of the messages I receive from bands include
  only a bio and some links. They don't say if they're looking for
  an agent, a manager, or if they just want consulting. It just
  looks generic and I can't figure out what they want. Make it
  easy on them, tell them what you are looking for, even if it's
  just a request for a short phone call.

- **Don't Forget:** Include your links, contact information, and
  give them a reason to call you or respond. If there's something
  of value that you can offer, it's more enticing for them to
  follow up with you.

Activity 1: Update Your Description

How do you describe your band? If you shared it with someone
once, could they memorize and repeat it easily? Could that description
fit in a tweet? If not, you might want to find a more succinct, catchy
descriptor for your music that has a stronger impact. How would your
biggest fans describe you? You might consider having each person in
your band write out 5-10 short descriptions each and select the best

one from the list. Don't pick one unless you have at least 25 different options to choose from.

Activity 2: Improve Your Ask

Pull up several of your key emails that you send on a frequent basis: the message you use to book shows, the email when you're interested in a label/manager/booking agent, etc., the letter you write to press who you hope will review your album, and the one you send to potential sponsors.

Answer the following:

- Is your pitch so unique to you that if you removed the band's name, they would still be able to figure out who is being described? Or could they substitute another artist in and it would still work?

- If you had limited time/resources, would you invest in you after reading that email? Or would you rather go with a "safe bet" from an established artist that you already know instead?

- If you showed it to a stranger, would they know exactly what you were looking for if they only read the first two lines?

- Have you tried reading the email on a smartphone?

- When was the last time that you updated the message?

Think carefully on each of these and see if there are ways to improve these messages. If there are, then that means it isn't the best possible ask that you could send. And if it isn't the best, you should ask yourself, why?

17. Increase Your Email Open and Response Rate

Despite all of the hype and attention on social media, the majority of business communication is still done through email. From introductions to pitches and proposals, chances are that your initial impression with someone will often be through this medium. Despite the importance of this system, few really take the time to learn it well in order to get better results.

Here are seven tips for improving your email open and response rates:

1. **State what you want, clearly and succinctly, in the first sentence, not the last.** After you state your goal, request or question, explain further. You hardly ever need to begin with context or an introduction. If you are emailing someone you don't know well, they're trying to figure out what you want as quickly as possible. In fact, the longer of an introduction that you have, the more likely the recipient will get frustrated or bored of reading your message first.

2. **Have a specific call to action.** It may seem obvious, but you

should have a specific next step or goal that you are looking for. In one sentence, you should be able to answer the question, "What do you want?" Do you want them to click somewhere, book your show, call you, answer a question, etc.? Then say so, directly.

3. **Write and rewrite the subject.** Websites like Upworthy write their headlines at least 25 times before publishing a story -- and it obviously works. Take time to keep subject lines interesting, short, and keep it free of spam triggering words such as "free" or "incredible offer."

4. **Test it on a mobile device.** The numbers say that more than ever before, we're reading messages on mobile devices like smartphones and tablets. This number will only increase. If you have an especially important email, then it's certainly worth your time testing the message on these devices first. This is another reason why the message should be as succinct as possible.

5. **Check who the message is going to.** This is another one that sounds obvious, but it is something that nearly everyone is guilty of. Email providers make things easy these days by having an auto-complete feature that will tag your frequent contacts. However, it's easy for things to be sent to the wrong recipient. Then, there's always the people who forget about the difference between "reply" and "reply all." Check the address: a misplaced period or letter can derail your efforts.

6. **End with a question.** I often like to finish emails with a simple question, especially one that can be answered in just a few words. Psychologically, it prompts a response from the recipient. The easier it is for them to answer, take action or address your need, the better. Sometimes, it can just reiterate the opening sentence.

7. **Read twice, send once.** There's an old carpentry adage that says, "Measure twice, cut once." It was intended to prevent costly and unnecessary mistakes. In the world of business communication, it can cost you the chance to make a good impression or even have your email address flagged for spam. Use a spellchecker. Check your links. If it's an important email, surely it warrants a second read.

These tips aren't exactly groundbreaking, nor are they particular to email. However, these basic principles are ignored all the time. As the world is becoming busier and more connected, we seem to have less and less time to be bothered with email messages that are long, boring, confusing or unclear with their intent. The easiest way to cut through the noise is to remove it from your own messaging. A little consideration in your email can go a long way -- certainly, much further than a long message can.

Activity 1: Dump the Traditional Auto-Reply

If you're using an auto-reply on any of your email boxes, whether it is an out of office message, something that lets recipients know that their message has been received, or a thank you when someone signs up on your email list, give the recipient something of worth or don't use the message at all. Chances are, you find these kinds of messages annoying (or certainly useless), so don't inflict the same thing on others. If you must use one, at least offer up a free mp3, a discount code for your online store, or something that will give them a laugh.

Activity 2: Slow Down Your Process with Mail Goggles

One way make ensure that you write the best emails is to slow down your process. If you are using Gmail, you can install a program called "Mail Goggles" which was originally designed to prevent users from sending emails that they'd later regret. It forces you to solve some simple math problems before the email is actually sent. By default, it turns on during late nights and weekends (a time where many might need it from being tired or drunk), but you can adjust the settings to keep it on - at least until you learn to read over your messages a few times before hitting send.

18. Book a Tour

Most artists who book their own shows have a general idea of how to book a tour but either lack the confidence or the initiative to do so. After all, it's very much like booking a single gig, multiplied by how many shows you want to do. However, there are some important questions that every artist needs to consider:

- **Why Do you Want to Tour?**
  What's the purpose of your tour? Is it to promote a new album? Get more exposure? To make money? Is it for fun? These are all acceptable answers, but it's important for everyone in the band to be on the same page so that expectations or attitude will be similar for what you'd like accomplished.

- **Where Do You Want to Tour?**
  What markets do you want to play in and why? Will playing shows in those markets help you work toward your S.M.A.R.T.E.R goals (Section 1, Chapter 9)? Don't just assume that larger cities will be better simply because more people live there - it's actually easier to have an empty show in a city of 3 million than a city of 30,000.

- **When Do You Want to Tour?**

  Is it the right time for you to be touring? When it comes to touring, timing is important. You have to consider a number of things. One of the more important things includes timing your tour with a benchmark event: new release, music video, major press/radio campaign, major music festival appearance or showcase, etc. If it's winter, you might not be able to drive in certain locations due to severe weather. In the summer, gas tends to be more expensive and college students are out. You also need to decide if you can afford to tour at all.

Once you have the big questions answered, you can begin by going through the next sections step-by-step.

1. Create a Budget

Touring can be very expensive, especially if you are not at a point where you can get some major guarantees. Plan your budget, but also include some emergency savings in case things go awry: tire blowouts and transmission fails do occur on tour. There's nothing worse than being stranded thousands of miles away from home with your gear and no money and no way to get back. Do you need to raise money in advance? You might need to launch a crowdfunding campaign or look for sponsors to help pay the expenses of touring.

2. Decide on a Date Range

I strongly recommend that you plan, at minimum, 4-6 months in advance. Booking a tour requires months of contacting promoters, follow-up work, and filling in gaps. Some venues book at least 6 months out in advance, some only one month at a time. You'll also need plenty of time to market, promote, and contact local press.

3. Choose a Route

After you decide if and when you can tour, decide where you'd like to go. I always believe in gradually expanding your reach: create a buzz in your city first, then the state, then your region. Slowly expand the radius of where you're doing shows by a few hundred miles each time you go out and build some new fans. Decide where you can go but keep a few things in mind:

- **Big Cities or Small Towns**: It's easy to just think in terms of large metropolitan areas but there are downsides to this as well. There's more competition with other bands/shows going on at the same time in the city, they tend to pay less (and won't provide guarantees if you don't have a solid draw), and venues tend to be more reluctant to book unfamiliar acts. However, larger cities have more opportunities for press: weeklies, dailies, radio stations, and TV shows. If you have a publicist or PR firm working these avenues, it can make your band look very good.

- **Your Fans**: Thanks to the insight tools of nearly every social media site, you can easily get a picture where your fans are. Search by city or zip code - if you don't have the data, try asking your fans directly to see where they'd like to see you play.

- **Towards the "Big Event"**: I get more requests for a "SXSW tour" than anything else. Touring there can be great: venues are more receptive towards touring acts at that time, many cities have their own music festivals before or after, and there's plenty going on outside of Austin. The downside is that no matter where you play, it will probably be on a bill full of touring acts rather than strong locals…so there's less of a chance for you to get the exposure you need.

- **An Anchor**: If you've received an offer for a large, well-paying show (such as a festival, college, or convention), you could anchor your tour around it by booking to and from that show.

- **How Large of a Venue?**: If you have never played a city before and have little to no serious press on you, don't contact the largest venues in town. It's a waste of time. Instead, realistically determine your career level and decide if you are more fit to play small rooms (100-200 capacity), medium sized venues (200-600), or larger.

4. Start Booking Venues

Begin looking for venues along your tour route. Websites like indieonthemove.com, byofl.org, and onlinegigs.com are free, searchable databases. You can also buy more details (and sometimes reliable) information from Billboard Music (they offer a touring guide for about $20), The Indie Venue Bible (about $100), and more. Most promoters prefer email. Some use social media or EPK submission sites like ReverbNation or Sonicbids, some use the phone, some have their own contact form. Whatever it is, find out their preference and stick to it.

Don't use one generic message or method (nobody likes spam). If you have a standard booking pitch, be sure to customize it with their venue, contact name, and the proper date.

Always answer the question on *their* mind: How will you make the venue money? How will you bring people in the door? No venue cares about how "good" your show is if you'll be playing for an empty room. Nearly every venue would rather hire a solid local band that can sell the place out over a touring band that can't even fill up their guest list.

5. Follow Up With Venues and Promoters

Most promoters are inundated with messages and are constantly juggling dates, bands, rentals, and other events. Get a confirmation, make sure that you are on their website. Check in to see if they want posters mailed to them, see if there are local media contacts you should be following up with. If a promoter gave you a "hold," find out what you need to make it a confirmed show. Follow-up again one more time before you leave for tour.

6. Filling in the Gaps

If a show doesn't pan out and you want to fill the date, start thinking creatively. You can contact nearby towns or check Craigslist to see if someone wants live music for their party or corporate event. If you're out of venues, try doing a search on Yelp or Google Maps for "live music." Contact local radio stations, morning news shows, record shops, bookstores, skate shops, church groups, roller skate arenas, restaurants, malls, any place where you might make a good fit. Hot Topic used to allow touring bands to do an acoustic set (some stores still do). Ask your friends/fans in the area if they want to do a house party. Or, begin contacting all of the venues you already reached out to and see if something opened up. Get in touch with bands in the area to see if they can help do a gig-swap.

The most important thing to remember is that this takes patience, consistency, follow-up, and a little bit of salesmanship. Keep at it everyday. Set up an appointment with yourself to contact venues, promoters, etc. for at least 1-2 hours per day (and more as you get closer). Never miss that appointment.

Activity 1: Write Your Tour Business Plan

The most important step for booking a tour is preparation. You want to have a clear goal in mind, a budget, a contingency plan, a measurement for success, and post-tour plan. By creating and sticking to a well-thought out plan, the tour moves from being an assortment of distant shows to being a strategic part of your band's career. Also, a plan can better help set expectations for your band members and to decide who is going to be responsible for what - that way, the burden isn't carried solely by the band leader.

These are the elements that you want to include:

- A mission/purpose for the tour
- Budget for the tour
- Market research - which markets are you playing and why
- Pre-tour work: finding sponsors or funding, booking, etc.
- Promotional plan
- Duties of each person helping with the tour (promotion, social media, driving schedule, merchandise sales, etc.)
- Expected outcome
- Post-tour plan (how you will leverage the tour)

Activity 2: Create a Detailed Budget

Any major endeavor should always include a detailed budget so you know how much to save for, determine the return on investment, and forecast any worst-case scenarios. A detailed budget should include the following:

Major Expenses
- Transportation - Vehicle purchase or rental, maintenance, and fuel. Determine the total number of miles and multiply by cost

per mile to help figure out the fuel costs. For example, $0.55/mile for a 2,000 mile tour = $1,100 in gas
- Accommodations - If you plan on staying in hotels, this can add up quickly
- Food - Create a food budget and stick to it. If you can get venues to provide meals, that can help save you quite a bit of money.
- Promotion - If you are hiring a publicist, printing/mailing posters, advertising, etc.
- Management or booking fees

Minor Expenses
- Toll fees - Use Google Maps to see if you'll run into tolls
- State Taxes - Some larger events (conventions, festivals, etc.) require you to obtain a state retailer's permit and pay taxes on any goods sold
- Parking - Parking fees are often levied in the city for larger cities or overnight at some hotels

Personal Expenses
- Strings, picks, drumsticks, or other equipment
- Clothing, sleeping bag, luggage, or other personal items
- Souvenir or sightseeing money

Once you detail the costs, project how much money will be coming in. You should create a best, a worst, and most likely scenario so that you have a good idea of what cash inflows can look like against your budget. You should include:

- Income from shows (guarantees, est. ticket sales, % of door or bar sales, etc.)
- Estimated merchandise sales
- Money from sponsorships, investors, donors, or crowdsourcing
- Money from busking or other activities (if you plan on doing so)

- Freelance money (if you will be working while on tour)
- Any other regular, dependable income that you receive (online sales, licensing, royalties, etc.).

Your budget will help you think of new ways to find income, areas where you can reduce expenses, prepare fiscal exoectations for the tour, and most of all, help determine your return on investment (ROI). Not everyone measures ROI solely on financials - you might still think it's worth it if it helps reach other goals, such as an increased fan base, performing at a specific event, personal fulfillment, etc.). Either way, you'll want a clear picture going in ahead of time.

Activity 3: Set a Booking Schedule

If you are booking a tour, you need to set aside at least one hour per day dedicated solely to booking (perhaps more if you don't have an extensive tour history). Set an appointment for yourself and keep it.

That time should be used for researching venues, sending emails, making phone calls, and updating your tour schedule accordingly.

You can get more detailed by setting goals for yourself: how many shows would you liked to be confirmed before X date, when your tour booking cutoff will be (if any), or confirming shows with X dollar amount for guarantees.

Activity 4: Create a Tour Booking Spreadsheet

If you create a document to help organize your booking process or list of confirmed dates, you will have a tool to show you the work that is left to do. When the sheet is completed, it can also serve as your band's tour itinerary - where you are playing, the details of each show, driving times between shows, etc.

A very simple version can look like this:

DATE	CITY, STATE	VENUE	DISTANCE TO NEXT SHOW	COMPENSATION	NOTES	LODGING
08/20 TUE						
08/21 WED						
08/22 THU						
08/23 FRI	Rockville, MD					
08/24 SAT	Breingsville, PA					
08/25 SUN	New York, NY					
8/26 MON	Philadelphia, PA					
8/27 TUE	Richmond, VA or Baltimore, MD, Washington, DC					

I also like to color-code my booking spreadsheets. It gives me a quick visual reading on the status of a tour:

- White - Nothing confirmed yet, but it is still 4+ months away (I usually use the "Notes" field to keep a record of who I contacted/when/any responses)
- Red: High priority - No show has been confirmed yet and it is less than 3 months away
- Yellow: A soft confirmation or hold
- Green: Confirmed show

Each person has their own preferences, you might find creating other fields will suit you better. Whatever you like, just be sure to have something that helps you stay on track.

19. The Ultimate Guide to Merchandise

These days, merchandise sales make up a pretty big portion of most touring acts' income. The staples of CD's, shirts, and stickers have become even more important as income from performing has gradually dropped. There are many tips out there of what bands should order and how they should sell their products, but there doesn't seem to be much on how to get the best possible pricing from vendors, how to calculate prices, or how much product should be ordered before a tour. This simple guide will save you money up front as well as help you earn more.

What You Should Order and Who You Should Order From

Your band's product mix should include a variety of items, with an emphasis on items that either have a good profit margin, help promote your band, or deepen the relationship with your fans.

The standard band mix of products should include:

- **Music** - CDs are generally the best option for most artists because fans like having something tangible that they can take home (as opposed to a digital download) and take up less room than vinyl. They also have higher profit margins. While many companies offer replication services, they aren't all created equal. Shop around and get quotes. If possible, ask for samples so that you can inspect the quality of cases, printing, and labeling.

Digital downloads are also another option. If you decide to not produce CDs, you should at least have download cards at shows so that people can still buy some of your music. Most artists have a harder time selling download cards than CDs, but they do offer higher profit margins and don't require a large upfront investment. Finally, you can also order custom USB thumb drives which can be pre-loaded with your music as well. That way, it can also double up for other purposes as well.

Viable, but often riskier choice.

- **T-Shirts** - The basic tee usually is a solid product to go with. You can usually get a better price and a more comfy product if you choose a lighter shirt, such as a Gildan 5.3 or 5.6 oz. While it's nice to have an assortment of designs, that requires more inventory management and higher investment for shirts (increased costs).

- **Stickers** - Stickers are cheap, easy to produce, and can be used for promotion or selling. When possible, order weather-proof vinyl stickers as opposed to paper ones. Most companies will make you order a minimum of 1,000. Some let you order smaller batches of 250 or 500.

- **Buttons** - These are another easy, cheap product that you can sell for $1 each. The most popular size and type is the 1" round button. These days, you can order larger buttons or get custom shapes as well. You might also consider ordering a button maker, which pays for itself fairly quickly.

- **Posters** - These are a staple. If you want a larger print, most printings companies will give you a 12x18 poster for the same price as an 11x17. But most of the time, an 11x17 on a heavy gloss print is standard.

There are many other options out there and I do recommend that you explore custom merchandise, but it's important to balance the "cool" factor of having variety with what actually sells and what you can make money on. These are other common products:

- **Bracelets/Wrist wear** - The most price effective bracelets are made of silicone. These can be imprinted with a limited number of fonts but are inexpensive and can come individually wrapped. Leather bracelets tend to be more expensive but are usually available in limited runs. Other popular options include slap bracelets, watches, charms, sweat bands, and nylon.

- **Shot glasses** - Shot glasses come in multiple shapes and sizes. They are easy to have custom screened so you can have your logo imprinted at a very reasonable price. They are tough to transport on tour though, so it's important to pack them carefully.

- **Beaniea/hats** - Beanies are generally less expensive than baseball caps and trucker hats. The appropriate style should reflect what your fans are most interested in.

- **Dog tags** - Metal dog tags are easy to make necklaces out of and some companies allow you to get a custom laser imprint for a logo as well. They go well with ball chain necklaces, which can be order in bulk and used for a variety of things.

- **Other** - If you want something really special, you'll want to get someone who specializes in custom work. If you can imagine your logo on it, it is probably possible. Just remember to carefully think about the available demand, any minimum orders, and the pricing.

How to Get Better Pricing From Suppliers

The internet makes it easy to shop for pricing because many vendors have prices published. However, there is almost always a local business who would like to earn your business as well - one who can offer better pricing, quality, service, or payment terms - if you know how to ask.

Here are some tips on how to get better prices for your merchandise:

- **Shop Around** - Take your time to compare pricing from multiple companies. Consider quality, minimum amounts ordered, payment plans, and additional costs that might not reflect the quote (screen charges, shipping, etc.). The internet is great for this!

- **Ask For a Better Price** - Most companies want your business and can work with you on your budget. If you find a better price elsewhere, they'll often meet it or throw in some incentives (free design work, waive screen charges, etc.). Often, they'll ask you to show proof of the lower price, so be ready with the quote.

- **Ask About Leftover Stock** - Many companies order large quantities of product to get a lower price but will have an assortment of odd sizes or colors at the end. Sometimes, you can get a great deal by asking for assorted clearance stock that can take the same design. The colors and sizes might not always match, but you can certainly get a great deal. You can pass the savings onto your fans.

- **Begin a Partnership** - Like getting a sponsor, you can find a long term relationship where you are both vested into the relationship. For example, I worked with a local vendor to get exceptional pricing and payment terms by committing to a long-term partnership. I agreed to always consider them first when pricing out options and to order a certain amount of business from them each year. In return, I get the best pricing around as well as net 45 day payment terms. In other words, payment for the products aren't due until 45 days after I pick them up. It's perfect when I don't have any available cash before I leave for a tour because I can pay for the merchandise when I get back - and most of the time, after I've already sold the products.

- **Order in bulk** - Most of the time, you start saving money on shirts when you order at least 48 of them at a time. With stickers, it's 250 (or 1,000 for full color). With buttons, it's usually 100. Get to know the optimal amounts to order so that you can save money. If you want to balance price per item and minimum quantities, talk to a sales representative from your vendor and see if they'd be willing to cut you a break by combining your order with someone else's (they get discount when more supplies can be order at once).

- **Order less designs** - If you reduce the number of different designs, you can order higher quantities of each product. This in turn drives down the price per unit. Variety is good but often gives you a much higher start up cost.

How Much You Should Sell Your Merchandise For

There are a few different camps on this one. Some people believe that you should offer your products up for a suggested donation; others believe in having set prices. How much do you want to make off of your merchandise? Is it more important for you to have more cash in hand or products in the hands of your fans?

If you want to run your band like a business, then you'll want to calculate things like ROI (return on investment), profit margin, turnover (how quickly the product sells), and keep track of your inventory. Translating that to the band world would look like this:

- **Return on Investment (ROI)** - This is how much would you make if you sold all of that product at your asking price subtracted by the total cost for ordering that merchandise. For example, if you had 100 shirts sold them for $20 each but they cost $5 each, your return on investment would be $1,500 ($20 - $5 x 100 = $1,500). To calculate the return on investment of your entire inventory, you would do the same calculation for each item, then add it altogether.

- **Profit Margin** - This is a percentage of how much you make per item. If a shirt cost you $5 and you sell it for $20, that's a profit margin of 75%. Every business has a mix of products that bring in different profit margins. The more items that you have with high profit margins, the more money you'll make (and the less upfront costs you'll incur). I recommend selling products in the 40-60% range. Try to avoid carrying too many items that have a very low profit margin because they tend to be more expensive and take longer to see a return.

- **Turnover/Turns** - Turns measure how fast you "turnover" your inventory. This number is usually measured annually, but this could also be a monthly number. For example, if you ordered 100 shirts at a time and sold 500 in one year, that would be a turnover of 5. The higher the number, the better. If you sit on some products for a very long time, that means that aren't making back the money it cost to make them in the first place.

- **Inventory** - Before ordering any merchandise, you should know exactly how much you have. It's important to break things down by size/color as well so you know which items move more quickly. Sometimes, inventory can be hard to track while on tour so it's recommended that you keep a running total on paper (or through a program like Square Register). If you keep a regular inventory, you'll know which sizes and designs sell faster than others, allowing you to be more accurate with product that moves.

As a general rule of thumb, you should have something in your interband agreement (Section 1, Chapter 14) about merchandise policies: who pays the for it in advance, how people get paid back, who is able to take/give away merch, and what terms are involved with that. Some band members sell merchandise to family and friends, others give it away. It's best to have an agreement in writing about how much merch can be used for promotion, how much is to be given to friends, or how much should be donated for charitable reasons. If you do decide to give some merchandise away, that should be factored into your costs and return on investment.

Once you have these important numbers calculated, you can determine the appropriate prices for your merchandise. It's better to calculate your selling price after figuring out your profit margin rather than simply selling an item for a price based on what others are selling their goods for. If you only compete on price, you won't be able to create a sustainable competitive advantage.

However, for general reference, this is how much I typically sell merchandise for at my shows:

CD - $12
Shirt - $15-20 (depending on design/type)
Hoodie - $3-45
Poster - $3
Sticker or Button - $1
Necklace - $5
Cell phone charm/Earrings - $3
Bracelet - $3
Water bottle - $8
Shot glass - $5
Lighter - $10

Finally, you can offer combination packages or specials in order to give a better value to fans. For example, I often offer a combination pack of a cd, shirt, poster, bracelet, sticker, and button for $25-30. Combination packages and specials also help steer fans towards buying more to get the better value as well. If you do sell in packages, keep track of how many you sell, as this will affect your return on investment, profit margin, and turnover rates as well.

How to Sell More Merchandise

In addition to making more on each piece of merchandise, you'll want to find ways to increase the overall quantity of merchandise sold (the turnover rate). Here are some tips on how you can sell more albums, shirts, and other items:

- **Focus on Quality and Design** - If you want to sell more, you have to give fans something worth owning. Sometimes, it's worth the extra cost of hiring a graphic designer to get more professional looking designs.

- **Get a Better Display** - Your merch setup should be easy to see, organized, clean, and in a prominent location in the venue. Invest in a decent display-it can go a long way. Buy some portable lights to help illuminate the merchandise as well, as many clubs are dark inside. Also, learn how to fold a shirt properly.

- **Accept Credit Cards** - Many companies offer convenient credit card processing services that can be used on a smartphone or tablet device. Each of these companies charge a small percentage of the overall sale, usually 3-5%. However, as it is becoming increasingly uncommon for people to carry cash, this ensures that you don't have to turn anyone who is interested in buying merchandise away. The two most popular companies who offer this service are Square and PayPal.

- **Man the Table** - Having the full band at the table makes a huge difference, especially if they have friends coming out to see the show who want to talk. Make the merch area the place to hang out. The more activity that is there, the more it will attract others to pay a visit.

- **Offer an Incentive** - You can give away low-cost items (sticker, poster, button) for the purchase a higher-ticket item like a shirt or CD, or combine it in a sales package.

- **Announce it** - When you're playing, let people know you have merch and where they can find you. In fact, you'll want to mention that you have merchandise available at least two or three times during a show, since people aren't always paying attention to chatter between sets.

- **Promote it Ahead of Time** - You can build up excitement about new merch by talking about it in your e-newsletter or social media sites. Get fans involved: ask for design ideas, favorite designs, and requested types of merch. You can also hold a contest where fans can submit potential new designs.

- **Out With the Old** - Give special pricing to older designs that you're trying to get rid of. Not only do older designs or odd sizes move more slowly, but they can take up room in your merchandise bins as well. Try to bring attention to older merchandise with special signage and/or pricing.

Supplies Every Merch Bin Should Have

In addition to the obvious (merchandise), your merch bin should have a number of things to help you create an attractive display, have some basic supplies to hang merchandise, and solve basic problems that might come up during a show. Here is a recommended list of items:

- A large vinyl banner with grommets
- Portable LED lights (battery powered)
- Powered lights or lamp and extension cord
- A locking cash box with plenty of change
- Binder clips and hangers for shirts
- A roll each of painter's tape, duct tape, and packaging tape
- Markers and pens
- Display equipment (folding shelves, CD display, grid walls, etc.)
- Blank sheets of paper
- Price tags and/or laminated signs
- Mailing list signup
- Extra credit card readers
- Scissors, pliers, and a basic tool set
- Table Cloth
- A set of bed sheets (to cover the table when you are away)
- Rubber bands, thumb tacks, and safety pins
- Hand sanitizer or handy wipes (some venues are gross)

Less Common Items Every Musician Should Own

In addition to the common set of supplies, these are some helpful items to have that will make life easier if you spend quite a bit of time on the road.

- **Laminator** - Laminators are pretty inexpensive, easy to use, and are very handy. If you need laminated items, these pay for themselves very quickly. With a laminator, you can create your very own tour ID placards, price tags, price sheets, and displays. In my band, I create tour badges for everyone in the band so they know the our day-to-day tour route. It also looks more professional because our crew members can be quickly identified.

- **Button maker** - A button maker helps increase profits because you can create your own merchandise. If you print out sheets of buttons in advance, you can make buttons during the longer drives of a tour, so that you'll always be fully stocked.

- **Silk Screen Press** - A silk screen press is useful for creating limited runs of merchandise, printing your own shirts, or getting your designs on almost anything. Some bands use these to put their logo on the screens of their guitar cabinets. In fact, with the right supplies, you can just create your own press.

- **Rolling Tool chest** - It's always easier to move things around when they are on wheels. Rather than using plastic tote bins, I recommend picking up a rolling tool chest to carry any merchandise and supplies. The model I recommend is a Stanley 29-⅞", 24 gallon mobile tool chest. It's large enough to fit most of our things, plus it can also double as a stage riser or merch table as well. It makes loading out much faster.

- **Projector** - You can make a dramatic merch display in a dark venue. A less expensive option is finding a slide projector and having your logo or backdrop made as a slide. Slide projectors are far less expensive than digital projectors and don't require a laptop or tablet to run them.

Along the way, you might find other things that come up. Get creative with meeting your particular needs. Sometimes, a quick trip to the hardware store can save you quite a bit of effort later on.

Activity 1: Calculate the Profit Margins and Inventory for Your Merchandise

Create a spreadsheet with your merchandise to calculate the profit margin, return on investment, and inventory levels of your merchandise. Here's a template that you can follow:

Item	Cost	Selling Price	Profit Margin	Qty. Ordered	ROI	Qty on Hand

Below are the calculations. If you are using Excel, you can use prewritten formulas in each of the cells.

Profit Margin:
Profit Margin = 1 - (Cost of the good divided by the selling price)

For example, on an item that costs $2 but is sold for $10, it would be:
1 - (2/10) = .80
.80 = 80% profit margin

Return on Investment (ROI):
ROI = (Earnings - Cost of Investment) / Cost of Investment

For example, if you made $1,000 total on merchandise that cost you $500, it would be:

($1,000-$500)/$500 = 1.
1 = 100% Return on Investment

You won't be able to calculate a true return on investment until you sell all of your inventory; the ROI might actually differ because of special pricing, sales, giveaways, etc. but you can get a pretty good idea of what it will be beforehand. When deciding what merchandise to order (and who to order from), you can use this sheet to figure out what kind of product mix will get you the most for your money.

It only takes a brief moment to set these calculations up, but once you do, it save you quite a bit of time and money later on. It also helps you decide where to put your focus and to make objective decisions of what to order and how many.

Activity 2: Create a Preferred Vendor List

I keep a list of regular vendors who supply my merchandise that I can count on. Like a venue database or any other list of contacts, this is an effort that is well worth the time spent in setting it up.

My suggestion is to create something similar to this:

T-Shirts	Price ea.	Additional Costs/fees?	Payment Terms	Special Services	Notes	Website
Company A	$3.99	$15 screen fee	45 day net		min. 48 shirts	COa.com
Company B	$4.49	Shipping	30 day net	Ringer tees available.	min. 48 shirts	COb.com
Company C	$4.75	n/a	Cash	Oversized prints	min. 24 shirts	COc.net

This is also handy when you're in between tours and doing research on potential merchandise because you have once place where you can easily compare the service and costs of multiple vendors for the same item.

Activity 3: Find the Lowest Price

Now that you have your preferred vendor list set up, you should spend some time every few months to look for updated pricing on merchandise. The shorter, online version of this merchandise guide on my website has many live links with some of the vendors that I recommend. You can access that here: http://bit.ly/18INDjj

In addition, you can simply use some basic terms on any search engine to find any number of companies that provide custom printing services. Also, many local and independent companies will post on Craigslist. Once you find some desirable pricing, you can call local printers to see if they're willing to meet or beat the prices that you find online.

Activity 4: Perfect Your Merchandise Display

For many bands, the merchandise display is an afterthought: shirts and CDs are casually arranged each night, depending on the amount of space. How it looks each night is roughly the same, but there is no consistency. Not only do they create the same display for every show, I make my band members practice setting it up as well - that way, any one of us can set it up if the rest of the band is busy with gear. It's always the first thing we set up at the venue (to make sure get the best selling space) and the last to be torn down (to make sure we get every sale). When it's the same setup at every show, the process is also much faster.

Take some time to think about how you want your merchandise to look. Do you want grid walls or a suitcase that opens up? How do you want it to be lit up? Do you want prices on each piece of merchandise or a pricelist? Would you like to build something yourself or order a custom merchandise case?

Whatever you decide to do, get a specific process in place so that it becomes a major priority in your band. If you get a consistent look/feel, it will be more natural for you to set up each time.

Activity 5: Get Some Inspiration From Fans

If it's about time to order some more merchandise, try launching a crowd-sourced campaign for ideas. You can either create several designs for your fans to vote on hold a contest asking them to submit designs of their own. Either way, getting fans directly involved in the process gets them excited about owning a piece of merchandise that they helped bring to life!

Section 2: Marketing as a Musician

Marketing is often defined as the act of promoting and selling goods and services. For the musician, it's really about building a special relationship between fans and your band. While marketing is definitely a function of having a full autonomous music career, I wanted to create a special section dedicated to creative ways that you can promote yourself as an artist. In fact, marketing is so important, you'll probably spend more time doing marketing-related activities as a professional independent musician than almost anything else, including performing music.

The way I approach marketing is through relationship building. I like to call it "organic marketing." In other words, I believe that you should get rid all of the artificial processes or trendy phrases that people use to try and make new fans. It doesn't mean that you shouldn't jump on trends, you should just do so from a sincere and authentic place. Marketing is so much more than advertising, it's any outreach from your band - social media, mailing list outreach, promotional efforts, press releases, and more. The more you do it, the more you'll learn how to do it naturally in a style that fits you.

This section contains a number of ideas to help get you started. Feel free to refer to these activities whenever you want to get some inspiration. If you'd like more ideas, feel free to visit my blogs, where I often over current trends in marketing for musicians (www.laststopbooking.com) and social media or strategic marketing for businesses and brands in general (www.simontam.biz).

1. Use Internet Memes to Market Your Band

If you use the Internet frequently, chances are that you've been noticing a few things on the rise: meme images or animated .gif's, certain types of videos, infographics, etc. This viral content is popular because it's easy to share, hilarious, appeals to emotions, or has an important message that people think is worth sharing. Popular examples include the "Gangnam Style" music video, the "Harlem Shake," and the "Brace Yourselves" meme.

Websites like TED, Buzzfeed, and Upworthy all specialize in delivering this type of content. However, sometimes the content spread organically on a random YouTube channel, Tumblr post, or a Twitter hashtag. Why not use these viral trends and put your own spin on them to create fun, engaging, easy-to-share content with your fans?

- **Memes**: Meme images have exploded online, especially in geek culture. These images have spread to billions, each with their own take of the images, from the "Y U NO" guy to the ever so lovable Nyan cat. You can create your own memes for free using generator sites like weknowmemes.com and memegenerator.net. Personalize your own images by referring to specific points in your band's history, favorite songs or themes, and also inviting fans to create some of their own. Most meme websites also provide multiple examples of each image in case you don't understand the logic behind that type of meme. Read a few, then create your own.

Here are some that I made for my band, The Slants, that generated some great buzz from our fans:

Two of these were based on some recurring themes in the band: our former guitarist, Johnny, always being asleep (and being victim to pranks) and our van breaking down frequently when on tour (we're always on tour).

- **Animated .gif's**: When the world wide web first came to rise about fifteen years ago, animated .gif images were all the rage (probably because XHTML, Flash, and Javascript weren't around yet). They quickly died out, but in recent years, they made a huge resurgence on the social media site, Tumblr. Many of them play off of Internet memes or pop culture references such as iconic moments on TV, but you could also create an animated .gif of your band playing, a video blog with the text typed below, or anything else that is memorable. Some social media sites, such as Facebook, will not play an animated .gif, so the only way to share them there is to use a link and have it hosted elsewhere (such as your website, a photo-sharing site, or social media sites like Tumblr).

- **Trending videos**: Sometimes, certain videos gather so much momentum that they not only gain a tremendous amount of views quickly, but also inspire dozens of spin-offs to be created as well.

In early, 2012, hundreds of videos were inspired by a video called "Shit Girls Say," most of which addressed social and gender stereotypes, each quickly gaining popularity since viewers were actively searching for new versions of the idea. Only a handful of bands jumped on this trend, but those who did received several hundred thousand views on their videos. For example, the band High received over 300,000 views on their "Shit Band Guys Say" video, as of this writing. The video also helped drive views to other videos on their YouTube channel as well. Other examples of viral content include Nyan Cat, dubstep and dubstep remixes, and parody videos of popular songs.

- **Infographics**: Infographics spread quickly because they take complex data, statistics, or trends and disseminate the information in a quick, easy to read manner. Why not make infographics with interesting data about your band to share with fans? You can also use sites like visual.ly to generate infographics that take information straight from your social media sites. For example, you can compare your Twitter account with anyone else's account: a rival band, the president, a band that inspires you, your fans, etc. Why not go the extra step and create an infographic to use as an EPK? Instead of a text heavy one-sheet, have one graphic that highlights important data (such as the number of fans, social media reach, online traffic, number of albums sold, etc.) in a dynamic-looking image that is easy to take in.

- **What's Trending Regionally:** Twitter allows you to see what is trending in specific regions (globally, by country, by state, and by city).

Have some fun with your fans by being a part of the new Internet culture. You should be especially aware of things that are special to your specific audience. For instance, in 2012, my band released a music video that was targeting a very niche audience: the anime convention world. Because we often play at conventions and many of our fans enjoy cosplay (dressing up as favorite characters from anime, video games, or comics), we wanted to have some fun with it so we invited them to dress up and be a part of the video. Since its release, the video has been shared by other anime fans, magazines, tv shows, and websites. The quick rise in popularity led to the video being picked up by an international tv show and it has been broadcasted in 82 countries worldwide.

Pay attention to the world around you and see how you can put your own spin on it for your music. If the content gets shared, you might be able to reach a new audience. If anything, you'll be able to enjoy some additional lighthearted engagement with the people that support you most.

Activity 1: See What's Trending

Get an early start on things trending online that pertain to your audience. Take a few minutes to look at content on the rise and see if you can put your own twist on it. Whether it is creating a video, sharing an image, or discussing a hot topic, this could be an opportunity take advantage of momentum on something that can be shared with your band

These websites can help give you a start:

- Twitter (Sort out which hashtags are trending by region). You can also follow @WhatsTrending
- http://www.google.com/trends/hottrends (the most searched items at the moment)
- http://www.youtube.com/user/Whatstrending (current trending videos) or http://whatstrending.com/
- http://currentlytrendingon.tumblr.com/
- https://www.facebook.com/TrendingNow
- http://www.ltsTrending.com (curated site that searches multiple platforms)
- http://www.buzzfeed.com

Activity 2: Crowd-Sourced Trends

The only useable trend is one that appeals directly to your target audience. What better way to find out what is trending with your fans than to ask them directly?

Code Switch, NPR's channel on race, ethnicity, and culture, asks the same question of their followers every Monday: "What stories about race, ethnicity and culture were on your radars this weekend?" It's a great way to get inspiration for content during the week.

Here are some ways to see what's trending with your fans:

- Ask them directly (i.e, "What're some of your favorite videos right now?" etc.)
- Follow them on Twitter and see what topics/hashtags they're actively using
- Follow them on YouTube and watch their activity (which appears on your YouTube dashboard).
- Use Facebook Graph Search to how many of your followers are engaged with a topic of interest, type "friends who like [insert band name here] and [insert topic here]."

Activity 3: Throwback Thursday

People often appreciate looking back on fond memories or reveling in embarrassing ones. In fact, many social media users have adopted a trend called "Throwback Thursday," which usually involves uploading an older photo, reminiscent from another era and using the hashtags #ThrowbackThursday or #TBT. If your band has been around for a while, has a new lineup, or the members have dramatically different look, try jumping in and posting photos across your social media sites with the tag. An unofficial rule is to post pictures 5 years or older.

You can also upload older photos of individual band members, past a few together to recreate a band shot, or give posts some flair by referencing the time period in which the pictures were taken. For example, if the photo was from 1994, you could include imagery or a quote from Forrest Gump (one of the most popular films that year). Finally, you can also use the post(s) as a conversation start, to ask for fans to post old pictures or videos of the band (or themselves), favorite memories from a certain era, and so on.

Activity 4: Return of the Living Meme

Some memes, laughs or videos are classic: people love returning to them over and over again because they never fail to deliver a laugh or fond memory. Sometimes, this is an oft-quoted scene of a tv show or movie, other times, it can just be an iconic image. When you can't find a current trend or meme to suit your needs, why not turn to something classic? In fact, some people might not even recognize a current trend, but can definitely relate to something that has been passed around or proven to create a reaction.

Here are some ways to get started on finding ideas that could work for you:

- Look through older social media or web posts and look for ones that have had the most engagement - if you are using a social content management system, you can often sort the data to find what has worked best in the past.
- Search YouTube for videos based on number of views and within a certain date range
- Use any of the online trend finding sites listed earlier and sort by date; some even have a "classic trends" list
- Simply ask fans for ideas, favorite videos or posts, etc.

However you find them, the idea is to bring back old favorite posts in order to use the momentum that recognizable memes can bring.

2. Learn When and How Often to Post on Social Media

How often should I post on Facebook? How often should I tweet? How many videos should I upload to YouTube a month? These are some of the most asked questions about using social media effectively – and the answers to them, usually in the form of blogs or online articles, tend to be all over the map. However, with the rise of enterprise social media management software and the analytics of tremendous amounts of data, we're starting to get better answers.

It's interesting that more people ask about the quantity of their social media posts rather than the quality of that content. In the world of social media, the quality of the idea (not necessarily the quality of the video, audio, or image itself) always reigns. If it is something worth sharing and the right people catch on, it will spread. However, the right quantity is also important because it helps people stay engaged, develop a relationship with your brand, and also keeps your content current. Yet, posting too often on some sites (such as Facebook) will dilute your message or create too much noise and make some people want to tune you out - even if everything you have to say is interesting, timely, and relevant to your audience.

Here are some tips to help you achieve the most appropriate quantity of posts:

- **Facebook's Edgerank System:** While no one knows the exact algorithm in Facebook's posting system, it's generally recommended to space out the number of posts by at least two hours. Otherwise, certain updates can be obscured. Besides, it's annoying to have one page constantly taking up space in a user's news feed. Remember, images and videos (hosted by Facebook, not by YouTube or Vimeo) get priority over anything else. They're also much more visual and engaging, especially for mobile users.

- **Don't Sync:** Don't allow your Twitter account to feed your Facebook page unless you do not use Twitter at all. It's a different system, different audience. In fact, it's generally not recommended to sync multiple social media accounts together because of the different formats and audiences. Imagine if you could connect your phone line to your email system. Does that make any sense? If you want to link the two, use Facebook or other social sites to help drive posts on Twitter but not the other way around. But that's only because it's generally accepted to have a Twitter account be as active as you'd like it to be.

- **Are They Online?** Thanks to social media metric service websites such as Tweriod, you can see when your followers are online. That's the best time to post because that is when your posts are most likely to be seen. If it's beyond your social media posting hours, then you can pre-schedule updates using services like TweetDeck or Hootsuite.

- **Are They Tweeting Back?** The outdated misconception that Twitter is a self-absorbed activity still persists but remember: social media is all about engagement. Conversations on

Twitter are just as important as responding to comments on Facebook, so if your audience is talking back, don't be afraid to jump into conversations. I've said it before, I'll say it again: treat social media like a telephone, not a megaphone.

- **Post Around the Clock:** If possible, try spreading posts out throughout the day to create a well-rounded account. Don't just limit yourself to certain hours. You can use a site like Buffer (bufferapp.com) to help stagger content time for you automatically. You can also pair it up with If This Then That (ifttt.com) to create your social media recipes on how things will post, when they will become public, and which channels you'd like affected.

- **Create Different Channels for Different Audiences:** Not all of your fans will be using the same social media channels. Some might prefer Vine to Instagram, some might use Tumblr or Wordpress. Whatever the preferenaces are, find the ones most used by your fans and consider focusing on those. When you do, you'll learn that it will be acceptable/expected to post on some channels more than others. Find the sweet spot by following your fans and learning from them.

There aren't really hard and fast numbers about how often you should post, but you should use analytics to guide you. How often are people responding, sharing, tweeting back, or liking your posts? Is it hard to find important updates because they're being obscured by other general announcements? How often does your audience want to hear from you? Just because they "like" you doesn't mean they're in love with you. And just because you have some followers, it doesn't mean that you're the only one leading the conversation.

Social media is very much like a science as well as an art. Learn the tools and then trust your gut.

Activity 1: Sign Up for Tweriod

Sign up for Tweriod (http://www.tweriod.com). Install their free application by signing in with Twitter. They will begin running an analysis of your Twitter account so that you can learn what times most of your followers are online. Once you know that, you can try a number of things: host an online chat using a specific hashtag, pre-schedule important tweets to post when your fans are online, host RT contests during those hours, and more. Best of all, Tweriod will email you on a regular basis so that you'll know if patterns change.

Activity 2: Regular Facebook Insight Check

When you sign into your Facebook page, click on "See Insights" on the top menu:

This should be something that you do on a regular basis - at least once a month, but weekly is best. I recommend looking at this every Monday morning to help plan out the week's posts.

Once there, click on "Posts" in the top menu. You'll see what days of the week your fans are online as well as the time of day:

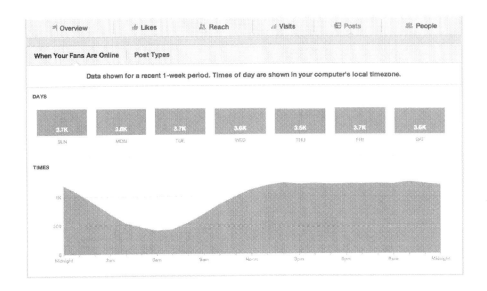

In the example shown above, the best time to post is any time after 2:30pm; the worst is between 5am and 10am. However, your page might be different. In fact, your page might change. It only takes a moment to check this data but it can drastically improve your Facebook posts.

Activity 3: Pre-Schedule a Few Messages

If you aren't able to be online during the same time period as your fans, pre-scheduling is often the best way to make sure that your updates are seen. This also helps ensure that priority posts (for example, promoting a show or new music video) aren't forgotten about either. Finally, pre-scheduling posts allows you to see what messages are being shared over a specific period of time, which will help you manage your outreach and messaging goals.

Many social media sites, such as Facebook and YouTube, have now included the ability to schedule posts in advance. For other sites, such as Twitter or Linkedin, you will need to use a social media management system such as Hootsuite, Tweetdeck, or Buffer.

Try scheduling a few posts in advance, while leaving some room to handle timely topics, news, trends, or other items that come up.

Activity 4: Scheduling for Tours and Appearances

Sometimes, you want to target a new audience that might not fit within the metrics of your current followers. For example, the late night crowd at your show or during a busy conference/festival weekend. Often, you'll be too busy with other things, such as selling merchandise or playing on stage, to be busy with social media posts. However, pre-scheduling posts can often help solve that. Here are several approaches:

- Schedule posts to appear before, during, and after you take the stage - to invite last minute people to the show, to let them know about the merch table or set, to thank people for coming, etc. You can promote your Twitter handle or hashtag during the show as well (or have a sign/banner) to try and get the crowd to engage with social media.

- During a busy conference or festival, use the event's hashtag and have continuous posts to let attendees know where to find you: in the vendor's area, at specific panels or shows, etc. Again, Twitter is often the most effective way to do this throughout the day. Pre-scheduling posts frees you up during the event itself - and when people respond, you can get push notifications sent to your phone so that you engage accordingly.

- Use IFTTT (If This, Then That), a simple task management program, to program specific triggered actions. For example, you can have social media posts automatically made when you arrive in the city or when you leave after the club(using the GPS locator on your phone). You can also have it automatically retweet, like, or post activity with other accounts. Be creative and see what you can come up with!

If you're ambitious, you could always try live tweeting or posting everything, but you might as well use the free tools at your disposal to help – especially because we tend to forget when we're tired, distracted with other tasks, or have more important things at hand (like figuring out where the next show is).

3. Master Twitter Just a Bit More

Twitter is one of the most polarizing social media channels out there - people seem to really love it or they can't stand it. For the latter, it's most likely because they don't understand it. However, those who use it well can often find an amazing resource for information, tap into an audience where things spread quickly, and can get an immediate feel for things happening at the moment. If you use Twitter in the way it was designed - essentially, the world's biggest cocktail party - rather than another platform to shout from, you'll get much more out of it than you thought possible. But before you dive in, remember to first see if your target audience is using it. If they are, then you better be as well.

Here are 62 tips for using Twitter, all written in 140 characters or less:

1) "Brevity is the soul of wit." -Shakespeare.
2) Keep it sassy, funny, or quotable.
3) Follow people by industry or interest, learn from them.
4) Listen before you post.
5) Be consistent, post as often as you can.
6) Timing matters more than grammar or spelling.
7) Watch for auto-correct. It's a sneaky beast.

8) Learn the language: Check a Twitter glossary.

9) There's room for 140, but try to keep it to 100-120 characters.

10) Connect it with Klout.

11) Don't tweet to enter stupid giveaways, it looks like spam.

12) Don't spam!

13) Begin w/your contact list. Sync those names first.

14) Use a URL shortner for all links that you post .

15) Use the search bar to find new people to follow.

16) Incorporate hashtags when possible, it's how people find you.

17) Get a great profile pic, the standard egg avatar looks like a spam account.

18) Avoid clicking on links sent via DM, too much spam there.

19) Give credit for others' ideas.

20) Keep calm when a crisis rises.

21) Use Tweetdeck or Hootsuite to help manage multiple accounts & searches.

22) Connect Facebook to Twitter, but not the other way around.

23) Keep things tweet-worthy; no one cares about boring updates.

24) Be passionate.

25) Find your favorite topics and stick to them (it defines your brand).

26) Don't overuse hashtags (2-3 most per post).

27) Use keywords in your profile but make it fun and searchable.

28) Spend more time talking about others than yourself.

29) Post your Twitter handle in your email signature, website, or other sites.

30) Be the kind of account that you want to follow.

31) Make people laugh.

32) RT good stuff.

33) Watch out for NSFW images in your feed.

34) Sign up for Twitter chats in your industry (best place to network).

35) Use the designated hashtag of events (also to network).

36) Share your best tweets on other platforms (blog, Facebook, website).

37) Post at different times of the day to see where your audience is.

38) You can tweet at people you admire, but don't badger them.

39) It's OK to post something more than once but don't spam people with it.

40) RT/link when low on content .

41) Use #FF for contacts that you like.

42) Don't buy followers, earn them.

43) Abbrev. when poss. 4 more space.

44) SHOUT SPARINGLY.

45) People like pet pictures.

46) Read tweets twice before posting.

47) The more you tweet, the more followers you'll have.

48) The more you use Twitter, the better you'll be at it.

49) Try using Tweepi.

50) Follow the recommended accounts, they're usually decent.

51) Treat Tweets more like text messages than phone conversations.

52) Be respectful, avoid tasteless comments in times of disaster.

53) Don't be a jerk. Avoid racism/sexism/or any 'ism.

54) Share life hacks, tips, and advice.

55) Ask for advice when you don't know the answers.

56) Google "facts" before posting them.

57) Avoid using automated, repeated, scheduled tweets.

58) Profile: Link to your own site, not other social media.

59) A little wit makes everything better: tweets, replies, bios, etc.

60) Answer this: Why should someone follow you?

61) Organize profiles you like by lists.

62) Give props to others, they like that.

A mastery of Twitter can do wonders for your music career. So why not learn how to be more effective at it?

Activity 1: Create Lists

Creating lists is often the best way to get started on Twitter. Lists help you organize users that you follow (or who follow you) so that you can get an overview of what is happening with that specific group (instead of just a barrage of all accounts that you follow). Lists are also a way to get tweets from certain users that you don't necessarily want to follow (for example, a rival company or band).

Some lists that you might consider making:

- Venues, Promoters, and Booking Agents
- Your fans
- Record Labels
- Music Industry Advice
- Media and Press (journalists and publishers)
- Other bands that you want to tour with

Whatever the topic or audience is, you can probably come up with a list. If you want some help getting started, try this guide: http://mashable.com/2009/11/02/twitter-lists-guide/

Activity 2: Create Something RT-able

One of the best ways of increasing your social media influence in Twitter is getting others to retweet (RT) you. In order to get RT's, you need to post content that is short (which allows room for a RT tag as well as any short quips) and lends itself well to retweeting.

Here are some ideas:
- Lyric lines (iconic ones from your catalog or others)
- Famous quotes
- On this day in history (both for your band as well as other events)
- Puns
- Images or short videos from Instagram and Vine
- Links to interesting articles

You can also participate in a hashtag game (there are numerous), which usually involves a clever play on words using a certain hashtag (@TheHashtagGame has many of them, most of which involves songs or music).

Activity 3: Changing Up the Voice

Another idea that you can use for social media (but especially Twitter) is to rotate featured different band members out to answer fan questions, post content that is interesting to them, and generally manage the account. This gives a different voice to the account that fans can interact with, as well as the opportunity to get to know each member of the band better.

Some bands rotate daily (certain members take on certain days of the week), others weekly. You can tag each post with initials, introduce the next member, etc. However you choose to approach this, just be sure that you have buy-in from each member of the band. If the account languishes due to inactivity or lack of response, that will make your entire band's Twitter account suffer. However, active engagement can bring something new and interesting to the platform.

4. Linking with Linkedin

Linkedin is a social networking site that has a specific focus on careers, education, and industry networking. It also happens to be a site underutilized by musicians.

Here are some of the key benefits for using Linkedin as a professional musician:

- The opportunity to network with people directly involved in the music industry
- Access to contact information for booking agents, labels, A&R reps, managers, and more
- Opportunity to engage with other musicians
- Access to potential sponsorships and endorsements
- Access to networking groups to get questions about the industry answered
- Get advice from others directly in the industry
- Find opportunities to showcase your music

Like anything else, the content on there should be taken with a grain of salt. You can also gain followers and influence in Linkedin Groups, which will ultimately be of use to you. Here are six proven ways to gain influence on Linkedin:

1) **By creating real value:** Actually participate in group discussions and add something meaningful, don't just use Linkedin Groups as a megaphone to promote yourself. This is the foundation of everything else here.

2) **Building up your brand:** Your Linkedin profile is part of your "brand" or how people view you. Look at the tip above: do you want to be associated as someone who only promotes their own products/services or do you want to be viewed as someone who contributes value to others?

3) **Make it two ways:** You can't expect others to blindly follow you if you aren't taking the time to follow them first.

4) **Create a niche:** Stand out from the crowd by offering unique insights, especially on something that you specialize in.

5) **Don't add to the noise:** Simply posting your twitter handle and expecting something to come from it isn't going to help you – if anything, it'll actually be counter productive.

6) **Get to know the mavens:** Follow and interact with the top influencers of each Linkedin Group. That will help build your credibility. See what kinds of posts they are making, how they are enriching the rest of the group. Learn from that.

Also, do not create a user account for your band - save that for creating a company page. Instead, you should create a profile for you as an individual. That's how the site is designed. Like Facebook pages, the Linkedin company page can post updates, services, have some branding, and contact information. Band members can all be tied to the account as employees.

Linkedin Groups can be a great resource for professional

networking. But the key is networking, as in working with others. Use it well and it will help open up doors for your music career.

Activity 1: Create a Band "Company Page"

If you already have a personal account, you can create a company page by listing the band as your employer or company. The company page will allow you to use custom graphics (banner, logo, etc.), have an "About Us" section, and a "Products" section where you can list information about the services your band offers (live performance, licensing, etc.

Activity 2: Create Projects on Your Profile

On your individual Linkedin profile, you have the ability to add special projects. While listing the band and its accomplishments is certainly useful, the "projects" section has certain advantages when properly used. Each project allows for a short description, the ability to tag other Linked members/connections involved with the project, and a URL. The URL provides a live link to your website, EPK, or project profile. Connecting the project with other members allows it to be listed on multiple profiles, this strengthening the connection and raising the visibility of the project.

Here are some ideas for projects and the other people that you can connect with outside of your band members:

- **Album or EP**: At the very minimum, you'll want to list each major release and include information about album sales, press received, or any other notable accomplishments. Connect with the audio engineer, mastering technician, producer, session musicians, publicist, etc.

- **Major Tours**: The description should cover major destinations, key venues or festivals, the amount of exposure/audience size, etc. Connect with promoters, booking agents, venue owners, publicists, festival staff, road crew, other bands/band members who shared the stage during the tour, press who covered the tour, etc.

- **Music Video:** Music videos are great addition to the profile because they are so visual. You can actually embed music videos into the profile's summary or company information, but use the project section to highlight any key points of the video. The project should connect with the video director, actors, extras, producer, film and lighting crew, and people connected with the location.

- **Key Sponsorship or Partnership**: If you launched a major campaign with a key sponsor or partner, this can be a great way to help pave the way for future sponsorships, especially for the Linkedin platform. You can include key staff that were directly involved with the sponsorship or partnership, vendors, press contacts that have covered the sponsorship, etc.

Activity 3: Get Active in Linkedin Groups

Linkedin Groups are one of the best ways to get more attention on your profile, make connections with people in a specific industry or company, and gain influence/credibility for your field.

To join a Linkedin Group, simply use the search bar at the top and type in any key words. For example, you could type in "music industry," "music sponsorships," "independent music," "music promoters," etc. Some groups are open, allowing you to join and begin participating immediately, while others require approval for admission. Try joining several groups in areas that you are interested in.

If you are a member of a few Linkedin Groups, try and post something of interest on a regular basis - whether it is a thoughtful article of interest, a question to be answered or debated, or a response to others' questions, being active gives your profile more visibility in the industry and within that group. The influence measurement is usually measured weekly, which means that you should try and post something at least once per week.

When you're active in the group, you'll notice a few members right away: those who post actual content of value and help answer others' questions, and those who post large quantities of "filler" in order to get attention. Focus on networking with those who add value and follow their example on how to thoughtfully engage with others.

Activity 4: Follow Thought Leaders

Linkedin allows you to follow thought leaders (called Influencers) who hold influence in their respective fields. Their posts, usually short blogs or articles, will show at the top of your dashboard's stream. Many of these posts will have thoughtful content that is worth sharing to your own audiences; they're often about leadership or inspirational and innovative content. It's also a good way to get to know these leaders.

You can view top posts from Linkedin Influencers here: http://www.linkedin.com/today/influencers

5. Using YouTube Successfully

Did you know that YouTube is the second most used search engine in the world?

Like any other social media channel, YouTube offers a tremendous opportunity for musicians to build an audience, market their music, and earn some revenue. Of course, there are several other video hosting channels available, but given YouTube's incredible reach and rich community, it is probably the one with the most potential.

There are no strict guidelines or instructions that will guarantee success on YouTube, but these are some best practices that you should be observing:

- **Post Content Consistently:** One of the most important tips for having a YouTube channel is posting on a regular basis. While you might not be able to release a new, fully produced music video that often, you can still create other interesting content to keep your channel active. For example, you can post video blogs, Q&A sessions with fans, footage from a live show, cover songs, acoustic or a capella versions of songs, discuss events, interviews, review music/books/film/food/etc., or any other content that is related to your niche, target audience.

- **Complete All the Fields:** Using a catchy video title can help drive more traffic. Additionally, you should use keywords to "tag" your video (they act like META tags for a website) and URL's to your website and other social media sites in the description field. Just as you want to write over dozen email subject lines, the same should be done for your videos to come up with the most intriguing, shocking, or interesting title...but always be sure to include your band's name. The tags should be specific since they'll often be grouped together with other videos of the similar tags.

- **Learn the Algorithm:** Videos that have high engagement (views, likes, comments, reviews, video responses, favorites, views outside of YouTube, and social media shares) are more likely to come up in search results. Leverage your other social media channels and get fans to interact.

- **Connect with the Right Audience:** If you have content that is relevant to a specific audience, promote on websites that are relevant to that audience's interests. For example, one of my band's music videos features characters in cosplay (costumes based on anime or geek culture), so it was a natural fit to share the video on anime and cosplay message boards. For another tour, we captured footage at famous restaurants and used Yelp to help promote those video blogs. Don't try and be all things to all people: find a specific niche and stick with it.

- **Create Teasers:** If you have a major video coming up, such as an official music video release, help prime your audience for it by posting teaser footage, a behind-the-scenes video blog, or blooper reel. The more related the content, the more interest and momentum that you can bring to your video.

- **Encourage Engagement:** In your video blogs and descriptions, get fans to participate: ask them to subscribe, post questions or comments, and share.

- **Create a Regular Schedule, if Possible:** Nearly every YouTube channel with high numbers of subscribers (1 million or more) has something in common: a regular schedule with certain types of content on specific dates/times. Geek and Sundry (www.youtube.com/geekandsundry) is a great example of a channel that has regularly scheduled content. Like a TV channel, consistent updates keeps fans coming back and lets them know they can always expect something new or interesting, which increases the incentive to subscribe.

- **Never Buy Views:** There are websites that sell "real views" to increase the number of views on your videos. However, these sites all use underhanded methods to increase views - bots, embedding on false sites, etc. - and can jeopardize your YouTube account to the point where YouTube will terminate your account.

Activity 1: Share in a Better Way

If you need some content for your other social media channels, consider sharing one of your YouTube videos. However, don't just post a link or announce it - give people an incentive to engage further. Here are a few ideas on how you can do this:

- Host a contest for fans to win prizes and/or recognition for a specific action - sharing your video, writing a review of it on their blog, tweeting the URL with a certain hashtag, or leaving a comment on the video.

- Ask everyone in your band to post the video at the same time: this dramatically increases visibility on your video, especially if you can get everyone to share the video from the band's post on Facebook or RT the tweet on Twitter.

- Share the video in a non-traditional manner if it ties in with a specific audience. For example, I once got the city of Baltimore to help promote a music video because it was shot in an area that they were trying to drive tourism to. That effort led to multiple shares/views from the official Visit Baltimore channels and staff, as well as Conan O'Brien Presents: Team Coco.

Activity 2: Create a Video Posting Calendar

Earlier in this book, I talked about the importance of having goals. This should also include your YouTube channel as well. Create a calendar where you can fill in specific dates on when you'd like new content: between music videos, covers, announcements, blogs, etc., how much content do you want posted? By creating a consistent schedule, it will help you stay on track with your goals as well as give fans a regular calendar to look forward to. You can even create excitement for the next video by having a countdown on your website or increase engagement by asking fans for ideas and/or contributions.

Once you have a calendar of when you'd like fresh content uploaded as well as a list of what the content is, work backwards so that you can adequately prepare for each video. Build time into the calendar so that you can film, edit, and promote your videos.

Activity 3: On the Cover

If you're running low on ideas, or just want to create some interesting content for fans to bite into, you could easily create an acoustic version of your own song or a popular cover. In fact, acoustic covers are some of the most searched for videos on YouTube. Look up any popular song on YouTube right now - chances are, the search will auto-generate acoustic versions of those songs. If you use an interesting arrangement, unique instruments, or create your own spin on it somehow, it will make your video more distinct.

Also, you don't have to focus solely on Top 40 songs. You could take on musicals, classical music, something outside of your genre, show tunes, or something reminiscent of a specific era. For example, the film *Pitch Perfect* featured a cover of 1931 bluegrass song called "When I'm Gone" that was inspired by a YouTube a cappella rendition using plastic cups. The original YouTube video went viral, inspiring dozens of others to produce similar videos.

Activity 4: Show Off a Skill

Does someone in your band have an unusual skill? Create a video blog based around it. You can tie it into with one of your songs, a tour, or just use it as a way for fans to get to know the band better. For instance, one of our band's most popular video blogs was our informal hot pepper eating contest that we held at a local Sichuan restaurant called "Lucky Strike." We chose that restaurant since we wrote a song in their parking lot and named it after the establishment. In addition to getting some great meals out of it, the restaurant helped promote the video with their customers!

Activity 5: Inject Some Comedy

Another way to create some content that is enjoyable for fans is to include something that makes them laugh. Whether it is a barrage of inside jokes, a parody of a popular cultural reference or hit song, or slapstick humor, audiences always appreciate some good humor. Comedy is often highly shared, so give people a reason to smile or laugh.

6. Sending Mail to Your Fans

One of my favorite ways of creating fans for life is exceeding expectations. These days, it is exceedingly rare for bands to send physical mail. With the cost of postage going up and the availability of email and social media tools, it's understandable that many artists only use fans' addresses to target show announcements by zip code. However, a little snail mail can go a long way in building a loyal army of fans - and it can also drive your social media engagement as well.

Here are some ideas for sending physical mail to your fans:

- **Show/Tour Announcement**: Given how seldom bands send physical mail, a simple postcard (or handwritten letter to your biggest fans) can really help elevate the visibility or importance of a particular show or tour.

- **New Release**: Releasing a new album? If you send a download code for a free song for people only on your mailing list, it could be an interesting way to generate some buzz for the music as well as serve as an incentive for people to join the mailing list.

- **Crowdsourcing Campaign:** One of the most effective, tried-and-true ways of fundraising is still the physical letter. Physical mail (especially personalized) has a higher open rate than email and stands out.

- **Postcards From Tour:** Sometimes it's best to not ask for anything, but instead to just surprise your fans by giving them something. For example, during every tour, I pick up postcards from different stops across the country. Our band signs them, writes personalized messages or artwork, and mails them out to random fans on our mailing list.

- **Holidays or Milestones:** You could send Valentines, Christmas cards, Halloween cards, or other milestones that tie into your band such as the anniversary of a first show or album release. These are ways to connect with your fans emotionally as well as provide them with something fun to reflect on and share with others.

When mailing things to your fans, here are some things to consider:

- **Cost:** While smaller/lighter items are usually less expensive, the Post Office does have minimum requirements. The smallest item is a postcard, which needs to be at least 3.5"x5"x.007. When in doubt, get an estimate from the Post Office.

- **Bulk Mail:** You probably won't be using bulk mail unless you have a large mailing list and send items out on a consistent basis. Bulk mail has a number of requirements that need to be met before you are allowed to receive the discount - for example, you need to send at least 500 pieces First Class, have a permit to do so, and strictly manage your address list. For more information, visit:

http://pe.usps.com/businessmail101/getstarted/bulkmail.htm

- **Delivery Time:** If you are sending mail for a specific campaign or show, add at least five days of lead time to account for mail and delivery.

- **Your Goals:** Remember the goals discussed earlier? Everything you do should fall into your objectives as a professional musician. How does physical mail play a role in meeting those goals? Can you think of ways to leverage mail to your fans in other ways? For example: having them post pictures of it, creating a contest, increasing sales, etc.

If you only send out one item per day for a year, that would be 365 delighted fans. What are some creative ways that you can surprise your fans with physical mail?

Activity 1: Complete Your Mailing List Database

In order to send physical mail to your fans, you're going to need their physical mailing addresses. Do you have a mailing list database? If not, read Section 1, Chapter 12: *Use an Email List Effectively* for ideas on a few. Any decent email contact service will also hold fields for physical addresses as well.

That being said, you'll want to provide fans with an incentive for sending you their physical addresses - you could launch a contest through social media, have a more detailed mailing list signup on your website or at your merch table, or simply ask everyone on your email list for the information. In return, you could give away a free download, a sticker, give a shout out, etc. Of course, the biggest incentive is actually receiving physical mail!

Activity 2: Surprise Your Fans

If you have a mailing list with some dedicated fans on it, take a few minutes out to send them something today. Whether it's a thank you card or letter, a postcard, or some goofy surprise, a small token in the mail can make a lifelong fan.

You can also schedule regular intervals of when you do this: for example, your band could have "5 Fan Friday" where you sign and send five pieces of mail after your rehearsal. You could either tweet at fans who will be receiving upcoming mail or leave it as a complete surprise. Either way, you'll get much more out of it than the small amount spent on postage.

Activity 3: Create Some Pen-pals

If one of your goals is to strengthen the relationship with your fans, why not create a pen-pal arrangement where you have a select group that you communicate with on a regular basis? This could consist of your biggest supporters, international fans or those who live outside of your normal touring region, or aspiring musicians.

Another idea is to create new fans from an actual pen-pal organization. There are numerous pen-pal organizations that are free, secure, and easy to use.

If you're looking for general pen-pals, try these organizations: PenPal World, InterPenPals, or PenPalsNow! You can also search for specific interest: student, prisoners, military soldiers, international, etc. Who knows? That might also help you land a gig in the future!

7. Write a Blog that Creates Conversation

Having a blog can be advantageous for a number of reasons: the content can help drive search engine optimization efforts and bring more traffic to your website, it can provide another way for fans to connect with you, it might reach a new audience or bring in new fans, it can inspire a song or story, and it can increase fan engagement. However, a successful blog requires dedication, consistency, fresh and relevant content, and a defined audience.

In other words, if you or your band are going to have a blog, you need to consider the following:

- **Purpose of the Blog:** What is the purpose of your blog? What do you hope to accomplish with it? How will you accomplish it?

- **Ownership of the Blog:** How are you going to divide up the responsibility of the band's blog? Who will be involved and what is expected of the commitment?

- **The Audience:** Who will be reading the blog? Who is the target audience and how do you plan on reaching them?

- **The Format:** Will the blog be written, in audio form (such as a podcast), or video (vlog)? Where will each post be posted? How often will there be an update?

- **The Message:** What do you want to say?

For some bands, this might seem like too much work. For others, they get a kick out of it. Before you commit to launching a blog, you might even just consider doing guest posts on other established blogs. This could be a great way to experiment with the platform, measure results, and see if it is a good fit for your band. Even if you launch a blog, guest posts can be a good way to gain exposure to new audiences.

No matter how you approach your blogging strategy, it's important to remember that like all social media, it should create conversation and engagement. If your blog is only a self-promotion tool, it will only be seen as that. But if the blog serves other purposes (a behind-the-scenes view of your music career, conversation starter on hot issues, allows fans a chance to contribute, etc.), then you'll get much more out of it.

The activities below will primarily serve as idea generators. It's up to you to answer the big questions about the blog and how to execute your plan.

Activity 1: Something Controversial or Remarkable

Posts that are about current, controversial topics or that have a remarkable insight tend to draw a lot of attention. Remarkable basically means something that is worthy of a remark, worthy of being shared - so that often means a unique perspective on something. Whether you choose to talk about something in the news, another artist, or a personal story, controversy often gets attention. If it is a sensitive topic though, you might not get the kind of reaction that you're desiring or expecting. Then again, that never stopped artists like Kanye West or Miley Cyrus, yet their controversial actions have only helped their careers reach new heights.

Activity 2: Embarrassing Story

Everyone seems to love self-deprecating humor. Some have made entire careers out of it. One share-worthy blog idea can be an embarrassing story: whether it's the worst show you've ever performed as a professional musician or a tale about falling off the stage, a little humor can show that you don't always take yourself so seriously. You could even ask fans for some of their most embarrassing stories as well. If you want to create some more relatable moments, share a funny story about your experiences as a fan.

Activity 3: Fan Guest Blog

If you have an active fan who is passionate about the band, you could ask them to write a guest blog. You might also ask fellow musicians in a local band, industry professionals, a sponsor or partner, or your parents. A guest blogger can help relieve some of the work that you're putting in as well as giving a new voice (and with that, sometimes a new audience) to your blog. They could share a story about meeting the band, their interpretation of a song's lyrics, a favorite live show, or even how they met someone else through the band.

Activity 4: Interview a Reader or Local Band

If you're ever short on ideas, you could always interview someone:

random fan, a local band, an artist who inspires you, a charity that your support, etc. Spend some time writing thoughtful or funny questions and treat it like a conversation so that the audience can get a pretty good feel for everyone involved. Remember, the most memorable interviews all begin with a good interviewer who carefully guides the conversation with consideration.

Above all, the interview should be interesting and entertaining. One of the fan-favorite blogs in my band, The Slants, is our "Moms of The Slants" series in which we interview the mothers of our band members in a candid and silly kind of way. But we've also been known to interview host hosts, promoters, sponsors, collaborators, and random people on the street as well. Keep it light-hearted, engaging, and fun!

Activity 5: A Picture Says a Thousand Words

If you're short on ideas or don't want to do a lot of writing, you could post a photo blog instead. Photoblogging is simply telling a story primarily through images. For example, a memorable show, a tour, a day in the life of, moments in the studio, etc. are all stories that could be communicated with several strong images and limited text. Photoblogs are dynamic, easy to share, and often make a good impact through social media as well.

Activity 6: Video

If a picture says a thousand words, how many does a video evoke? It doesn't matter as long as each one is interesting and engaging.

Video blogging, or vlogging, can be great way to meet the purpose of a blog without all of the heavy writing. However, if you decide to make a blog post in video form, be sure to spend time carefully working on the title, description, and video tags so that you benefit from the keywords involved. You can create a video version of any of the ideas above (including a photo slide show). You could even just post a candid "check in" with fans from a tour, from a band rehearsal, or from your living room.

8. Creating a Niche

One of the most important things you can do for marketing your music is to create your own niche market. It's far easier to market yourself when you have a specific angle rather than a generic or broad one. By carving out a niche, you can reach audiences who are more enthusiastic about what you have to offer and set yourself apart from the rest of the market. In fact, you might create a few niche markets for yourself with different audiences that may or may not be related to each other.

Here are different areas that you can create niche for your band:

- **Your Sound:** Do you have a new approach on the type of music that you're playing? Perhaps a new fusion or spin on a type of sound? You could create your own genre or subgenre of music.

- **Your Lyrics:** Do you have a new approach to lyrics? Do you have specific content or themes that would be of special interest to a certain crowd? The subject matter or delivery method could reach a very specific crowd.

- **Your Image**: Perhaps you have a specific type of fashion, a certain look, artwork, or unique costumes. Maybe your band uses specific props or theatrical elements for your live performances? The visual image that you convey can help distinguish your act.

- **Your Business Approach**: Do you have a unique approach to the music industry, touring, creating music, or marketing? That in of itself can help define your niche.

- **Your Fans:** Maybe you have a unique group of followers who have their own identity or a special relationship with your fans. Your fans help embody who you are.

Here are some examples of artists who have created their own niche:

- **The Misfits**: They were a pioneer band in the "horror punk" genre, with a very specific image and lyrical content.

- **Kiss:** This band was probably best known for their makeup as well as their hardcore fans, dubbed the Kiss Army. They also had an incredible business approach, dominating nearly every type of merchandise product possible.

- **Bruce Springsteen**: Among many things, "The Boss" is recognized for lyrics that represent the working class of New Jersey.

- **Postmodern Jukebox**: This band made headlines in 2013 for their unique, 1920's renditions of popular songs.

- **Lady Gaga:** Lady Gaga takes on the niche approach in numerous areas but she probably gets the most media attention for her outrageous outfits.

- **Johnny Cash**: The "man in black" was not only known for his all-black attire, but also for performing for prisoners serving time at famous state penitentiaries.

- **Daft Punk**: While this duo is certainly respected for their music in their own right, they have a defining look and feel for all of their artwork and photos. Their custom helmets are highly recognizable and often imitated.

There are many ways to create your own niche. Whether it is a severe deviation from the norm or just your own spin on things, you should define who you are in a way that stands out. This gives a specific angle or press to grab onto and help you narrow down your target audience.

Your approach doesn't have to be outlandish or campy, it just has to be unique and focused. Once you work on a niche, you can broaden up or diversify from there. For example, when I started my band, I focused on an Asian American audience (our band has an Asian American theme). From there, we worked on markets interested in Asian culture: cultural festivals, anime conventions, diversity events, etc. The press wrote many stories on us because of our unique approach and for being the only Asian American dance rock band in the world. But over time, we began expanding, playing at rock clubs, military bases, prisons, and more.

Activity 1: Finding a Niche Based on Existing Characteristics

Think of how you can find a unique angle for your band based on your sound, lyrical content, image, business approach, or your most enthusiastic fans. Create a list of any unique identifiers about your band, themes or subjects in your lyrics, etc. Even though you might be known for a specific niche, this might help generate ideas for new angles, stories, audiences, or marketing materials that you can concentrate on.

Activity 2: Creating a New Niche

There are a number of ways to create your own niche. For example, you might already be thinking of taking your band or music in a new direction, working on a concept album, have new lineup, or are working on a licensing project. These are all activities that lend themselves to new possible frontiers. Furthermore, these new endeavors don't have to be permanent or a complete reinvention of who you are as an artist. It could just be for a specific music video, a special tour playing unique venues and events, or a new look. Think about how you can incorporate a unique and cohesive theme for the sound, look, and/or delivery.

Activity 3: Finding the Niche Audience

If you have carved out a niche or multiple unique identifying traits, you can find more ways to reach audiences who are specifically interested in the niche. Try to think of as many different types of individuals who would take interest as possible. For example, if you were singer-songwriter who decided to tour only using a bicycle or public transportation, you could tap into numerous micro-markets: bicyclists, ecological conservationists, fitness enthusiasts, professional bus drivers and bike cabs, explorers, campers, etc. Of course, each of those audiences have their own markets, festivals, retailers, websites, message boards, or networks that can help you land a sponsorship or enthusiastic fans.

It helps to imagine specific individuals rather than broad demographic groups. Think about specific individuals who might be interested in the niche, what their lifestyle is like, and what would appeal to them. Then, reach out to that audience!

Activity 4: Reach Out to Niche Media Sources

The Internet has allowed many niche publications, websites, and interest groups to flourish. Do some searching about your niche and see if there are clubs, magazines, podcasts, radio shows, tv shows, or online channels that are related to the topic of interest. For instance, if your music has many surfing references, you can reach out to surfing magazines, videographers who shoot professional surfers, surfing industry organizations, and TV shows that cover the sport. You also find and reach out to related media sources, such as oceanography media sources, travel magazines and websites that highlight tropical areas, or even media sources and organizations talking about protection against too much sun exposure. If you can find a way to tie it back in to that publication's audience, you might just have a chance.

9. Let Your Fans Do the Talking

The best way for any company or new artist to grow their fan base is through referrals. People trust their friends and family significantly more than any brand. You earn referrals when someone enjoys your music so much, they can't help but share. But you can also increase referrals by asking and giving incentives to those who share.

To get fans into the sharing mentality, you first need to build their loyalty and excitement. The combined energy from a hardcore fan base can create some serious momentum (just look at the career of Justin Bieber or even the popularity of the book *50 Shades of Grey*, both were launched by obsessed fans).

So how do you create that kind of loyal army? Here are some tips:

- **Always Over-Deliver**: Always take the time to get to know your fans: online, via social media or email, and especially at the show. Turn your fans into friends. When people order merch from you or book you for a show, over-deliver by doing more than promised.

- **Get Creative**: Find new, fun ways to surprise your fans. You can try sending things in the mail, recognizing their birthdays, bringing them on stage, getting them involved with your album or music video, baking them cookies...you get the idea.

- **Get to Know the Mavens**: Malcolm Gladwell writes about how things go viral. One of the key concepts is getting the social "mavens" (or leaders/influencers) on board with what you're doing. These are the trendsetters, the people who are hip to what's cool. Think about your target audience and who influences them. Music blogs? Skateboarding icons? Guitar gurus? YouTube cover artists? If you get these influencers on board, they'll help you spread your music to target audiences in no time.

- **Consistency, Consistency, Consistency**: When you start something, you have to consistently follow up on it or it'll fall through. When people sign up on your email list at a show, get them into your database ASAP, then write them and thank them for coming to the show. If you have a mailing list, send out a newsletter on a regular basis. If you are on social media, update on a regular basis. Don't spam them with an overwhelming amount of updates, just be consistent with your updates for show announcements, new music, or other fun things.

- **Think Telephone, Not Megaphone**: Who do you pay more attention to, the guy standing on a street corner yelling into a megaphone and holding up signs or your friend on the telephone? Think of your e-newsletter and social media as a phone, a prompt for a two-way conversation and not simply as an information/propaganda service. If you have a personal relationship with your fans, they'll feel more inclined to treat you as a friend - and friends help each other.

- **Rethink the Relationship:** Think of creating fans in terms of the golden rule. How would you want to be treated by your favorite bands? How do you want your fans to treat you? Go and do the same.

As you build the relationship with your fans, you'll want to have a few different ways to approach them about sharing your music. Here are a couple of ways to accomplish that:

- **Simply Ask:** The most straightforward way is to just ask. This is pretty common on social media - you'll often see messages like "Please share this," "RT this," or "Help us get to X number of followers." If you have fans who are eager to help, they will. Asking is a good way to initiate the process.

- **Competition**: Many people are driven by competition. Making a game out of things can help - you can either create some friendly competition with a rival band or even amongst your fans (i.e., "Who is the biggest fan?" "Who can bring the most friends to show," etc.).

- **Incentive**: Reward fans for their support and they will support you some more. You can provide some recognition, donate to charity on their behalf, feature them on your site, or send them some goodies for doing things like promoting your band and writing about you on their blog.

- **Campaign**: A specific movement can often mobilize fans to take action - whether it's getting people to vote for you or to share your Facebook page, tying actions to together in a campaign can create some more momentum. This will make efforts even more effective.

- **Assign a Leader**: If you do have a "super fan," you can ask them to help rally others to the cause. Often, people who are in a position such as fan club president will take their duties seriously and are eager to help. Give them some authority and see what they can do.

- **Shareworthy**: Provide your fans content that is worth sharing. This could be a good cause, a funny story, or a catchy song. Whatever it is, it should be something that also delights the people that they share it with. How do you know what that is? Well, just focus on the niche (Section 2, chapter 8).

Your biggest supporters want to help your band anyway that they can. You just have to provide them with a little direction. When you let your fans do the talking, you can make a lot more noise.

Activity 1: Recruit the Team

You probably already know who your biggest supporters are: they go to most of your shows, they are the most active on social media, they've introduced everyone in their social circle to you. However, it's sometimes easy to lose track.

Use tools like www.crowdbooster.com and www.commun.it to see who your most engaged followers are on Facebook and Twitter. Create a list of your super fans in your email database and ask these fans to help lead the charge in spreading the word about your new album, music video, tour dates, or other efforts.

Years ago, it was popular to create a street team. The idea is actually very good but many artists failed to execute it well because they didn't stay organized or have clear goals. You can create a street team 2.0: rather than having them put tour posters up, give specific tasks to complete online. When people take action on your behalf, thank them and recognize their efforts.

Activity 2: Create a Social Conversation

One of the greatest things about social media is its social aspect: as people engage with you, their followers will see. This is the case with almost any social media channel - Facebook, Twitter, YouTube, G+, etc. It's an easy, natural way of exposing your brand to your fans' followers without even asking them to do so.

Create a fun or interesting conversation that your fans can take part of. This could be a game, debate on a hot topic, or even an interview with fans. The idea is to just get them interacting. For example, every few months, I play the word association game with my band's fans. I'll start out with a word and then just ask people to post the first word that comes into their mind. From there, fans just continue to play the game on our Facebook post with each other, dramatically raising the profile of our page.

Activity 3: Launch the Operation

Create a campaign that your fans can rally behind. Some ideas to get you started include: reaching a certain goal (number of views on a video, number of plays on a song, number of fans on a social media channel, etc.), getting the attention of someone who you want to notice you (celebrity, media source, industry person), starting a hashtag trend, a crowdsourcing campaign, welcoming a new band member, or voting for you in a contest...you get the idea. If your goals become their goals, it will give them a reason to take that action.

If you give the campaign an identity, it will be more obvious to fans that it is something they should take action on.

Activity 4: Give a Fan the Helm

In 2012, the nation of Sweden gave a different citizen control of its official Twitter channel each week. Why couldn't an artist do something similar?

Facebook allows you to give "Moderator" admin status to users. This will allow them to post content, respond to comments, and view insights, but it won't allow them to edit the page. You could ask your most dedicated fan to lead the conversation/posts for a week (I would recommend that they sign each post so others know it is from them and not the band). You could also have a fan create a video blog or interview them - if they're involved in a special way, you can be sure that they will brag about it to their friends.

Activity 5: Make the Ask

Sometimes, it is good to just ask for a specific action. It might be to share a post, watch a video, or to tell five friends about you. Whatever it is, just be clear that you would love some help.

Today, ask your friends, family, and fans to take action on your behalf. Remember, until you ask, the answer is always no.

10. Stand Up for a Good Cause

It is worthwhile to give back to the community. However, you (and the causes that you support) stand to benefit much more from your involvement when it is done with thought and purpose. This kind of thoughtful involvement is called strategic philanthropy.

Strategic philanthropy is the type of giving that maximizes the positive impact for the community as well as the organization giving. It can help drive engagement, strengthen the brand, reach new audiences, and improve morale, all while helping a cause that is important to you.

When you find a cause that resonates with your audience, they'll be even more engaged and loyal to your band. A 2011 Cone/Echo Global CR Study showed that 93% of customers want to know the brands that they support are making the world a better place. 91% of these customers want to hear about those efforts, but most of those are confused by the messaging shared. In 2013, a Nielsen study found that 50% of customers are willing to reward companies who support causes that they're passionate about by paying more for goods and services.

So you'll see a much greater return when it is a cause that you are passionate about and something that connects personally with your band's audience. For example, wizard rock band Harry and the Potters often raises money for the non-profit group, The Harry Potter Alliance. Fans love it and both groups benefit from the exchange.

There are different ways that you can stand up for a cause with your band:

- **Fundraise**: The biggest need of nonprofit organizations is funding. Whether you choose to run a 5k, hold a bake sale, or even lead a crowdfunding campaign on behalf of a cause, funding is often the best way to make an impact.

- **Volunteer**: Most organizations are understaffed and rely on volunteers to help with some of the heavy lifting. Sometimes they need specific skills (office work, construction skills, etc.), but other times they just need general labor. Either way, it usually only requires a few hours of your time and could make a positive impact.

- **Donate**: If you don't have time to lead a fundraising campaign, you might consider donating some money. You can pool together money from the band, donate a portion of your proceeds, or even have a donation jar at your merchandise table. If you are giving to a 501(c)3 organization, the money is also tax deductible.

- **Advocate**: Often times, organizations need people who are willing to speak on their behalf. Sometimes it involves mobilizing people to write to their elected officials, other times, it's to bring awareness to an issue. You could be that advocate by highlighting the needs of a specific issue.

- **Partner**: A long-term partnership will give the most return on investment for time, money, and resources. You can contact an organization to think of some unique campaign projects. For example, if you're going on tour, you could distribute information and collect donations at every show as well as visit the local chapters of an organization and interview their staff/volunteers for a video blog.

- **Songs**: Most bands can easily could release a record or write a song about an issue. My Chemical Romance, an American rock band, has taken on cancer as something that they've wanted to work for. Not only have they written several songs about it, but they have a special t-shirt to raise money for the issue, participate in fundraisers, blog about it on their website, and do PSA's about it as well.

A partnership will help you by getting you more press, interest from volunteers, staff, and donors of the organization, and realize the full effects of a strategic philanthropy initiative.

Activity 1: Find a Charity

If you don't already have a specific cause or organization in mind, here are some ways to find a cause that your band can champion:

- **Check with your band**: Is anyone in your band or their family members already personally involved with charity? Pulling the rest of the band in can be an easy transition.

- **Ask your fans**: Getting your fans involved is advantageous because they'll be more personally vested in your strategic philanthropy projects. You could hold a poll for which organization to support through some kind of a charity-of-the-month (or tour) program.

- **Work with your sponsors**: If one of your sponsors has a strong strategic philanthropy or corporate social responsibility (CSR) program, your involvement could further strengthen the relationship with them. They might also have additional resources, contacts, or ideas to give to help you get started.

- **Charity match program**: There are numerous charity match programs online that let you find organizations based on interest, location, or need. Charity Navigator (charitynavigator.org) and Charity Watch (charitywatch.org) are two of the largest resources for this.

Create a list of possible organizations and then work with your band to sort out the best fit for your group. You can consider a number of factors: a personal connection to the organization or cause, a good match for the brand, location of the organization, fan involvement, co-branded or partnership opportunities, their charity rating, fundraising or advocacy activities, type of need, etc. Whatever your criteria is, carefully think through your selection and find something that aligns with your goals.

Activity 2: Start a Fundraising Team

Most charities have fundraising events with an online component. For example, the American Cancer Society is known for their Relay For Life events. Participants register on a team and use the site to measure the amount of money that they raise. Top teams earn recognition online, at the local event through an awards ceremony, and in the community where the event takes places. Your band could start a fundraising team with your fans - not only is this a great way to reach all of the participants involved with the event, but it is a great bonding experience with your supporters as well.

To begin, simply ask your chosen charitable organization or find one that supports fundraising teams. Some sites, like Crowdrise

(crowdrise.com) are comprised entirely of team fundraising opportunities. All of them feature a leaderboard of sorts - it's an excellent way to get some additional attention while helping your favorite cause.

Activity 3: Have a Volunteer Day

Plan a day to volunteer with your band and your fans to volunteer at a local organization. Some examples include: cleaning up a neighborhood, feeding the homeless, handling the phones during a telethon, acting as guides at a museum, or just general help during a fundraising event. Often, fundraising events like to have live music - it's an opportunity to donate your services in exchange for a tax deduction and get some exposure with a new audience.

To get the most out of it, just follow these guidelines:

1. Try to plan something at least 1-3 months in advance.
2. Once you have a date and a cause identified, find the key stakeholders (people involved - your band, friends, family, fans, etc.) and personally ask them to get help.
3. Promote your appearance while recruiting for volunteers - list the date on your website as you would a show, issue a press release, and promote on social media. You might even be able to have the organization help by promoting your involvement as well.
4. Work with the organization's community relationship manager or volunteer coordinator to get the details about the opportunity and share that with all if your volunteers.
5. On the day of volunteering, assign someone to take photos and videos so that you can share the experience online in your blog, video channel, and social media. Post on social media throughout the day with a unique hashtag and asking volunteers, the organization, and people online to post using

it as well.

6. Collect all social media posts about it using Storify (www.storify.com) and creating an online article about the day. Then, share that article!

Activity 4: Give a Fair Share

One of the easiest ways to give is to donate a portion (or all) of the proceeds to a charity. This is something that you can do for a limited time, such as a weekend sale, or it can be a normal part of your business (X percent of every sale goes to a cause).

You can try it out by announcing a sale for an upcoming weekend. Be sure to support it with plenty of social media posts, web and email announcements, and letting the organization know that you are fundraising for them so they can help promote. One of the organizations that my band is involved with will notify all of its 60,000 social media followers every time we do plan something for them. It helps us sell merchandise, get publicity, *and* help a good cause!

Activity 5: Launch an Awareness Campaign

Some organizations will hold an awareness campaign and ask participants to take specific action on their behalf.

For example, 1-800 RUNAWAY asks volunteers to wear green socks as a conversation starter during National Runaway Prevention Month. People will also share photos on social media using a specific hashtag for the campaign as well.

You can launch an awareness campaign in a number of ways:

*   **Creating or collecting signatures for a petition:** If there is

some change in the world that you'd like to see, you could create a petition on Change.org or We The People (http://petitions.whitehouse.gov) and even get the attention of the U.S. president!

- **Ask the organization**: Check with your charity of choice to see if they have a specific awareness campaign coming up. If they do, they'll often have plenty of materials and ideas to share with you.

- **Get visual**: Post a link or host a banner on your website and social media sites. Consider dedicating part of your merch table or banner on stage to promote an organization or cause that you're supporting.

- **Share your story:** If the organization that you're involved with has a personal connection, consider sharing your story and explaining what it means to you. It's easy to create a quick video and most of the time, the organization will share it with their audience as well.

Activity 6: Build a Partnership

The most effective strategic philanthropy effort is a partnership. It often requires more involvement and resources but it also gives the biggest return on investment as well. So what does a partnership look like? That's really up to you and the organization that you are working with.

Meet with someone from the organization and brainstorm ideas on what you'd each like from the relationship. What kind of opportunities do you want to pursue? What are some of their big goals or needs? How can you help each other to become successful? Whatever you choose to do, dream big and inject some creativity into the process.

This is how my band, The Slants, approached a strategic philanthropy plan with a nonprofit organization called Liberty in North Korea:

- Created a campaign to raise money and awareness for a campaign they launched called "SHIFT." We filmed videos talking about why we were getting involved, shared about the organization in our newsletter and social media, and created a fundraising team.

- One of their donors pledged $0.25 for every view received on a campaign video that was uploaded. Our followers helped spread this and got over 20,000 views on the video within 72 hours, which raised enough money to rescue a family of four. We also helped recruit 7,000 volunteers, fundraisers, and people who committed to sharing the video.

- We proposed creating a "Nomad" campaign to travel with some of their interns across the country, bringing the message about the organization to venues, colleges, conventions, and other appearances for the band.

- Furthermore, we discussed the band visiting the organization's offices in Korea as part of an Asian world tour. This would include meeting with volunteers and staff in the field and interviewing the people being served by the organization.

- Finally, we proposed working with other artists for a fundraising concert, video series, limited-edition merchandise with a design related to the cause, and other possible campaigns.

There are no limits to the potential or creativity that you can bring to the project. In fact, the bigger and more creative the partnership is, the more opportunities that there will be for press, reaching new audiences, and to do something special that you care about.

11. Facebook training: better headlines, engaging links

Like learning your music instrument, it pays to invest some time into being more effective with social media. I often say that you should only focus on the channels where your audience is - but given the size and reach of Facebook, it is extremely likely that a good number of fans will be there as well (unless they are anti-Internet, in which case you can just skip this section entirely).

One of the most important (but underappreciated) skills to learn on Facebook is being able to write more effective posts that serve as an impetus for conversation. This is especially the case when posting links to content outside of Facebook itself.

When you share a link on Facebook, you can rewrite most of the content that pops up automatically in the share box:

image courtesy of Upworthy

As you can see, you can control the headline, the description, and the image as well as the normal Facebook share text that goes along with it all. Sure, it takes extra time to carefully think through each of these steps, but when it is more interesting, it ensures that more people will see - and hopefully, interact - with your post.

If you don't take the time to edit each of the areas, it's likely that the article you're sharing will end up looking like this:

image courtesy of Upworthy

Sites that have extremely high click through rates like Upworthy and Buzzfeed often spend more time working on their headlines than anything else. In fact, the editors at Upworthy write no less than 25 headlines per post before sharing something. After writing 25 headlines and choosing an image, their curators and editors ask:

- Does it leave them wanting more?
- Is it framed to share?
- Is it ready to go?
- Do we need an A/B test?

The extra time spent is definitely worth it: Upworthy will often get up to 25 times more traffic and activity on a post simply because of a better headline.

It's a good habit to fall into for any subject line or headline on any platform: Facebook post, YouTube video, email, etc.

Activity 1: Share and Rework a Link

Follow these steps:

1. Find a webpage that you'd like to share. It can be an interview or review of your band, your tour dates page, an interesting article, or even something from Upworthy. Just remember to keep it relevant to your target audience.
2. Paste the URL into the Facebook share box.
3. When the description box appears, delete the URL from your post and replace it with your own share text. Remember to add your call to action: ask fans to like, comment, share, or whatever you'd like them to do.
4. Try reworking each of the elements in the description box: the image, the headline, and the description. But remember, write out multiple versions of the headline before you post!
5. Measure and test the results. Use Facebook's Insight tools

afterwards to see the number of views, likes, and shares as well as the click through rate.

The more that you practice this, the better that you will get. Try sharing links at different times of day with different content to see what sticks.

Activity 2: Keeping Up with the Changes

You'll notice that underneath every post, Facebook will let you know how many people have seen that particular update (at the time of this writing, the message is on the bottom left-hand corner and says "X number people saw this post"). Facebook often adjusts its algorithm which can affect how effective your posts will be. As such, you'll sometimes see dramatic increases or decreases with each post - most of the time, the number will decrease because Facebook wants to encourage you to pay for boosted posts.

Today, search for any new articles relating to Facebook Edgerank, increasing engagement on Facebook, or Facebook's feed algorithm. Give higher priority to be credible sites and the date of the published article. The newer, the better.

Use search terms like "Facebook algorithm," "Facebook affinity, weight, and time decay," "Facebook Edgerank," and "Facebook post visibility."

It's easy to get into routine habits with Facebook and just catch up to the changes later. But I you stay ahead of the curve, you'll be able to have a more engaged audience.

12. Use your Facebook to subscribe to and engage with others

When it comes to social media, engagement is key. When you join any social media site, you become a part of a community. The more that you participate, the higher the visibility and engagement of your social media channels. This is especially true with your band's channels: your Facebook page, Twitter account, Pinterest, YouTube, Tumblr, or whatever site that you use.

Most social media channels let you interact like any other user when it comes to your band's profile. Facebook is an exception: there are some limited functions. However, you can use your page to "like" other pages and interact with them (leave comments, etc.).

To do this, click on "Use Facebook as:" under the settings wheel in the top right hand corner of your personal profile.

If you manage multiple accounts, you'll see several options available.

When you use Facebook as your page, you'll start on your Admin Panel and your band's profile page by default. To see the posts of other pages that you like and follow from your page (a view like your personal account's News Feed), just click on "Home" in the top right hand corner.

From there, you can like, comment, and share the content of other pages that you follow. They can, in turn, interact with your page - either on their own posts or on your wall if they do the same thing.

Think of social media as the world's largest networking party: if you only interact with a certain group of people, you'll miss out on opportunities to meet everyone else there. However, if you walk around the party and connect with everyone else who is in your target audience, you'll get much more out of it.

Using your band's account to subscribe, post comments, retweet, pin, etc. is the equivalent of being the social butterfly at the networking party. As you are looking for other channels to interact with, just remember your niche (Section 2, Chapter 8) and when appropriate, your pitch (Section 1, Chapter 16). That way, you can make the most of your efforts.

The advantage of using your channels to interact with other bands, celebrities, news sites, sponsors, or whatever content that you follow is that those interactions are visible to the public. In other words, your activities will be seen by those respective channels' followers. It's another way to be seen on social media in other places. However, don't spam the walls of others with only self-promotional content. That isn't appreciated and it certainly doesn't count as engagement.

One other note about using Facebook: the "Pages to Watch" feature is not the same thing as using your page to interact. You'll see that module in your Admin Panel like this:

The intention of "Pages to Watch" is that it allows you to compare against competitors (or others) in your industry. At the moment, it doesn't measure anything else other than the total number of likes for those pages and any changes each week. Facebook will recommend some similar pages, but you're also able to type in and follow your own choices. It's also important to know that when you add someone else to the "Pages to Watch" section, it notifies that page's administrators.

Personally, I don't find the feature that useful yet (you can look up each page whenever you like just as easily – and engagement matters more than the number of followers anyway). If Facebook adds more functionality, it might be helpful in the future.

Activity 1: Find your allies, influencers, and niche audience

Conduct an asset inventory of your social media channels. Ask yourself the following: What are your main, active social media sites? Where do you want to be seen or what pages' audience do you want to interact with? Once you have the general idea of what you want to accomplish, follow these steps:

1. Make a list of your most active social media channels and the

other brands that you want to interact with. This could other bands, media sites, celebrities, local businesses, etc. There isn't a limit to how many you can subscribe to but it's best to stay focused on other channels that are related to your niche.

2. Subscribe to and follow each of these brands' pages. Some sites have better tools than others for this process. For example, Twitter allows you to organize users by lists. You can create lists of your sponsors/partners, your super fans, venues and promoters, media contacts, or any other group of contacts that would be useful to keep together. Google plus allows to organize contacts into certain "circles." Most other sites (such as Facebook, YouTube, and Tumblr) will just consolidate all of your subscriptions into one feed.

3. Make it a habit to interact with these channels when appropriate - remember, you are representing your band so interactions should be appropriate to the voice or vibe that you normally have with your own followers.

    With Facebook, you have to take a few extra steps before you can see the content being shared by other pages.

4. In similar fashion to your own channel, you want to focus on creating conversation that's of interest to the audience - talk about your own music when appropriate, but don't force it. Find things of interest to that brand's audience and they'll engage with you/explore your channels on their own.

13. How to Use Facebook Events Effectively

Facebook Events is a useful tool for getting a gauge on what kind of response your show can expect . It will also send a notification to each person invited about the show. When used properly, it can create excitement about your show, update everyone when there is a change, and motivate people to invite others to the show.

The problem is that most people don't use Facebook Events well. Many blanket everyone on their contact list, including those who don't even live near the show. Those individuals just end up blocking or ignoring you. That's what happens when they feel like what you are doing is spam.

Some people use Facebook Events for other purposes as well: to invite people to watch a music video, for a crowdfunding campaign, or other online activities. However, this chapter focuses exclusively on using it for physical events.

Here is a step-by-step guide on how you should use Facebook Events:

1. **Have the event details set before you create the event**: Make sure that you have everything confirmed first. There's

nothing worse than promoting a show only to have it relocate or change times (people don't always go back to the event page or see the notifications). Be sure to have an appealing cover graphic, that always helps in raising visibility.

2. **Log in as your page to create the event**: If you log in as your band's page, the show will automatically populate under your page's "events" tab. After creating the page, you'll have to log in as your personal account to invite your contacts. At this time, there's no way for a page to invite its followers to an event, you can only share the event on your page.

3. **Sort the list before you send invites**: When you are inviting people to the event, don't blast everyone on your contact list. Spam is the quickest way to get ignored. Only invite people who you know who are in the area. In other words, don't bother inviting your friends in New York to your Los Angeles gig unless you absolutely know that they'll be in town.

   Facebook does not offer a very good way to do this but you can use graph search: in the search bar, type in "Friends who live in [enter city name here]" The downside is that if someone identifies their area with a county instead of a major city or uses a nickname for the city (i.e., Portlandia), they won't show up unless you search for it specifically.

4. **When possible, follow up with a personal message**: Most people don't like an anonymous invite, especially from someone that they haven't heard from in a while. It's best to send a message personally inviting them out and telling them how much it'd mean to you if they would show up and/or pass the word on.

5. **Use your email system**: If you use an email management system, then target a message to people specifically in the zip

code and send the link to the Facebook events page. The more people that are shown as attending, the better.

6. **Use your page to make updates**: "Share" the event on your page as well as on your personal profile (have your bandmates do the same). You can even target updates by location, so it will only be seen by fans in that specific area. As people RSVP, ask questions, or information gets updated, use your band page to respond to comments. As you get closer, leave a comment saying how excited you are or post a reminder (that kind of activity shows up under "notifications" for people connected to the event).

As an alternative, you can create an event page for your tour instead of individual shows. While I've used this method in the past, I don't recommend it. However, if you're short-pressed for time, create an event for your entire tour and invite everybody to that. List all of your show dates and link to your band's website so people can get more information, buy tickets, etc.

Having an active events page can appease promoters, especially if there's a good number of people RSVP'd. If you have some budget, you might also consider using a Facebook Ads campaign to support the event.

Remember, this still has to do with your music's branding so take the extra time to do it well. Whenever you use a tool like Facebook Events, put some extra thought into the process. If you respect your friends enough to not drop spam on them for every show, they'll pay more attention to your updates/invitations.

Activity 1: Best practices on Facebook Events

If you have an upcoming show, you should go through each step in this chapter and practice using Facebook Events effectively.

If you already have some events on your page, you should comb through your Facebook contacts based on their locations and invite them to their respective local shows. But don't just blindly invite them - send a personal message, post on their wall, text them or email them...you get the idea. The personal touch makes a tremendous difference because it shows that you care enough to put some thought into the process.

Activity 2: Create a Friends List Based on Area

You can export a list of your email list by zipc ode (fan management systems such as Fanbridge or Constant Contact are great for this) and find people in your personal network. Alternatively, you could create Facebook profile lists of people who live in certain cities that you frequent. That way, when you create an invite and need to invite contacts, you can quickly identify the people who should be getting an invitation and eliminating those who don't need to hear about the show.

14. Upload Tour Dates

You probably have multiple band websites (or at least should): your own website, an EPK or two, several social media sites, and an account with a band management website (such as Sonicbids, ReverbNation, Fan Bridge, Tour Command, etc.). Then of course, there are show databases as well (SongKick, Gigpress, etc.).

One of the least glorious but important tasks is to make sure that your tour dates are updated across all of these sites. Some will use a widget and can sync across multiple systems for you. However, you'll most likely have a few accounts that don't work well with each other so you will have to put things in manually. If you want to use the proprietary functions of a site (such as Facebook Events), you'll definitely have to enter those in separately.

There are a few different ways to reduce the amount of redundancy:

- **CSV File:** Most sites allow you to upload your calendar using a common-separated values (CSV) file. It's a pretty common type of form that can be created with Microsoft Excel or other table-based programs, such as Google Spreadsheet.

- **Use One Source:** Some sites, such as ReverbNation, allow you to export a widget of your calendar that can be embedded in other sites. It's not uncommon to see artists' websites or Facebook pages to have a ReverbNation calendar built-in. Most of these tools are free and easy to use. Unfortunately, none of these tools have an application that can cover all of the bases.

- **Reduce the Number of Sites:** Some believe that having too many websites or EPK-type accounts can fragment your brand - especially if some (or all) are suffering due to the lack of resources to dedicate to them. By limiting the number of sites down to the absolute essential and those used by your target audience, you can decrease the amount of sites needed to be managed.

- **IFTTT:** ifttt.com (If This, Then That) has a few pre-programmed functions, or recipes, based on Google calendar. For example, if you update your shows on a specific Google Calendar account, IFTTT can automatically create a post on Facebook, add the event to a Google Drive spreadsheet, tweet using a certain hashtag, or any number of other things.

Of course, you could always divide up the work among bandmates as well. If two or people were in charge of updating the calendar, it can reduce the amount of work quite a bit. However, if someone falls behind, it hurts the overall impact of the band.

Finally, don't forget about your partners. You should always have people like your publicist, manager, sponsors, fan club manager, street team(s), distributors, label, road crew, etc. be up to date when it comes to your upcoming appearances. That way, each of these partners can help look for opportunities to promote, introduce other business relationships, or to network at your show.

Activity 1: Have your bases covered

Do you have someone responsible for updating each of your websites and social media accounts for any changes to your calendar? Do you have someone in place who holds that/those person(s) accountable for keeping the information accurate and up-to-date? This could be something that you add into your inter-band agreement.

The business of the band is important: staying on top of your calendar should be considered a fundamental part of your operation. If you don't have some kind of agreement in place of who will update what information, how often it is updated, and which sites should be updated, then you should decide that immediately.

Activity 2: Increase Efficiency and Automation

You might spend some time learning about CSV files or IFTTT automation to see if it makes sense for you to set up a system for your tour dates. This can save quite a bit of time (after the initial learning curve and setup time).

15. Breaking Into New Markets

One way to grow your music's reach is to break into new markets. This could be taken a number of ways: new geographical areas (cities, states, countries, etc.) or simply new audiences in general (by demographic, interest, psychographic, etc.). Before you try and expand your reach through new markets, it's important to take a few things into consideration:

- **Return on Investment:** What is the cost or effort required to break into this market? Is the return on investment worthwhile or would you be better off using those resources to grow an existing market?

- **Goals:** What kind of role will this market play in your S.M.A.R.T.E.R Goals? (look at Section 1, Chapter 9)

- **Barriers to Entry:** What are the biggest challenges or costs that you need to overcome? Examine the economic conditions, competition, and openness to what you have to offer.

- **First Mover Advantage:** If there's no one else with a similar product/service, you'll enjoy what is referred to as "first mover advantage," or FMA. In the world of music, this usually is attention (from press and fans) for doing something new or different. For example, Elvis Presley gained FMA for his unusual style and gyrating hips, "Weird Al" Yankovic for his satiric songs in a time where few were making careers out of parodies, and DJ Kool Herc is often known as the father of hip hop. While you don't always have to be first in a market, it certainly helps - nobody wants to be known as the act that copied someone else.

- **Target Audience:** Who is the target audience in this market? What are their interests, habits, dislikes? How will you reach this audience?

Musicians traditionally break into new markets through one or more of the following ways:

- **Touring:** Most musicians try to break into new markets through touring, with the idea of playing in new cities and venues as a chance to build an audience. Often referred to as "paying dues," the number of shows per year and number of cities played is still considered a standard in the industry by which most artists are measured. When you're submitting to major festivals, record labels, booking agents, or other professional opportunities, most (if not all) will evaluate how often and how effectively you are touring.

- **Media Play:** When radio, TV, or internet media broadcast music, it's usually an effective way to get exposure in other regional markets without even performing there. These days, it's becoming more common for music media channels to expand the type of genres that they play or cover (radio, TV, and internet). Also, with the popularity of Internet radio or video sites such as YouTube, it's even easier than ever to get media play in front of new audiences.

- **Compilations**: Years ago, it was popular for record companies and magazines to give out compilation CD's to bring exposure to many different artists. Some magazines still offer this by charging bands to participate on a CD that is given out with the magazine, though it's much less popular now.

- **Remixes/collaborations**: Another way of getting media play outside of one's audience is by having someone else cover or remix the song. Sometimes artists collaborate on projects together through co-writing songs and guest appearances as well.

- **Press:** Getting unconventional press coverage (outside of your genre, region, etc.) is another way to expose your band to a new audience. This is usually achieved when something is particularly noteworthy. Note: this is different than growing an audience in your current market(s) that you are working for, which is why for the press to be interested, it needs to be something press worthy (Section 1, Chapter 3) in a manner that interests that audience. Sometimes it involves scandal, sometimes it is a major breakthrough.

- **Word of Mouth:** Fans usually don't fall neatly into categories or markets, but they often have contacts that may fall outside of a target audience. The most enthusiastic fans will often be the first to begin sharing outside of the market - telling friends in other cities or who have other similiar interests.

- **Advertising:** Those who have a marketing and advertising budget can reach new markets by buying ads (or sometimes media plays) in other markets.

Additionally, you can break into new markets through using some of these less common methods:

- **Marketing in Unexpected Places:** When you really understand the target audience of a new market, you can find ways to market to them in way that most musicians don't. An easy way to do this is to focus on specific interests, habits, or behaviors. For example, piano-rocker Matthew Ebel began playing at furry conventions (a subculture involving animal characters with human traits) and found an energetic, excited audience who immediately loved his quirky music. Playing just one of these events opened the door to many more across North America.

- **Responding to Controversy:** If you're able to write a quick, clever song about a hot topic, you can often get quite a bit of press from doing so (especially if you're one of the first to do so). For example, there was a huge controversy over someone making racist comments in a YouTube video titled "Asians in the Library." Rather than responding with anger like most people, singer-songwriter Jimmy Wong wrote a snarky song in response called Ching-Chong. The video immediately went viral, getting millions of views and national TV interviews, and helping launch Wong's career.

- **Sharing Your Expertise:** You probably have interests, skills, or experiences as a musician that could be shared with audiences outside of your own audience. For example, I often respond to calls for interviews from magazines looking for world travelers. When I interview as a professional musician on behalf of my band, they're always happy to print our name (and sometimes a link). It's even better when I can share an amusing story or interesting factoid. We've received press- and new fans- from exposure in Travel & Leisure Magazine, USA Today, Yahoo! Travel, and more simply from this.

- **Strategic Philanthropy:** As mentioned earlier (Section 2, chapter 10), connecting with a cause that you are passionate about can help you reach an entire audience. For instance, the artist Jon Davidson often performs for many charities, including at the American Cancer Society's Relay For Life events throughout the Pacific Northwest. His dedication to the cause has made many new fans of participants in these events - fans who otherwise would have never heard his music.

Whatever you decide to do, just make sure that it fits with your goals, will provide a return on your investment, that it is focused on the target audience, and that you use some creativity in the process.

Activity 1: Research New Markets Based on Geography

Spend some time carefully looking at new prospective markets that you'd like to break into. Gather as much information as possible and measure it against the checklist provided earlier (ROI, Goals, Barriers to Entry, etc.). The more time that you spend getting to know a target market, the more effective you will be.

It's easy to think in terms of geographic markets. It's also how many booking agents and most promoters think. When you're booking a tour or out-of-town shows, you'll need to consider the geographic market to some extent: how well you can draw at the show, what the audience and local press is like, what other local acts are based there, etc. Doing extra research ahead of time will not only help you book better shows, but also reveal if it is worth playing there to begin with.

When researching a new geographic market, you should look for the following:

- Venues: their size, genres that they cater to, their booking

process
- Local artists: Who frequently plays at the venues that you'd like to book, those who get local press, market themselves well
- Local music industry contacts: Promoters, booking agents, labels, managers, talent scouts, etc.
- Media: local weeklies that feature an Arts & Entertainment or live music section, local radio stations that cater to your genre.
- Events: Local festivals, conventions, cultural gatherings, etc.
- Schools: Colleges and universities in the area, their proximity to local venues, programs or clubs that are offered that relate to your music, etc.
- Record Stores: Which retailers offer in-store performances or meet-and-greet events, which offer consignment, will allow posters/promotional materials, and any that your distributor recommends that you contact.

Helpful tools for this information include: Yelp, Foursquare, Indie on the Move, the local papers, the local chamber of commerce, venue databases, Google Maps, etc.

Activity 2: Research New Markets Based on Market Segmentation

Market segmentation involves breaking down a broad audience into a smaller subset of customers. You can divide along demographics (age, gender, ethnicity, etc.) and/or psychographics (values, lifestyles, interests, etc.). The more that you can segment a market by narrowing it down, while still having an audience large enough to offset any investment, the better. Broad marketing is not only very expensive, but generally ineffective as well.

Example of Poor Segmentation (too broad):
I want to target the young (ages 12-25) Christian market in the Midwest.

The above example can be improved by narrowing and/or adding additional qualifiers. For example, this could be re-written to: *I want to target male Christians, ages 18-25, who live in the Midwest and are interested in bluegrass music.*

Here are some guidelines on finding new markets based on segmentation:

- **It Requires Experimentation:** You will need to try out different combinations of demographics and psychographics before settling on some. Researching different groups will help give you an idea over the size of the market that is available to you.

- **Don't Rely on Stereotypes:** People are often complex and have varied interests or habits. Sometimes, you'll seemingly contradictory values, traits, or interests - in fact, those are often the best niche markets because they are often ignored. For example, there are many Buddhist Christians and vegetarians who eat bacon. By trying new, unique combinations, you might find a new niche.

- **Have a Minimum:** You'll need some standard to measure by in order to see if there is enough of an audience in a particular market. Some examples include: number of websites or interest-based magazines, followers or groups on social media, message boards, subculture-based videos, books, and the amount of other musicians targeting this same market, if any.

- **Connect the Pieces:** It's best if you have a direct connection with that new audience, even if you aren't actively targeting it. You might have a song, imagery in a music video, certain fans, personal values, or other things related to the interest of the new market already. Coming from a place of authenticity is going to be much more effective than if you are only pandering to that market.

You can't effectively market yourself to everyone so it's important to be strategic about the process. Do some research, look at the potential, and find ways to connect. As you collect this information, save your notes so you can compare the pro's and con's of each potential new market.

Activity 3: Introduce a New Product for a New Market

If you've done your homework and know the interests of a new market, then you should begin working on a product that would appeal to this audience. This might involve re-packaging an existing product or service (live show, song, merchandise, artwork, etc.) but it could also mean creating something new (song, cover, music video, merchandise, etc.). If you work with someone else (such as an established artist or maven in that market), that could also mean collaboration, licensing, co-branded marketing campaigns, or other things.

Whatever you do, it should be based on research and done with your S.M.A.R.T.E.R goals in mind (Section 1, Chapter 9).

Activity 4: Connect with the Mavens of a New Market

One of the most effective ways of breaking into new markets is to reach the mavens (also known as influencers) of that particular market. In fact, author Malcolm Gladwell argues that this is the most important ingredient for a movement to go viral. For example, Rebecca Black's infamous "Friday" music video didn't get much attention until a few select mavens (such as the TV show Tosh 2.0) got a hold of it.

When you are researching new markets, you should have the

information that you need to see who wields influence over that audience. Generally, it's local media, bloggers, celebrities, and other tastemakers, so you will get the most return on your investments by focusing on those individuals. However, they probably get approached often so it's important that you've perfected your pitch (Section 1, Chapter 16) and that you explain how your work would appeal to *their* audience. How do you know it appeals to their exact audience? Well, all of the research you've done will tell of course.

Activity 5: Connect Your Current Market(s) with The New Market

Sometimes, you can reach an entirely new audience from making a connection with your existing market through an alliance or common bond.

In eras past, entire empires would make this kind of alliance through marriage. Today, some artists still are. For example, when cabaret pop/rock icon Amanda Palmer married novelist Neil Gaiman, their two distinct audiences merged together like extended family meeting for the first time. The support for both artists grew exponentially and they became royal icons for a sexy/geeky movement. While they certainly aren't the only entertainment power couples that exist, it definitely made an impact on their respective careers.

Of course, marriage isn't the only option. Sometimes, artist collaborations are another way to achieve this same effect, especially when they are unexpected. For example, over the years, we've seen pairings such as Garth Brooks and Kiss, Nelly and Tim McGraw, Weezer and Lil Wayne, and Elton John and Eminem. The cross-genre and cross-cultural exchange can be an effective way to get exposure to a new audience.

Finally, don't think that all collaborations have to be made solely with other music artists. The same effect can be achieved with visual arts, authors, theater, or any other possible partnership. For instance, my band, The Slants, has worked with wushu martial artists experts, trapeze and aerial artists, and cosplayers to reach new audiences.

Activity 6: Breaking Into a New Region

Playing a show in another town is a great way to get introduced into the market, but how often does a single tour date (or even repeated shows) make a city or state-wide impact? The reality is that it takes much more than a good show to move the needle. So how do you make a lasting impact?

If you really want to break into a new region, you should create a deliberate and strategic plan about how it will be done. Some ideas of what you should include: trading shows or collaborating with a prominent artist in the area, touring and performing frequently (if it's within range), getting press coverage, working with an established entity (such as securing a residency, working with an organization like a college or indie record store), focused and regular advertising, festival appearances, developing a fan-led street team, or most likely, a combination of the above.

If you already have a target audience, you can use that to your advantage. For example, if you have a connection with the roller derby crowd, you could contact leagues in that city, either to invite them to a show or to perform at an event. You can often turn personal hobbies, interests, or contacts into opportunities to reach multiple audiences in a geographic area.

Finally, when you do play, you need to develop relationships. That might mean getting them signed up on your email list (Section 1, Chapter 12), connecting with them on social media, and/or finding ways to make them feel special (Section 5, Chapter 11).

Activity 7: Create a New Market Out of Old Ones

Related to Activity 2 (researching new markets based on market segmentation), you can often focus your promotional efforts on a more specific part of your audience. The more targeted a message, marketing effort, or idea, the more it will appeal to that specific niche. That in turn increases response rates, return on investment, and for organic marketing processes to occur.

The easiest way to do this to create a Venn Diagram of your different audiences that you're currently appealing to, then finding ways to specifically target the people in the intersecting points.

The more intersecting points, the more specific the audience that will be interested. For example, if you played in a female-fronted band that plays in bars across New York City, but also have a song about magic inspired by Harry Potter, the Venn Diagram for the fans would look like this:

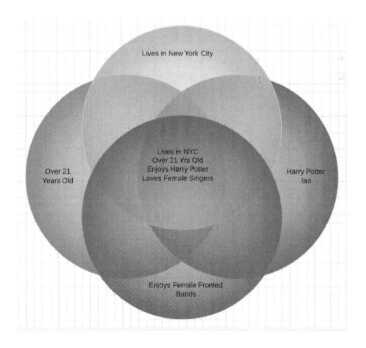

Each of the circles represents different audiences:
- Those who love in New York City
- Those who are over 21 years of age
- Harry Potter fans
- People who enjoy female singers

While a band in this situation could easily target any of these groups individually, the categories are so broad that it would be very expensive to get any decent response. If you combined any two of these, it would still be difficult or feel too generic. However, the center section offers a much more precise market to target - and helps narrow down an audience that would be most interested in the band.

If you add some additional qualifiers or circles, it could help narrow it down even more. For example:

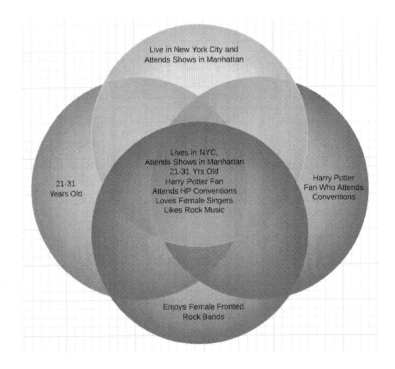

In this example, the interests are narrowed down so it's even more specific. If you had a show booked at Fontana's (venue in the Manhattan region of New York City), you could focus on the fans of adult-themed Harry Potter conventions (in fact, there is one in the Northeast called Misti-Con), and work with other female-fronted acts. Furthermore, you could design a social media ad campaign with each of these interests in users' profiles. However, you can see that the combination of the overlapping circles represent some opportunities for defining new, niche markets.

Many online ads work this way. If you have a Facebook ad campaign, you'll essentially create your own intersection of interests, demographics, and location.

In both of the Venn Diagram examples, the band wasn't working with the intersection of all the groups. They might have marketed to Harry Potter fans separately from their live show endeavors. But the new, niche market created would offer an extremely high return on investment for fans who sat in the center of all of the circles.

Of course, your diagrams will look much different. You don't necessarily have to have a location and you might even list specific social media sites. Whatever you do, start out broad, then narrow it down. As you do, look for websites, magazines, fan clubs, other artists, or festivals that may cover the intersection of several of your circles. When you do, look for new, specific markets that you can target that all originated from existing ones that you've been working with.

Section 3: Developing Your Musicianship and Songwriting Skills

When most musicians work on their craft, they often focus on "hard skills" or technical abilities. This can include extending vocal range, the ability to play certain musical phrases precisely, finger placement, and more. While these skills are fundamental, it's also important to develop musicianship as well. Musicianship involves the "soft skills," or intuitive abilities. Musicianship includes things like the having a musical ear, the ability to sight read, and being able to recognize melodies or rhythm. The former deals with being able to play an instrument, the latter deals with the ideas of being a musician.

A good analogy would be mastering the use of language. Hard skills would include vocabulary, grammar, and sentence construction whereas soft skills would be the ability to use language for expression or poetry. While the two are definitely related, training in both areas would be necessary to achieve true proficiency. Being a musician is no different: not only should you master your instrument, but you should also master the overall concept of music as well.

Songwriting is definitely a part of musicianship, a soft skill that should be developed with specific training and education. And of course, songwriting is an essential part of having a successful music career. Even if you plan on hiring professional songwriters, it's important to have musicianship abilities to not only recognize appropriate material, but to be able to fully express it as well.

Finally, like the business side of your music career, it's also important to be strategic about the musicianship side of things. Do you pick up your guitar or some drum sticks only to practice certain songs or are you challenging yourself and have a growth plan for your skills as well? The very best musicians are constantly developing and expanding upon their craft in a very deliberate manner.

1. Musicianship Through Scales

One of the best ways to practice is to work both your hard as well as the soft music skills simultaneously through the use of music scales.

Major scales, arpeggios, and music exercises can help further skill with an instrument while developing harmony recognition and deeper melodic understanding. To further develop musicianship, you can practice with variations in timing and intonation. For instance, many jazz pianists actually practice scales in harmony form through transposing or performing in different voicing registers:

Learning concepts like the Cycle of Fifths is essential for this (more on that in the activities section). Memorizing the relationship between notes in the chromatic scale will help you develop your own scale exercises to challenge and increase your skill.

Additional exercises can be added through the use of different time signatures or rhythms, such as swing eighths (every other eighth note as a slightly different length but still lands on the 2nd and 4th downbeat).

Practicing scales also develops your aural musicianship skills, especially when you learn the types of relationships between notes in non-traditional or Western scales. Not only can these musical relationships inspire new music ideas, but it will deepen your improvisational skills as well.

Here's what jazz legend Chick Corea says about scales:

1) **Learn all the scales you can find** - from books, from recordings, from listening to live music, from questioning other musicians—and especially from transcribing from recordings any scales that sound interesting to you.

2) **Take these scales (you can start with just one or two) and start experimenting with them.** Play them—fool around with them. See what music you can make with them. See how they may fit into songs or improvisations that you like. Make sure you continue to use your own judgment about what works or doesn't work—what sounds good to you and what doesn't.

3) **When you find some scales that you really like and the music starts to flow, write songs and phrases with the new scale**s. Improvise with them. Perform the songs. See how it goes. Then write some more.

4) **Once you see that you can do these first 3 things (and you can do them over and over again)—then begin creating your own scales.** Try a series of notes that sound good to you. Write them down. Even give them names if you want to. Write songs and improvise with these. Combine them with other scales you've learned.

4a) By the way, you can do the same thing (1 through 4) with chords and voicings.

5) **And finally – forget all about "scales" and "what chords and notes fit into them"—and just play what you hear!**
You can do 1 through 5 over and over and over – - and build up your "repertoire" of scales, chords and various techniques—and keep inventing new ones. Eventually these "techniques" become part of you because you are now "inventing" them—therefore you now never need to rely on "memorization"—it's all just a flow of creation, always in a new unit of present time.
Ahhh—easy to say—but—the test and the fulfillment is in the ACTION! Good luck—and many happy (and/or grueling) hours of searching and creativity—and making Music!

(from http://www.chickcorea.com/ask-chick/47-your-questions/132-what-is-your-approach-to-scales.html)

Activity 1: The Cycle of Fifths

The Cycle of Fifths is both a visual as well as aural tool to help understand the twelve tones of the chromatic scale, their key signatures, and their associated major and minor keys. Every musician should memorize the concept in order to help transpose songs, compose, produce harmonies, and understanding key signatures.

Every note has an equal interval of a tempered fifth with the next note. If you visualize it on the wheel, as you move clockwise to the next fifth's key signature, the number of sharps increase. Conversely, if you rotate counter-clockwise from a note's fifth, the number of flats increase. For example, in the key of C major, there would be no sharps or flats. However, its fifth, G has one sharp, D has two sharps, A has three, and so on. Moving counter clockwise from C, F has one flat, Bb has two flats, Eb has three, and so on.

This is a visual representation of the wheel itself:

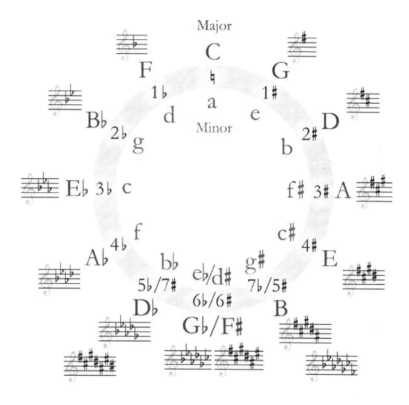

Learning the order of sharps and flats is a fundamental, but often ignored skill outside of those who have been classically trained. Study it to become a better writer and performer.

Activity 2: Learn Other Related, Advanced Circles

If you have mastered the Cycle of Fifths and are able to not only play but recognize the musical intervals, consider looking up and learning other important musical concepts, such as:

- The Cycle of Fourths
- Diatonic Circle of Fifths
- Chromatic Circle
- Enharmonics
- Pitch Constellation

Activity 3: Learn Every Scale That a Musician Should Know

Below are the most common scales that are used to construct chords and also are the foundation of many songs:

- All 12 Major Scales
- Modes of the Major Scale
- Minor Scales
- Natural Minor Scale
- Harmonic Minor Scale
- Melodic Minor Scale
- Chromatic Scale
- Pentatonic Scales
- Whole-Tone Scale
- Octatonic Scale

Additionally, there are essential scales specifically used in jazz music as well. Below are several popular examples:

Dominant Bebop Scale

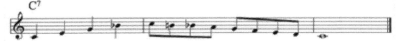

Minor Bebop Scale

Major Bebop Scale

Harmonic Minor Bebop Scale

Lydian Dominant Scale

Most people are only familiar with those musical ideas of the genres or cultures that they're used to. Learning scales from other genres or music of cultures can help you produce more interesting sounds, chords, and musical phrases, especially if you've only trained with traditional Western scales. It's a great way to not only stand out, but expand your creative horizons as well.

For instance, the Phrygian Dominant Scale is especially common in Arabic and Egyptian music.

Here it is in the key of C:

The Double harmonic is another popular, slightly different variation:

    When practicing your instrument(s), familiarize yourself with all of these scales. Obviously, there are many more that aren't even listed here so if you have these down, feel free to explore and grow your musical horizons. You can also expand your practice repertoire by incorporating swing time signatures, harmonies, and other variations as well.

Activity 4: Write Your Own Scales

    When you consider the core concept of a scale - any series of notes that go up or down, you can create your own scales be putting together a series of notes that sound good to you. Write the scale down, transcribe it to other keys. You can also program that scale into a synthesizer or music composition program to use as an arpeggiator or the start of a song.

2. Learn/Understand a New Instrument

One way to develop your musicianship skills is to gain the perspective and experience that comes from learning the hard skills of another music instrument. This is especially true when you learn from an instrument of a different classification (strings, woodwinds, brass, percussion, or even vocals). Understanding how each instrument works, especially how it works in an ensemble, will give more depth to your songwriting as well as help you communicate your ideas to your band members more effectively.

In a way, music instruments are akin to a toolbox when it comes to building a song. The more tools that you master, the more quickly you can work without relying on someone else. Yet, even if you are working with others who specialize in other tools, you will have an understanding of how things work, what step in the process they come in, and how things should all work together in tandem.

Of course, learning a brand new instrument - especially one from a different classification - can often take some time and dedication. However, I've found that it is not only a fulfilling endeavor, but it also helps you master your primary instrument(s) better. For example, when I started learning how to play the drums, it helped me be a better bass player who could work with drummers in a tighter, more effective way. Similarly, when I learned chords on the guitar, it gave me a better understanding of harmonic structures on the piano.

Activity 1: Master Your Natural Instrument - Your Voice

Whether you sing in your band or not, learning how to use your voice as an instrument is an important part of being a musician. Learning how to sing teaches you how to inhabit your space, develops self-confidence, has positive benefits to your health, and allows you to develop your own personal, unique instrument: your voice. Additionally, singing helps your memory and can reduce stress and anxiety as well. Finally, singing helps you develop your musician's ear and trains you to listen to tones.

If you're able to, I recommend taking singing lessons from a vocal instructor. However, if you don't have the time or resources to dedicate to that endeavor, there are many free videos available on YouTube to help you get started. When you're learning to sing, you should especially focus on your posture, your breathing, how to safely warm up (and cool down), and of course, pitch.

Activity 2: Step Into a Band Member's Shoes

Begin learning another music instrument that's played in your band. Not only is it useful for developing your musicianship abilities, but you can sometimes cover for a band member who is sick or unable to make a show in a pinch.

Bonus points if it is an instrument entirely different than your own. For example, if you are a guitarist, learn how to play drums. If you play drums, learn the guitar. And so on.

If you don't have access to the instrument, ask to borrow or trade between rehearsals.

Activity 3: Step Out of the Band and Into a Different Classification

This one might be a little more difficult since it requires access to an instrument that you might not already have, but you should try learning a music instrument from an entirely different classification.

The four major music instrument classifications are:

- **Strings:** Instruments that produce sound from vibrating strings. It includes guitars, piano, the violin, etc.

- **Woodwinds:** Instruments that require the flow of air for sound that are played in a particular manner (flutes or reeds). For example, the flute, saxophone, oboe, and clarinet are all woodwinds.

- **Brass:** Instruments that produce sound from the vibration of the player's lips. They usually have a specific mouthpiece and includes devices such as the trumpet, trombone, or bugle.

- **Percussion:** Instruments that produce sound from striking or scraping. Most people think of drums but it also consists of xylophones, bells, whistles, and the dulcimer as well.

It definitely helps having an instructor, but if you have a fundamental understanding of music instruments, you can probably teach yourself using a variety of resource - books, videos, and so on.

Also, remember that complete mastery of the instrument isn't the goal (though proficient playing can be a benefit in a number of ways). The goal is to learn the overall concepts, approach, and perspective of that instrument in an ensemble setting. Having a good understanding of the tonal and dynamic range, sound qualities, and style is more important to the development of your musicianship.

3. Dissecting Song Structures

One of the most important skills of any songwriter is the ability to develop successful song structures. The components of a song are like building blocks: they ultimately comprise the core of the anatomy. Mastering the techniques behind different song structures allows you to fully develop a creative idea without hindering your creative abilities.

If you are playing pop music - or almost any genre other than improvisational jazz - there are actually very few song structures that are used in hit songs. These song structures can all be learned and implemented effectively. Also, contrary to what some may think, it is possible to apply a primary structure without affecting the creative integrity of the song itself.

Most radio-friendly songs are built on the following components:

- Verse
- Pre-Chorus

- Chorus
- Bridge

The most four basic (and most popular) structures:

- Verse - Chorus - Verse - Chorus
- Verse - Chorus - Verse - Chorus - Bridge - Chorus
- Verse - Chorus - Verse - Chorus - Verse - Chorus
- Verse - Verse - Bridge - Verse

While there are certainly variations out there, most "hit songs" are based on these main music ideas. Some also involve other components such as introductions, instrumental solos, or turnarounds, but those usually only serve as a function of arrangement than song form.

Learning popular song structures will not stifle your creativity. Instead, it will help put your music in a format that is radio-friendly and approachable to larger audiences.

Activity 1: Identify Song Structures in Your Genre

In *6 Steps to Songwriting Success* by Jason Blume, he offers the following songwriting exercise:

Write out the lyrics to three of your favorite songs...if you are writing for yourself, with an artist (for his/her project), or for your own band, choose songs that were written by the artist and/or producer in genres similar to your own. Answer the following questions for each song:

- What structure did the writer employ?
- Can you identify the sections of the song?
- Where does the title appear?

- How many bars make up the introduction?
- How many lines are in each section of the song?
- How many bars are in each musical section?
- If there is an instrumental solo section, where does it appear, and how many bars is it?

After, compare the songs selected with your own.

Activity 2: Identifying Song Structures Outside of Your Genre

If you've mastered the basics of song components and song structures, I recommend dissecting top songs from artists outside of your genre. You can either turn on the radio station or look at the top 3 songs on Billboard or Spotify right now from artists outside of your genre. Then, ask yourself the following:

- What structure is being used?
- How soon is the chorus introduced and how does the writer reinforce it through the song?
- How are turnarounds used (melodic hooks that follow a chorus and leads back into the verse)?
- How many bars is the bridge and where is it used in the song?

The more you do these exercises, the more that you'll notice almost every pop song on the radio fall into these major song structures. These structures should come as second nature to you to help you better communicate your musical or lyrical ideas.

Activity 3: Use a Song as a Template

Follow these steps to help you apply a successful structure to a new song. First, choose a favorite song of yours and dissect its parts. Then, use the anatomy of that song and fill its components in with yours. For example, if the song format is Verse - Chorus - Verse - Chorus - Bridge - Chorus with a turnaround after the first verse, then use the same structure for your song but fill it with our own chord progressions, melodies, and lyrics.

The simple re-arranging of a song can sometimes lead to more interesting or approachable structures. Try it out and see what can become of your own songs!

4. Build Sight Reading Skills

Sight reading, or *prima vista*, is an important skill that every musician should have. If you are regularly auditioning for roles or are a studio/session player, sight reading is an absolutely essential. While the ability to read music is very much a hard skill, the benefits of developing sight reading will allow your musicianship to flourish. It helps you develop better concentration, increases recognition of musical phrases and patterns, enhances your rhythm, and improves your improvisational skills.

Below are some tools that can help you improve your sight reading skills.

Activity 1: Sight Reading Websites

There are several sight reading websites to help you master the craft (some are free, some require a subscription). Most involve an online library of composed musical phrases and exercises that you can practice on. Advanced sites offer some degree of control or have additional features, such tempo, and key and time signature searches.

Take a look and find the one that best fits your needs:

- http://sightreadingmastery.com
- http://thesightreadingproject.com/home
- http://www.sightreadingpractice.com

Activity 2: Construct Your Own Sight Reading Book

You can put together your own collection of sight reading exercises to practice through. Here some general tips when constructing the book:

- Find shorter music pieces so you can still practice when you're short on time
- Mix it up with exceeding simply pieces to extremely challenging ones
- Organize them by difficulty level (easy to hard)
- Include multiple genres, time signatures, and keys
- Include music written for a different instrument on your own

If you want to add an additional challenge, try transposing the musical phrases into different keys or tempos while you run through them.

Activity 3: If You Can't Read Music...

If you can't read music, you can still practice the general concept by trying to sight read tablature. The same general concepts apply: play pieces unfamiliar to you (especially in a genre other than your own), practice live transposing of keys, play a variety of key signatures and tempos in order to get used to learning new songs on sight (and on ear).

Activity 4: Sight Singing

Another activity that is extremely helpful is to sight sing music pieces that you have. In fact, you can still use your sight reading book (from Activity 2) or download a variety of music available online. Not only will this help strengthen your vocal abilities, but it will also improve your musical ear as well - especially if you can learn to find proper pitch ranges without a tuner or another source.

5. Transcribe Your Music

Transcribing your music involves translating everything from a piece of music that is performed to written form. Think of it has dictation for music. If you have intricate pieces of music, time signature changes, instrument solos, or other frills, it can make the task much more tedious. However, there are a number of benefits for taking the time to transcribe your music:

- It sharpens your musical ear and sense of relative pitch.
- It will help you recognize, learn, and dissect ideas such as reharmonization, embellishing chords, good bass-line movement, voice leading, and riff construction.
- Transcribing improvised solos will further enhance your improvisational skills.
- It helps you become a faster and more accurate reader (develops sight reading skills).
- It strengthens your musical memory.
- You can sell the transcriptions to publishers, fans, etc.

If you aren't well-versed with reading/writing sheet music, you can still enjoy some of the benefits from tabbing your music as much as possible - even for instruments other than your own (including vocals).

Some general tips:

- When transcribing, **use a chordal instrument** such as a piano or guitar in order to recognize and duplicate types of chords in music. Sometimes the variations are subtle and requires careful listening.

- **Begin with the key signature**. If you know the key signature, you can already eliminate an entire set of notes that won't be present in the sections of the song that uses it. It could very well be the entire song, if they don't change keys.

- **You don't always have to start at the beginning**. Initiate the process in whatever area you're most comfortable with.

- **Loop it.** Use a playback method that is friendly to repeated playback, especially the ability to start/stop in exact moments.

- **Use Software**. There are programs such as *Transcribe!* and *Amazing Slow Downer* that can help you with loop sections and slow down sections to hear intricate parts without affecting their pitch You can also use software such as *Finale* or *Sibelius* for playing back transcribed music to make sure that you have it correct. They also keep track of time (bpm) and make editing much easier.

- **Begin by mapping out the song's sections**: intro, verse, chorus, reprise, bridge, etc. Include the key signature and tempo. Then transcribe repeating elements before moving to complex, individual sections. As you transcribe, sing the parts to see if they sound correct (or if you are using composition software, simply play the written music).

Activity 1: Start With a Song

Begin transcribing one of your shorter, more simple songs. Deconstruct it in every way possible through the art of written music. If you have access to transcription or music composition software, you should definitely use it. If you have trouble with sheet music, you can begin by tabbing each of the song's parts.

You can either use a pre-recorded song or one that is in the works. In fact, transcribing songs as you write them can help tremendously before you record them in the studio. Not only will it tighten the overall song, but it will help you completely think through each of the parts involved in the song.

Activity 2: Change It Up

Add some challenge and variation to your transcribed music. Not only will this help grow your overall musicianship skills, but it can also help with your songwriting, production, or creating additional renditions of your song (for remixes and so on).

Take your transcribed music and try some of these additions:

- Add a harmony or counter melody to some of the parts
- Change the tempo or key of the song
- Find specific sections to add breaks (music rests), tempo changes, or key changes
- Strip away sections of the song, change out the instruments
- Record improvisational playing to the song and see if they fit

Activity 3: Try Another Writer's Song

Another good exercise is to transcribe a song that has been

written by someone else. If you're looking for an activity that is aimed at helping your band or career in a direct way, you can focus on a song that you're thinking about covering (or at least a song from a writer that is considered a primary inspiration). If you want to specifically focus on personal growth and the development of your musicianship skills, transcribe a song from an unfamiliar genre.

6. Create a Better Melody

It's often said that all songs on the radio sound the same. To a certain degree, that's partially true many are based on a similar format, key signature, tempo, vocal cadence, and sometimes, the main melody. However, learning how to create slight variations in a signature melody or musical phrase will help you explore some of the key concepts in musicianship: developing variation, understanding sound patterns, and assisting with improvisation.

Many artists initiate writing a song by beginning with a main hook or melody already in mind. These exercises challenge you to do the opposite: begin with the foundation and work your way up. To begin, simply create a specific chord pattern, something that can serve as a chorus or a verse (approximately 8 bars in length, but no more than 16). If you'd like, you can begin with an idea that you've already worked on. Just keep the chord pattern underneath the melody but leave out the rest. It's nice to have several foundations or patterns on hand to work from in order to generate new ideas.

When writing melodies, there aren't hard and fast rules - it tends to be subjective and relies on intuition. However, you should keep the following tips in mind:

- **Repetition.** There has to be some degree of repetition in the music phrase (but not to the extent where it eliminates variety and becomes boring or annoying).

- **Dynamics:** Have some play with the volume and intensity of certain notes.

- **Harmony:** Adding a harmonic parallel or counter-melody could help give the main idea some additional depth or strength.

- **Rhythmic Variation:** Slight changes in rhythm or speed while keeping the same general note pattern can make things more interesting.

- **Shape:** The rising and falling of notes will have a certain flow, but if it only rises or falls, it will sound more like a scale than a tune. Most of the time, the melody will stay within one octave range so that it's more accessible and memorable. But more than anything else, it should flow.

If you're reading this book, you probably already have a good sense of how to write music and know how to write a catchy melody. At the same time, you'll also recognize the importance of a strong melody and know that it is one of the most important skills that any songwriter should posses. The following exercises help you expand your current skills.

Activity 1: As Many Melodies as It Takes

This is all about creating as many melodies as possible in order to create variety, spontaneity, and develop improvisation. It might also lead to developing a new, usable song as well! Grab a recording device (either a portable voice recorder, your smartphone, or studio setup) and simply follow these steps:

1. Take your basic chord pattern or structure (approximately 8 bars in length, but no more than 16 and no less than 4 bars) and set it up to loop with a 2 bar break between each set.
2. Sing a vocal melody to the pattern.*
3. Sing another. Then another. Then another. The idea is to record as many ideas and variations of the idea as possible in 10-15 minutes. Some of this might be terrible, but just keep going.
4. You should have at least 15 ideas recorded. If you feel like you need more, just repeat the process.
5. After you have collected at least 15 ideas, save the recordings and walk away. Wait at least 24 hours before listening to them.
6. After the waiting time, if a certain melody stays in your head, that can definitely be a good sign of a winner. Either way, review all of the ideas and pick out the parts that are the most useable. You might be able to combine ideas or even use a variation as a counter melody or reprise.

*The same activity can also be adapted for creating guitar or keyboard riffs and leads as well.

Activity 2: Drop the Base

This is a variation of Activity 1 - rather than working off of a foundation or base chord structure, you simply record yourself singing/playing as many melody ideas as possible. Record for at least 15 minutes.

By eliminating the repeating structure, you'll get much more variety in tone, shape, tempo, and cadence. For some people, it's actually more difficult since it involves complete improvisation without any base to work from. However, the free-flowing nature might generate more ideas that you can work with.

Again, wait at least 24 hours before reviewing, then transcribe or record the ideas

7. The Art of Remixing

Remixing is another activity that involves deconstructing and reconstructing songs in order to improve the fidelity, adapt it for a different audience or genre, and to create new versions of the composition. While this type of work will involve greater lengths of time, it is an activity that will help you consider new points of view when approaching a song.

Sometimes, a remix becomes more popular or well received than the original version of a song. For example, R Kelly's *Ignition (Remix)* completely overshadowed the original to obscurity. Canadian DJ A-Trak's remix brought new depths to the song *Trying to Be Cool* by Phoenix. In fact, some artists build entire careers simply from remixing others' works, especially in the electronic/dance and hip-hop genres.

For artists who want to showcase some depth, market their songs to new audiences, or simply surprise existing fans with new renditions of classics, remixing can help provide a tangible option.

How to Create a Remix

These days, digital audio workstations (DAW) make it easier than ever to create a remix, especially of your own songs (assuming that you have all of the raw tracks available to you). For those who can't afford a premium program such as Ableton Live (http://www.ableton.com), Audacity is a free option that can help you get started (http://audacity.sourceforge.net/).

It's best if you have the separate tracks of a song available to you, especially the vocals. If you only have final versions or complete versions of a song, most DAWs have tools to help you extract vocals - either to completely isolate or remove them from the song. These tools are rarely perfect and usually require a bit of reworking but they are worth a shot if they're your only option.

Once you import all of the tracks, you can begin by dissecting the song down to the parts that you like best. This could be a certain vocal melody, a guitar riff, line in the song, or a repeated element that you find interesting. You'll also want to isolate any rhythmic elements that you'd like to keep - drum loops, percussion, beats, and so on. To test the rhythmic elements, turn them into loops and see how they fall into place when placed in a full bar of music- are the beats landing in the right place? Are sounds getting cut off (cymbal crashes are notorious for this)? You might need to edit the sample or loop created to make sure that it feels right.

Adjust the BPM to a tempo that you like and make sure the your rhythmic loops line up properly (DAWs usually have editing windows to get precise measurements of time). If you decide that you want an entirely new beat, you can usually construct one using the tools of a DAW or download other drum samples and loops for your song.

Begin to add the other elements that you've kept or create new ones that you believe will work for the song. Many DAWs cater to electronic and dance remixes so they'll usually have on board virtual synthesizers or other tools to work with. You can also record new parts (matched to the new tempo) and import the sounds in.

After you reconstruct the song with the new, time-corrected

pieces that you like, begin experimenting or adding in effects. For example, you'll probably need to EQ certain tracks over again but they might benefit from delay, phasing, flange, reverb, modulation, or other effects as well. Again, these are usually found in the DAW itself.

After you finish, you'll want to normalize the audio and export it. Of course, if you end up remixing a song and would like to release it, it's recommended that you have it tested out on multiple systems, then professionally mastered, before it is shared.

Activity 1: Dance Dance Evolution

Because the art of remixing naturally lends itself to electronic/dance music, try creating a dance remix of one of your songs. If you're unfamiliar with the genre, take some time to listen to popular dance remixes of songs that you're familiar with or are in an inspiration for your music. You might even approach the project by dissecting the song structure that they use and base yours off of it. The primary goal is to create a remix that makes people want to dance!

Activity 2: Create an Ambiance

Ambient music is a subgenre of electronic music that focuses on sound patterns rather than traditional compositional elements in music. For ambient music, it's all about evoking a certain mood. It can be minimalist in nature, musically descriptive, or even avant-garde. The pieces tend to be longer in length and can be ignorable while interesting - a balance that can be surprisingly difficult to achieve. Noted artists in the genre include Brian Eno and Aphex Twin.

Try deconstructing one of your songs in order to focus on the emotional or atmospheric elements that you'd like to emphasize. Take the time explore songs by other artists to get a feel for the genre and begin experimenting with songs, forms, and layers of sound. While it is definitely a departure from the traditional pop song, learning about ambient music with your own songs can be a great way to pull new, emotional content and inspire additional ideas.

Activity 3: Get Remixed

Sometimes, it's best to let a pro handle things and see how they interpret your songs. If you work with someone who is much more experienced and fluent with remixing tools, you'll often find a number of tricks that can assist you with the production of your own music, no matter what genre you perform. Also, giving someone else complete creative control over your songs can bring out some interesting ideas that you might not otherwise hear in your own music. Finally, working with another artist can also help you reach a new audience. You might consider remixing or covering each other's songs to make each of your catalogs more accessible to a new market or audience.

8. Find New Sources of Inspiration

As a creator of artistic works, it's always important to have new sources of inspiration. Some like to think of it as a cup or bowl: if you're constantly pouring ideas out (composing songs, creating art, writing lyrics, etc.), your vessel will eventually become empty unless you replace it with something else.

Here's a simple list of places that you can turn to in order to find inspiration for new songs:

- A personal experience that is relatable to your target audience (this is why heartbreak and love are the most popular themes for songs - they're themes that many people can identify with).
- Favorite film or TV show
- Spiritual, faith-based book, or sacred text
- Poem
- Favorite (or random) book
- Inspirational quotes
- Historical event
- Current item in news headlines
- Other songs that you enjoy
- Nature/landscape

- Old photographs

Once you have a general idea of what you want to write about, you should narrow it down to a specific emotion or perspective expressed in a way that an audience can relate to. If it is a common emotion or idea, such as love, try to find a new way to express it.

Whittle the emotion/idea down and begin with the song's title and wrap everything else around it. Like a book, song titles that are intriguing are going to be more effective in attracting attention than ones that only sound generic or trite. One word titles can work as well. While a catchy title alone won't sell a song, it can certainly do a better job of eliciting attention.

Learning to discern good song ideas from mediocre ones is like any other skill: it takes practice, consistency, and feedback to help develop a sense of what works and what doesn't. When it comes to songwriting, one of the best ways to help with this is to continually find new sources of inspiration and to keep writing.

Activity 1: Create an Idea Book

When inspiration strikes, it's important to be able to jot the idea down. Whether it is with a pen and paper, a voice recorder, or your smart phone, you should keep a collection of ideas handy for you to develop later. I like to keep a small notebook with me at all times. However, some people like to use their phones, laptops, or tablet computers and use a program such as Evernote (www.evernote.com) to organize everything.

You can also use the idea book to collect sources of inspiration to help generate new ideas for songs. This can include photos, news articles, receipts, quotes, or anything else that might be of interest for a song later on.

Activity 2: Learn to Write Stories

Some of the most successful songs create ways to involve the audience (usually by engaging them emotionally). The best way to do that is to learn how to tell better stories. By sharing the experience rather than telling the direct feelings, it brings the audience into the song - as if you're singing directly to them or that they're actively watching a scene unfold before them.

You can learn how to write better stories in your songs by incorporating tools that writers use:

- **Detail:** Use specific details about the scene to paint the picture: colors, smells, sounds, etc.

- **Research:** If you're singing about a specific topic, you might do some research on the idea. Not only can this help bring out additional detail, but it might provide some inspiration for verses.

- **Tense:** Try to use only one tense in the song - if it is in the past, use past tense. If it is a song about the present, use the present tense. Consistency in tense is important to make the song more accessible.

- **Metaphor/Imagery:** Sometimes the best way to tell a message is to show it through the use of imagery.

- **Perspective:** Who is singing the song? Who is the intended recipient? By keeping that clear in the song, the message and story can remain consistent.

- **Pacing:** Develop the idea throughout the song in order to maintain interest. If you reveal the ending or crux of the story is too early, there won't be a satisfactory payoff for the listener.

One of the best ways to learn how to write good, succinct stories is simply to read and listen to as many as you can. Whether those stories happen to come by the way of songs, books, or stand-up comedy, you'll notice that great stories have all of the characteristics listed above.

Activity 3: See What Songs Are Selling, Then Do Something Else

If you are looking to write songs specifically for commercial success, you try applying your own twist to other commercially successful songs. Try looking at the Billboard Top 100 - both the "hot" list (http://www.billboard.com/charts/hot-100) as well as the lists specific to your genre. You don't need to emulate song content, but it might provide some ideas, especially if you see a common theme running through them. In fact, if you notice that themes that aren't relatable to your target fans, you might even take on the opposite perspective.

For example, there are many popular songs about breakups - most are written with general themes such as "I miss you" and "I still love you." Fewer are written with a "good riddance" attitude. However, songwriting duo, The Civil Wars, created an even more interesting angle with their hit single, *The One That Got Away*, by singing about the regret of staying with the person that they are with:

Oh, if I could go back in time
When you only held me in my mind
Just a longing gone without a trace
Oh, I wish I'd never ever seen your face
I wish you were the one
Wish you were the one that got away

One of the top songs of 2012 was Lorde's *Royals*, which specifically calls out and preaches against the ostentatious lifestyle that is sung about in most pop songs:

But every song's like gold teeth, grey goose, trippin' in the bathroom
Blood stains, ball gowns, trashin' the hotel room,
We don't care, we're driving Cadillacs in our dreams.
But everybody's like Cristal, Maybach, diamonds on your timepiece.
Jet planes, islands, tigers on a gold leash.
We don't care, we aren't caught up in your love affair.
And we'll never be royals (royals).
It don't run in our blood,
That kind of luxe just ain't for us.
We crave a different kind of buzz.

Visit Billboard or other charts and find ways to put your own perspective on subjects that you feel passionate about.

9. Train on Music Software

When it comes to creating music using software, there are a two main types that you'll most likely be working with: digital audio workstations (DAW) and composition software. DAWs are production programs with the primary purpose of recording, editing, and sequencing audio for playback. Music composition software focuses on the ability to compose, arrange, and notate music specifically for sheet music. Unless you're composing a score, you'll most likely just be using a DAW on a regular basis.

Some of the most popular DAWs include:
- Ableton Live
- Cakewalk SONAR
- GarageBand
- Image-Line FL Studio (also known as "Fruity Loops")
- Logic Pro
- Pro Tools
- Reason
- Steinberg Cubase

For many years, the industry standard for professional recording studios has been Pro Tools. Some data shows that in 2013, FL Studio surpassed Pro Tools in popularity, but that is generally only based on the popularity of search engine searches, not actual units sold. While each DAW offers its own set of tools or caters to specific types of music, the reality is that any musician working in the studio should really have a basic working knowledge of Pro Tools. It's also good to be familiar with a few types of software so that you can understand how they work on a general conceptual level.

Activity 1: Learn Digital Audio Workstation Best Practices

The Producers and Engineers Wing of the Recording Academy (of The Grammys) publishes a work called the Digital Audio Workstation Guidelines for Music Production. It covers best practices for using DAWs, has excellent recommendations for managing files, and assists with the labeling or MIDI instruments. Best of all, it's free (at least at the time of this writing).

Download this guide, read through it, and keep it nearby when you are preparing to go into the studio: http://www.grammy.org/files/pages/DAWGuidelineLong.pdf

You can also download the quick reference guide here: http://www.grammy.org/files/pages/DAWGuidelineShort.pdf

In fact, you can check out other resources for producers and engineers at: http://www.grammy.org/recording-academy/producers-and-engineers/guidelines

Activity 2: Learning Hotkeys

Hotkeys are combinations of keys that perform specific functions within a program. For example, in most software, CTRL+ S is the shortcut for saving whatever file you're working on. Hotkeys in DAWs can adjust playback, toggle selections, create timestamps, and other useful functions that would otherwise require navigating through several windows and menus.

If you do any direct editing of your music in a DAW, you should learn the hotkeys for the functions that you use the most. In fact, many audio engineering courses for certified studio engineers now require a class solely dedicated to learning the hotkeys in programs such as Pro Tools, Ableton Live, and Waves. Like many other skills, hotkeys are best learned through repeated use - memorizing them can save you many hours in the studio.

Here are links to hotkey guides for several of the most popular DAWs:

- Ableton Live: http://bit.ly/1faKWri
- GarageBand: http://bit.ly/1jHrXpb
- Logic Pro: www.logicprokeycommands.com (online trainer)
- Pro Tools: http://bit.ly/1hQvdOu
- Reason (v.6): http://bit.ly/KOcW8i

If you are involved with actively recording or editing, just a few minutes per day learning the hotkeys of your DAWs would definitely be time well spent.

Activity 3: Learning Advanced Techniques Online

Whether you are a novice or an advanced pro at using DAWs, chances are there are still many tricks for you to learn. There are numerous free, online tutorials to DAWs offered.

If you would like a 4-8 week, college-level crash course, I would recommend taking a Massive Open Online Course (MOOC). For example, the prestigious Berklee College of Music offers a free online audio production course through Coursera (coursera.org). FutureLearn (futurelearn.com) offers a course on critical listening for studio production.

For a regularly updated list, visit:
http://www.mooc-list.com/tags/sound

On the other hand, if you just want to know specific techniques or tricks that you can use in your DAW of choice, a good resource is YouTube. Many engineers have posted videos sharing shortcuts, advanced options, or other studio tricks on the social video site. Simply search using the name of your DAW and see what options are available.

Activity 4: Write Using Recording Software

Surprisingly, there are many musicians who only turn to DAWs when recording their music. However, they can be extremely useful for writing music as well. Not only can a DAW help record ideas when inspiration strikes, but they also offer some other benefits as well:

- **Allow Immediate Demo-Creation:** Some songwriters have an easier time developing hooks and melodies in the context of other music. Using a DAW, you can quickly drop in drum loops or other tracks in order to hear an idea in context.

- **Multiple Takes:** It's easy to set up a continuous loop on a specific section of music so that you can try out different melodies, harmonies, riffs, and solos. Most programs let you revert to any number of your previous takes so you don't have to worry about stopping and starting the recording process each time.

- **Easy Arrangement:** One of the biggest advantages in using DAWs for songwriting is the ability to quickly cut and paste different sections of the song together to test for flow, pacing, and transitions between parts of the song.

A DAW is simply another tool available to you to use. If you've only used them for recording and production, you might try using your favorite program to start the writing process itself.

10. Improve Your Rhythm

Timing and rhythm are two of the most important skills for any musician. The better you and your bandmates are at timing, the tighter you will sound. This is helpful for the studio (cuts down on recording time) and improves your live performances.

These activities are designed to improve your sense of rhythm and timing.

Activity 1: Metronome/Click Track and Scales

It might not be the most exciting exercise, but it is one of the best for developing several aspects of musicianship: practicing your scales to a metronome or click track on varying speeds. Simply play one note per strike of the metronome or click. Playing straight notes is more effective than playing to a song because it helps you tighten your playing to exact counts at varying tempos without background noises or other instruments that can bury your playing in the mix. By using scales for this, you can reinforce special relationships with notes simultaneously. You can also begin to incorporate 8th notes and 16th notes as part of your routine as well.

Activity 2: Record Yourself

Recording your rehearsals (and performances) is one of the best ways to get feedback on your rhythm. Recording with a straight click track will make it easier to hear your timing abilities, but recording rehearsals with a full band can help you hear performances within context.

If you are recording using a DAW, you can create a visual grid with the bars of music so that you can see where your notes are landing in the music. This is especially helpful if you have trouble discerning the beat or want to get a visual confirmation on what you're hearing.

Activity 3: Rhythm Trainers

There are several online training programs and apps that are designed specifically to help you practice and learn rhythm, different time signatures, and rhythmic dictation.

Try some of these programs to help improve your sense of time:

- www.therhythmtraining.com
- www.teoria.com/exercises/ritmo-ear.php
- www.rhythmtrainerapp.com
- www.worldjazz.ch/rhythm_training.htm

11. Improve Your Vocals

Whether you sing or you simply want to be able better express yourself vocally, there are a number of exercises available to strengthen your tone, improve your range, and help you find your pitch more quickly. While there is quite a bit that you can do on your own, serious vocalists should consider getting professional training through private lessons. Either way, it is important to treat your voice as you would any other instrument: with regular practice, investing in tools to help you improve, and with care.

Activity 1: Learn How to Warm Up and Cool Down Properly

Just as a weightlifter or professional athlete warms up prior to strenuous activity and cools down when they're finished, singers need to protect their most important asset: their voice. When you sing, you use a combination of soft tissues and muscles that needs to be stretched and warmed up before any performance. By warming up properly, you can reduce the risk of injury as well as remove excess mucous, which will also help improve your tone.

A good warm up will gently use the muscles, loosening them up and allowing air to enter in. Most vocal trainers recommend humming, though lip trills can help as well. As you progress through the warm up exercises, you'll steadily move closer to actual singing (both in volume and in range). You can find a number of great warm up exercises from professional vocalists on YouTube. There are also some excellent apps that you can install on any smart device. I recommend VocalCoach (by Singing Success), Voice Tutor (by Impack Productions), and Vocal Ease (by On Cue Productions).

After a singing performance or extensive speaking, it's also important to cool down the vocals as well. Cool down exercises help avoid fatigue or the raspiness that many singer experience after performing. Most warm up exercises actually work well for cooling down as well. You don't need to worry about volume or range as much as simply walking through the exercises - lip trills and short, five-note scales work well for the purpose.

Find some exercises that you like and implement them before and after each concert or rehearsal to prolong the life of your voice, improve your performance, and to keep sounding great. If you make a habit of this through daily practice, you'll see growth and a positive impact on your performance.

Activity 2: Learn the Singer's Diet

There are some food and drinks that are much better for your vocals than others. Protect your voice by keeping it hydrated and building healthy habits to keep it in top-shape. Just as professional athletes adhere to rigid diets, professional singers need to do the same.

Food and drinks every singer should stick to:

- Plenty of water, at least 64 oz. per day (especially at room temperature)
- Simple foods with high water content (fruit and salads with

light dressing)
- Fresh, non-processed foods
- Leafy greens - watercress, kale, spinach (raw), romaine, mixed greens, etc.
- Celery (helps with nerves)
- Bok Choy
- Melons
- Avocado (helps lubricate vocal chords)
- Broth soups (but not a tomato or creamy base)
- Lean sources of protein
- Healthy carbs, such as sweet potatoes, the day before a performance

Food and drinks that singers should avoid:

- Caffeinated and alcoholic drinks
- Very hot or cold drinks
- Candy or foods with high sugar content
- Fried foods
- Juices or foods high in citric acid
- Salty foods
- Overly spicy foods
- Dairy products (cream, cheese, milk, ice cream, etc.)
- Bananas
- Nut and crunchy snack foods prior to a performance
- Foods with high vinegar content
- Peppermint

Activity 3: "The Instant Fix"

This is a tip from acclaimed vocal coach, Cari Cole (caricole.com):

Say A-E-I-O-U (watch your jaw movement in the mirror). Did your jaw close on any of the vowels? Chances are your jaw closed on the E and the U – and most likely on others too, if not all of them. Take your first two fingers and pull your jaw down 2 inches (or even better – use a plastic bottle cap or a cork (wine) to prop your jaw open). And speak the vowels again. And repeat again (we're trying to re-program muscle memory – so the more the better). Now sing the vowels on one pitch. A-E-I-O-U.

Your goal is to keep your jaw open (long not wide) without closing for all of your vowels. Repeat until you can do it. Now sing a phrase of one of your songs – and make sure your jaw opens to the same position on all of your vowels. You have to practice this a bunch before it becomes natural – but the more you do, the sooner this new movement is programmed into your muscle memory. And you might be one of those lucky ones who notice the improvement in the sound right away (it will sound louder and more resonant with less vocal strain). If you don't – don't sweat it – you will. It just takes a little practice. (You might have some unwanted tension in your neck, jaw and throat muscles – try loosening them up and try it again.) The next time you perform open your jaw more on your vowels — it's a quick trick that makes you sound better instantly!

12. Ear-Training Exercises

Ear-training helps you recognize tone, pitch, note intervals, melodies, chords, and rhythm simply by listening. It's usually a part of most formal music-training programs and is an important part of musicianship. Think of it as deconstructing a song, piece-by-piece, simply through listening. Most professionals recommend that ear-training be done daily.

Some exercises are designed specifically to develop pitch recognition, others concentrate on intervals. Advanced ear training can also focus on chord recognition (learning the harmonic structures that support a song). Create a training program for yourself that can develop numerous facets of ear-training over time.

Activity 1: Ear-Training Software

In the past, ear-training would often require the help of a partner to play and test different musical intervals and chords. These days, there are many software programs that can help you develop your ear. Most of these not only test your ability, but also keep track of your scores over time to measure progress as well.

Some of the most popular professional programs include:

- Auralia
- EarMaster
- MacGAMUT

There are also open-source and free ear-training programs accessible online, including:

- Good-Ear (www.good-ear.com)
- Music Theory's Interval Ear Training (www.musictheory.net/exercises/ear-interval)

Some training programs also offer a free trial, such as:

- Berklee School of Music: http://online.berklee.edu/music-theory-harmony-ear-training
- Thea Music Trainer: http://trainer.thetamusic.com/en/content/music-training-games

Finally, there are numerous apps that can be downloaded to your smart devices to help develop your musical ear. These are the most popular options:

- EarBeater
- myEar
- Piano Ear Training
- Sharp Ear

Activity 2: Use Your Voice

In addition to recognizing musical notes and intervals, it's also important to be able to reproduce those same notes and phrases. The best way to do that is to use your natural instrument: your voice.

You can also use a digital tuner to play a note first, then try to replicate it with your voice. Or you can set the tuner to specific notes and try to find them with your voice, using the tuner to help you determine if you happen to be sharp or flat.

Activity 3: Bad Tuning

This is a great exercise for performers on stage who break strings or need to tune often. While you always hope that your instrument will constantly stay in perfect tuning, the reality is that external conditions can often shift the tuning slightly. This exercise helps you train and learn how to deal with mistuning until you get a chance to adjust - it also helps sharpen your pitch recognition as well.

When practicing, alter the tuning of your instrument to be slightly incorrect. Then, as you play, carefully listen to hear how it impacts each note in a melody, in a chord, and how it clashes with accompaniment.

Before you fix your tuning, try adjusting your playing style to help compensate for that pitch variation. You can try a number of things:

- **Pitch Bend:** A pitch bend can help slightly alter a note to help it reach target. Practicing pitch bends will help you develop a natural feel for how much the string needs to bend in order to slightly move a note up or down the scale.

- **Slides:** If you think of a pitch bend a something that moves the string up or down, the slide is when a note is moved side to side, in a slight motion to change pitch.

- **Vibrato/Tremolo:** Vibrato is another technique that can slightly alter pitch as well, depending on the instrument.

- **Alternate Notes:** As long as one of your strings is in tune, you can continue to play. Sometimes, you can play the same note, other times, it might involve playing something an octave up or down. One of the best ways to train for this is playing scales that involve multiple hand positions and strings - simply playing the same scale as many ways as possible.

- **Harmony:** If you can't play the same exact note, you might learn how to create harmonic notes that offer a good substitute - thirds, fifths, etc.

By learning and practicing the different techniques available to you, you'll not only improve your musical ear, but be able to compensate for tuning accidents on stage during a performance as well.

Section 4: Improving Your Live Appearances

Most artists depend on their live performance. In fact, the stage is where the majority of acts make new fans, drive record sales, and build alliances. But more than anything else, performing is one of most rewarding aspects of being a musician.

What's interesting is that most bands aren't trained for playing live or for touring. Most learn along the way by watching or asking other acts. While there really isn't a standard procedures manual, there's definitely an unspoken code between bands, promoters, stage managers, live sound engineers, and the audience. Each of these people have their own expectations of how a show should run and what they think of as success. The more that you can do to exceed these expectations, the more you'll get out of each live performance.

If you're a touring veteran, this section might primarily serve as a good set of reminder or it might help spur new ideas. However, if you've only got a hundred shows or less under your belt, these will be the rules, guides, and best practices that no one bother to ever tell other aspiring musicians.

So read carefully, apply the lessons and share with other aspiring artists that you know so that we can all grow together.

1. Making Rehearsals More Effective

Perhaps the biggest impact on your live performance is how you approach practices and rehearsals. Many artists use the two terms interchangeably even though there are some differences.

Practice is usually what is done individually, it is the work that is prepares someone for a rehearsal. It's used to improve your technique, musicianship skills, and ability to perform certain pieces of music. Practicing is generally better done as an individual because parts can be isolated and carefully examined without being drowned out by the band. In a plan, practice would often be considered a tactical activity.

On the other hand, a **rehearsal** is usually what occurs in a group setting - for the band to improve tonal balance, timing with each other, and learn the material in an ensemble setting. Rehearsals are usually strategic in nature because of the wider effects. In other words, it is not the place for a band member to get their individual practicing done.

To make band rehearsals more effective, each band member should be practicing for the rehearsal. That way, more time is spent focusing on improving the overall live experience rather than learning individual parts that should already be known.

Bands often ask how often they should rehearse. The answer will vary depending on the group, especially since most people have varying schedules and responsibilities. Most bands aim to rehearse 1-2 times per week for 3-4 hours at a time. No matter what though, band members should practice at least five days per week on their own.

My band only rehearses 5-6 times *per year* for about 3 hours at a time. While we'd like to increase that, we're busy with 100+ live appearances throughout the year as well as our individual pursuits (not to mention the fact that we live across three cities and two states). But we do just fine because of how we approach practicing and rehearsing.

It can be done, it just requires thoughtful planning and discipline.

Activity 1: Plan Your Next Rehearsal

As you schedule or plan your next band rehearsal, be sure to to do the following:

- **Set Goals:** Have a specific set list or list of materials to be learned. If it is a new song or cover, send the file to band members in advance so they have time to learn their parts. Remember, this time is for rehearsing, not practicing.

- **Plan Breaks**: Set aside a few minutes each hour for short breaks and a longer resting point mid-rehearsal so the vocalist(s) can recuperate.

- **Account for Setup/Tear down:** Those who need extra time to set up or tear down their gear should show up early - you might even consider a different start/end time for those members. That way, time isn't wasted for other members who will end up just sitting around and there is greater focus on time dedicated specifically for rehearsal.

- **Business**: If there is band business to be discussed - (such as touring or album plans), schedule time specifically for that after the rehearsal. Stick to getting the work at hand finished first.

- **Send a Schedule**: Send a schedule and reminder to the band. If you want time set aside for writing, auditioning a new member, testing equipment, or whatever else, put it in the schedule so people know exactly what to expect.

Activity 2: Rehearse Like a Live Show

In almost every professional arts organization, the rehearsal leading up to a performance is known as the dress rehearsal. It's a full-scale production that is supposed to replicate the live performance. It is a full run through, with as much of the set design as possible, to identify and address potential problems, to help reduce nerves, and to test the material.

For a band getting ready to tour or perform, a dress rehearsal would include:

- **Playing a specific set list**, start to finish, with planned breaks for talking and tuning instruments. Other than those planned moments, there should be no stopping between songs. Band members should have the set list memorized, know when to start/stop, and know how long their set is.

- **Setting up like your stage plot**. Most bands rehearse facing each other, allowing band members to hear/see each other. However, that's a different experience than being on stage, where everyone faces the crowd instead, and the monitor mix may change each night. Practice performing in that kind of arrangement.

- **Performing like there is an audience**. Musicians should practice moving around comfortably with their instrument, replicating positions or moves on stage. Knowing where people are going to be during key moments (guitar solo, crescendo, break, sing-along chorus, etc.) can bring dynamics to the song without bumbling around.

- **Recording:** If possible, set up a multi-track recorder or video camera to capture the rehearsal. Go over the footage to see what works, what doesn't. Whatever your show's running time is, figure out how you would adjust it if you were running 5 minutes late, 10 minutes late, 10 minutes early, etc.

- **Setting Up and Tearing Down**: Practice quickly setting up and tearing down. Time your band to see how long it takes to get on or off the stage. Think about tasks that you can consolidate to make the process faster so that you have more time performing and less time sound checking. For example, you could set up drums in advance and move entire pieces as opposed to adding/removing cymbals right before playing.

- **Practice Stage Banter:** A few years ago, I met with a marketing executive who used to work with bands who'd perform for audiences of 10,000+. They would set those bands up in a room with footage of a fake audience, then teach them how to talk to an audiences. While you don't need to plan out every word that is said on stage, it's definitely helpful to rehearse those moments as well.

Remember, your show isn't just the playing of a few songs. It's the entire thing, including everything from the moment that you begin setting up on stage for a line check to the moment you leave the stage. As such, you want to be professional and entertaining while under the spotlight to give fans and the staff a good experience.

Activity 3: Set Rules for Band Rehearsal

Expectations for rehearsal should be outlined in some form - whether it's in your interband agreement (Section 1, chapter 14), posted in your rehearsal space, or shared within the group. You might set up some basic rules to make rehearsals go much more smoothly.

Here are some recommendations for band rehearsal rules:

1. **Show Up on Time:** Respect each other's time by showing up on the agreed time. If someone takes longer to set up, show up early.

2. **Come Prepared**: Everyone should show up with the material practiced and memorized ahead of time.

3. **Communication**: When someone is talking, don't be playing guitar or drums - it makes it hard to hear.

4. **No Distractions:** Treat rehearsal like a job - leave distractions at home.

5. **No Alcohol, Smoking, or Drugs:** Smoke is terrible for the vocals, keep it outside. Alcohol and drugs are a distraction, not to mention hamper the ability to focus.

6. **Clean Up:** If you are rehearsing in someone's else, show some respect and clean up after yourself - throw away any trash, bottles, snacks, etc.

7. **Food:** Plan to eat before or after rehearsal, not during the time where everyone should be working.

8. **Feedback:** Find ways to deliver constructive criticism.

You might have other rules more appropriate to your situation, band members, or equipment. Whatever you decide to do, be sure that it is in writing and something that each person in the group can understand and follow.

2. Learn How to Soundcheck

One of my biggest pet peeves as a performer is a band who doesn't know how to soundcheck properly. It shouldn't be - it usually reflects inexperience and ignorance rather than disrespect and apathy. The truth is that most bands are not taught how to soundcheck, it's just a skill that gets picked up along the way. Despite this, the soundcheck is often an indicator of the professionalism of the band.

Here's a lesson on how to soundcheck the right way:

Before the show

Once you have a show confirmed, you should send a stage plot, technical rider, and input list to the sound and lighting engineers. Having detailed needs spelled out in advance can help overcome any issues early on, including deficiencies in equipment, limited inputs or monitor mixes, etc. For larger shows, you could send audio tracks or performance footage showing the kind of mix and light design that you'd like for the show (assuming you don't have your own sound/lighting crew).

You should be prepared to bring everything needed for your instrument: the instrument, cables, adaptors, amp, stands, microphones, batteries, etc. Unless you have a detailed list of what is being provided by the venue, assume that you are responsible for your own gear. I also recommend keeping a backup set of power strips, extension cables, strings, drum sticks, gaffer tape, set lists, sharpies, DI boxes, power cables, and vocal microphones. These days, many bands travel with a portable P.A system as backup. Things should be clearly labeled so that they can be quickly identified - something that is often useful on dark stages.

The biggest issues with soundchecking that are under your direct control include:

- Weak or dead batteries, especially in wireless systems or electronic pickups
- Loose or damaged cables
- Poor mic technique (standing too far back, holding the mic improperly, etc.)
- Noisy channels caused by effects, grounding, or wireless systems
- Over-aggressive padding or attenuation of devices (mixers on stage, DI boxes, etc.)

The more that you can take care of these common problems ahead of time, the more time that can be spent making you sound good.

When you arrive

Show up at the designated time (or earlier if you need more loading time) and ask the sound engineer where they would like you to place your gear. When loading onto the stage, begin with the larger pieces of equipment - the drum set, amp rigs, etc. but watch out for the mixer snake, power outlets, or areas where XLR cables will be run. Find a place for "dead" or empty cases to be stored off stage.

Whether you will be getting a full soundcheck or only a line check, prepare your gear in advance so that you can be ready at a moment's notice. This includes setting up the drums, positioning stands, tuning, etc.

The soundcheck

Most shows will soundcheck in reverse order of the show. In other words, the headliner will soundcheck first and the opening act will soundcheck last. Sometimes, the acts in the middle will only get a quick line check right before their set. Whether you get a full soundcheck or not, the process is generally the same.

The sound engineer should guide you through the process, asking for one instrument at a time. No one else should be playing or testing their gear at this time, only the person being addressed by the engineer.

Most of the time, engineers will check in this order: drums, bass, guitar, keyboards or electronic samples, horns, lead vocals, backup vocals.

When your instrument is being checked, play a quick sample at the intended volume and test any gear that might increase that volume (pedals or effects). Usually, as each instrument is being checked, the engineer will ask which band members require it in their monitor - simply gesture whether you want it up, down, or not at all in your monitor. This is also the time to address any mixing requests for the house as well (e.g., "we'd like stage right guitar louder in the mix").

After all of the individual channels are dialed in, you'll be asked to play a song. Play one that incorporates all of your instruments and vocalists if possible, so that the engineer can get a good mix for the house. In fact, try to play the same song every time you soundcheck so that you can listen for consistency.

Band members can also walk through the front of the house (one at a time) or have a member of the road crew listen for any abnormalities or changes.

After the soundcheck, if you're requested to move your gear (such as sliding it back to make room for the next band), try and mark the positions of amps and stands with brightly colored tape so that you can quickly re-set the stage.

After the soundcheck/show

If you have another act coming on after you, clear off your equipment as quickly as possible. Try and get the larger things out of the way, such as drums or amp stacks, so that the next band and can load their gear on stage. Tasks, such as breaking down drums, wrapping cables, putting things in cases, etc. should be done offstage. A quick tear down is a courtesy both to the act following you, the sound crew who needs to set up for the next band, and the promoter who is trying to run a show on time. Before the act begins playing their set, do another quick walkthrough to make sure that you got everything.

If you don't have another act following you, there isn't as much of a rush to clear the stage but you should still ask the venue when they'd like you to tear down. The last thing that you want to do is to keep up any staff waiting to close and who want to go home for the night.

Finally, be sure to thank the sound engineer. You might even consider tipping them or buying them a drink so that you can develop a good rapport.

Activity 1: Make/Update Your Stage Plot

If you don't have a stage plot, now is the time to create one. A stage plot is a visual representation of your band's setup when you perform live. It should include:

- All of the music instruments and their relative positions on the stage
- The gear being used
- The names of the musicians and their roles
- A list of equipment that you are providing
- A list of equipment or inputs that you'll need to be provided (mics, DI boxes, etc.)
- Whether items will be mic'ed or using a direct input.

If you do have a stage plot, it might need some updating. Stage plots should be reviewed or updated whenever:

- The band lineup changes
- Music instruments are added or taken away
- Band members update their music equipment
- The positioning of equipment changes

There are numerous tools available for creating stage plots, such as Stage Plot Pro (www.stageplot.com), ReverbNation Pro, and Sonicbids. Alternatively, you can create one in Word, Powerpoint, Photoshop, Corel Draw, or other graphic programs. See next page for an example of a stage plot.

A stage plot can also be paired up with a technical rider (often referred to us a "tech rider" for short), which might have some more information about your sound/lighting needs, general provisions, or other requirements for the show.

Stage plot example:

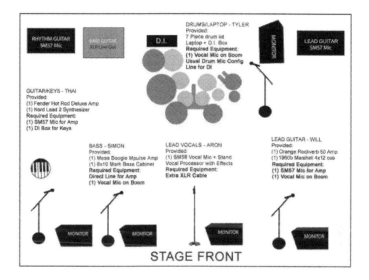

Activity 2: Create an Emergency Kit for Shows

Sometimes, things don't go as planned: the venue doesn't have enough microphones or monitors, strings break, there isn't enough power on stage, etc. For those moments, having an emergency kit can help make the show run more smoothly.

These are some things that you might consider carrying with your band at all times:

- Additional vocal mics
- Extra XLR cables
- Extra ¼" guitar cables
- DI boxes
- Power strips
- Heavy and medium duty extension cables
- Gaffer tape and masking tape
- Strings, picks, drumsticks, and other common accessories

- Velco strips
- Flashlight
- Batteries (9 volt, AA, and AAA)
- Additional copies of the set list
- Sharpies

These items aren't as common but are also helpful to have on hand as well:

- Mic stand
- Guitar stand
- Keyboard stand
- Powered stage monitor
- Portable PA system
- Fuse kit
- Basic tool set
- Power cable (for amps)

The idea is to be prepared so that you can minimize downtime and focus on making the show run well.

3. The Post-Show Plan

Do you have a post-show plan? Is there a set of procedures that you work on after each performance? Or, does your band simply work on the next event - the next show, the next rehearsal, time in the studio, etc.?

In almost every professional endeavor, there is some kind of routine or review period to measure performance or follow-up with customers.

- In sports, the coach diligently sits down with the entire team to review footage of the previous game. Team members celebrate successes and most importantly, look for areas of improvement.

- In corporate business, the board of directors and executive staff look over stock performance and make decisions to keep their shareholders satisfied.

- In the arts, performers carefully review each element of the show to see what delighted audiences and what could use work.

- In retail, after Black Friday and other large sales events, stores do a quick inventory and review of the schedule to make sure that they are prepared for the rest of the season.

Of course, in any situation involving customers, there should also be some kind of follow-up as well. They need to be properly thanked! Coupons and surveys are sent out, appreciative messages are broadcasted across social media, some even take ads out just to show their gratitude towards supporters.

With your music career, you should be thinking about how you can make the most of each show, which includes a post-show plan that you follow. It should have some routine elements that have details of what will happen, when it will happen, why it should happen, and who will make it happen.

Here are some suggestions on what you could do after each show:

- **Share Gratitude**: Thank the promoter, venue, sound engineer, fans who attended, other bands - basically, anyone who was involved with your show. This can be through social media, email, or even physical thank you notes. Whatever the method, it should be sent within 24 hours of the show.

- **Review the Performance**: You should record each performance (especially with something that has decent audio) so that you can highlight good and bad moments from the show. Review the show as a band and look for areas of improvement: stage banter, certain moves, flow of the set, audience involvement, lighting, set design, etc. Even if you have nothing to improve, you'll still have some good footage that you can share online.

- **Update Your Contacts**: If you have new contacts to add to the mailing list, try adding them within 48 hours of the show. Thank the people for coming to the show.

- **Social Media/Blog**: Share any highlights from the show - photos, videos, quotes, funny moments, etc. across your social media channels and/or band blog. You could send out quick updates or a full write-up/video review.

- **Contact the Press**: Did something newsworthy happen at the show? It could be positive (your band got signed) or negative (your band got banned), but either way, you might have more opportunities to get some press coverage. For more on press-worthy material, see Section 1, Chapter 3.

- **Order Merchandise**: If you noticed that certain items were running low or high in demand, it's best to place orders in as soon as possible so that you'll be completely restocked before the next show.

- **Equipment Maintenance:** Frequent playing can really wear down your gear. From old strings to action resetting, missing bolts to dying batteries...it's better to take care of issues offstage rather than to deal with problems on stage. Doing a spot check can make sure everything is ready to go for the next performance or rehearsal.

- **Proof of Performance**: If you have sponsors or investors, consider delivering a "proof of performance." In other words, provide a recap specific to their interests: where their logo was displayed, what the attendance was like, how your brands were connected or marketed to the audience. You can also show web visits, social media engagement, or any other statistics related to the show that can continue to show value for their investment.

Whatever you decide to do, just make sure it's done with consistency and purpose. You might spread the responsibilities around and charge certain members or road crew with certain tasks. By building these regular habits into your routine, your band will have greater professionalism, be working towards tangible goals, and you'll be able to leverage the benefits of performing live to a much greater degree than just playing show after show with no post-show procedures at all.

Activity 1: Develop a Post-Show Routine

Now that you have some ideas on what you can include in a post-show plan, you should create your own routine. Sit down with your band members and decide what you want to accomplish with each show and how you can take advantage of the momentum from a show to develop a set of procedures that will make future performances better. Create a checklist of specific tasks with responsibilities assigned to each person and a schedule of when things should be completed by.

Activity 2: The Play-by-Play Recap

Find a way to record every performance on video. If you don't know someone who is willing to film your shows, buy a solid tripod and set up the camera in the back of the room - you might even be able to get a direct audio feed from the mixing board. Just make sure that you can capture the entire show, start to finish.

Then, after every show, watch the video at least twice. Spend time analyzing the footage with your band. Focus on things such as:

- **Set length**: How much time did you use up from what was given to you?

- **Pacing**: How was the pace of the overall show? Were there lulls between songs? Should the order of the songs be changed?

- **Audience response**: What songs/moments did the audience react to the most? How can you create more moments like that?

- **Performance**: How did each member of the band do in terms of performing the songs? Is more practice needed? How was the energy on stage? Is it exciting to watch?

- **Set Design**: How was the layout of the stage? Could the band be positioned better? Do you have set pieces, banners, or decorations on stage that could be better used?

Reviewing the footage as a band also helps you point out errors in a very objective manner - people can't claim that they didn't make certain mistakes if it was caught on film. Take the time to carefully review the footage from every show to find ways to improve the experience for your fans. Then, make the changes.

4. Learn How to Work the Crowd

When you are on stage, your main goal isn't to play a good set, to sell records, to overcome nervousness, or to impress someone in the industry. When you are on stage, your main goal is to entertain the crowd. By meeting this goal, you'll be able to meet the other objectives that you probably have for the show as a whole: make new fans, sell records, and so on.

You can entertain a crowd in a number of ways:

- Performing well
- Adding creativity and spontaneity to the show
- Interacting with the audience
- Creating memorable moments
- Giving your show dynamics
- Controlling momentum and pacing
- Adding crowd pleasers
- Having a distinct personality on stage
- Reducing down time between songs

Often times, there should be a distinct amount of confidence and charisma, especially from the lead singer. All members of the band should be comfortable with maintaining eye contact (as opposed to only looking down at their instruments), moving around on stage, and giving attention to multiple sections of the audience.

Here are some tips on how to improve your ability to work a crowd:

- **Practice:** Plan specific moments in the set to talk to the crowd. Everyone in the band should know exactly when the pauses will be so they aren't starting the next song or fiddling with their instruments. In fact, tuning breaks should be scheduled in the set (unless it's absolutely necessary) so that they occur when someone is doing the talking.

  You should also plan out specific talking material - short stories, song introductions, jokes, merch announcements, etc. so that you have a good feel for the timing and delivery. Stage banter isn't necessary - people came to see you play, not lecture, so keep it limited but entertaining.

  Also, practice speaking into a microphone. Annunciate. It's annoying when people talk into a mic but can't be understood.

- **Dynamics:** Create a song where songs can flow into each other - both in terms of their key as well as their tempo. Provide reprieve at appropriate moments by finding songs to change up the volume, mood, and tempo - don't keep the same feeling throughout the entire set. By giving your overall set dynamics, it can give the bigger, energetic moments more power.

- **Once Voice**: Limit the number of people whoaddress the crowd (try to keep it to the band leader). Crowds usually don't enjoy hearing band members talking to each other or telling inside jokes.

- **Improve Set Design**: The tasteful use of stage effects, lighting, or props can enhance the overall show. What are some things that you can incorporate into your show to make it more fun or exciting?

- **Interaction**: Some of the best shows include some kind of interaction - simply maintaining eye contact or creating an emotional connection is one way. But you can also take this to another level. For example, cabaret pop rocker Amanda Palmer will sometimes have the crowd write down intimate, anonymous confessions during her show - then read them and loop that audio into one of her songs. Punk band Peelander-Z has members of the audience come on stage to play their instruments. In fact, the lead singer will also dress up as giant bowling pin and have the crowd "bowl" other band members into him. Other artists have been known to project a live tweet stream and have the crowd tweet words or lines to do a freestyle rap around in real time.

- **Crowd Pleasers**: Many bands who have hits save them for the end of their set in order to keep the crowd waiting for those moments. Other bands selectively use popular covers to get the crowd worked up. Use crowd pleasers strategically in the set to build momentum during the show.

- **Formal Training**: If you're really serious about working a crowd, you might take a speech, communications, or theater class. You could also join a group like Toastmasters to help improve your public speaking skills.

Whatever you decide to do, do it from the perspective of the audience. Ask yourself, how can the show be enhanced? How can you create climatic moments during the show?

Activity 1: Study a Little Theater

If you want to improve your performance, watch other live performers in other arts - theater, ballet, opera, ballroom dancing, the orchestra, etc. Study how they use dynamics in the performance to create memorable moments, what captures the audience's attention, and what accentuates the moments of the performers. How can you apply some of those techniques into your show?

You'll notice that with any fine art performance or live event, there is almost no talking to the crowd until after it is complete (if even that). They truly adhere to the adage, "less talk, more rock."

Many events (as well as films) follow the dramatic structure, with distinct sections: a beginning, middle (climax), and end. The more modern version of this structure, often known as Freytag's Pyramid has several other sections to create greater emotional range:

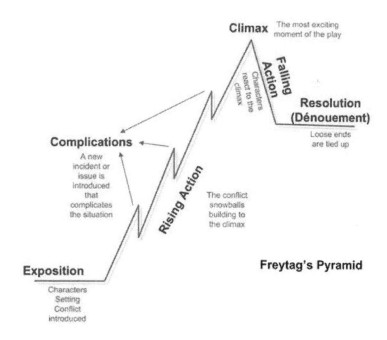

Think about how you can replicate a similar feel with your show: increasing energy throughout the performance to set the stage for highlight moments, changing the pace or flow, creating sonic dynamics (louder/softer) to keep the audience interested. The climax, or most exciting part of the show, doesn't necessarily have to be the loudest or most energetic - sometimes, it can be the most intimate or passionate.

Approach your performance as it truly is: a set, a complete work. That work should have rises and falls, peak moments of energy or emotion, and resolution.

Activity 2: Write a Set List with Breaks

You should design your set with breaks. It's inevitable that you'll need to stop for any number of reasons: tune guitars, drink water, talk to the crowd about your new album, etc. However, those moments should be planned so that the rest of the band can use the downtime as effectively as possible. The musicians should be tuning at the same time (preferably while the singer or band leader is addressing the crowd). You should plan any needed vocal breaks in advance. If you have specific jokes, stories about a song, announcements, etc. those should be planned in the set.

What I often do is write out a set list with specific breaks in the performance highlighted so everyone in the band knows their task (tune and/or talk). I also include specific announcements in certain areas of the set (i.e., "Announce new album," "Reminder: merch in the back," "sign up on email list," "Happy Birthday to X," etc.). It keeps everyone on task and reduces dead time for the crowd.

Write out a set list - and practice it with the breaks - so that everyone in the band knows this process.

Activity 3: Practice Your Stage Banter

It might seem cheesy or unnatural, but you should practice your stage banter, especially things that are more than a simple announcement (such as a story or a joke). The talking between songs is still a part of your performance and offers a distinct opportunity to connect with the audience in a different kind of way.

As you practice jokes, stories, or your sales pitch for merchandise, keep these things in mind:

- Level of confidence
- Stage personality and passion
- Inflection of your voice
- Ease of understanding through a microphone
- Length of the joke, story, pitch, etc.
- Is what you're saying something worth repeating?

The idea is to try and frame things up in a way that is relevant to the point of view of someone in the audience: it should be interesting, funny, or memorable. The more that you practice this, the better you get at it.

5. Overcoming Obstacles

Things rarely go exactly as planned on stage. There are often setbacks - instruments get knocked out of tune, the monitors don't sound right (or the venue lacks monitors entirely), someone forgets their parts - you got the idea. However, many of the typical obstacles can be overcome with the proper attitude and a little preparation.

Often, the biggest source of stage setbacks is the lack of communication. Many musicians have different experience levels and expectations when it comes to performing. So when things go awry, each member of the band might deal with those issues differently - this can be a big problem when it is an issue that affects the entire band.

For example, imagine that you are the guitarist of a band on playing a show at a dive bar with bad monitors. Most of what can be heard on stage will come from the amps and whatever is reflected off of the walls. In the middle of one of your songs, you notice that the lead singer begins singing the verse too early. However, you're not sure if anyone else has noticed - you're not even sure if the drummer can hear vocals. What do you do?

I've seen it many times before: some of the band continues to play the song as written, some of the band adjusts to the singer's mistake. This of course, causes more mistakes, resulting in a complete mess on stage. Sometimes, the band stops the song entirely and tries playing it over again (another mistake in my book).

Mistakes will happen - how you deal with mistakes will be a testament and measurement of your professionalism. When mistakes do happen, the band should be ready to:

- **Play on:** If it is a relatively small mistake and one that the band/song can recover from, the band should continue to play as if nothing amiss occurred. Most of the time, the audience won't know that you messed up anyway.

- **Follow one voice:** If something happens on stage, there isn't time to argue about what to do next. There should be an appointed bandleader, acting like a conductor, who can quickly guide everyone on what to do next.

- **Know when to stop:** Some setbacks are too large to recover from (power outage on stage, no point of recovery in a song, broken strings with no spare, etc.). Know when to call it quits on stage.

- **Prepare in advance:** Have extra gear on hand to deal with common onstage problems, like dropped drumsticks or broken guitar strings, as well as a plan on how to deal with issues that come up. For example, a spare guitar that's already in tune is much better than an extra set of strings because it can be swapped out much more quickly.

- **Have a good attitude:** I've been to a few shows where someone gets upset, throws a tantrum, and storms off stage. That's no way to deal with problems. Whether you're mad at the venue, a bandmate, or yourself, the stage isn't an appropriate place to deal with those issues. Instead, take things in stride - humor is usually a good way to disarm the situation and let everyone know that you can move on without being a jerk.

While you can't always choose what happens to you on stage, you can certainly choose how to react to situations on stage.

Activity 1: Make a Band Contingency Plan

It's good to have a routine or plan in place in case something goes wrong during the show. While you don't necessarily have to have a written plan (though that wouldn't be a bad idea), you should at least have a conversation on how to approach common issues that might be experienced on and off stage.

For instance, you could decide how to handle or prepare for the following:

- Insufficient sound system - not enough microphones or monitors, not enough channels to have everything mic'ed, etc.
- Last minute shortened set - who decides what songs to keep/drop?
- Song falls apart on stage, someone gets lost, etc.
- Guitarist breaks strings and there is no backup
- A DI channel (such as keyboards) isn't available
- The club is almost completely empty
- The crowd is booing or clearly wants you to leave the stage
- The stage is too dark to see the fretboard/instrument clearly
- You can only hear drums
- The stage is too small to fit the entire band
- The sampler/click track or other main instrument isn't working
- An amp shorts out
- Your wireless systems are creating too much interference

- The drummer plays the song at the wrong demo
- Someone begins playing the wrong song

You get the idea - think about your situation and what a worse case scenario would look like. Usually, the more complex your setup is or the larger your band, the greater the chance of something going wrong. However, some thoughtful preparation or discussion will help you overcome these obstacles and making you a better, more professional performer.

6. Stage Effects/Set Design

Many bands don't think of set design unless they're touring large venues on a regular basis. Even then, some only go as far as putting a large backdrop or banner. However, touring acts have the ability to kick things up a notch by applying some creativity, lessons from theatre, and special effects from magic shows to really enhance the performance. Good stage design can help transform mundane rock clubs into unique experiences that help the band stand out. Many of these things don't even require a large budget to start out with - just some forethought and a little preparation.

These are some of the things that you can enhance your stage with:

- Custom lighting
- Projections (or LED wall)
- Art pieces/sculptures/banners
- Pyrotechnics
- Confetti and streamers
- Fog/smoke
- Bubbles/stage snow
- Wind/air movement

- Phosphorescent paint or materials
- Fabric
- Custom instruments
- Strobe lights
- Balloons
- Height (ramps, risers, etc.)
- Costumes
- Dancers
- Other theater effects

Stage elements should be thoughtfully added to enhance, not replace, your live performance. You can get ideas from high-profile touring acts, theater productions, dance groups, or other performing artists that use a lot of set design. From there, you can adapt ideas to suit your particular needs.

Most of the above items can be ordered from theater effects production companies, especially things that require a specialized machine (such as a confetti canon or LED wall). Others need to be custom built by someone who is experienced with set design. Bu others are projects that you might be able to take on yourself.

In fact, there are many instructional videos and websites that teach you how to create various stage effects using common items found at your local hardware store. Instructables (www.instructables.com) has multiple, detailed tutorials on building stage risers, lights, and other items. I've created stage lights, risers, custom lights for amps and mic stands, and backdrops just from looking up ideas and finding creative ways to approach them.

You don't have to have a grand-scale project to make it special. It should just be unique and reflect your band.

Activity 1: Get Some Ideas and Sketch Out Your Set Design

Take out your band's stage plot and look for areas where you can add something to the stage. It might also help to watch a video of your performance or browse through photos of your live show to see what can be added.

If you want to get an idea of what is possible, do some searching for band stage designs online. You can also get ideas by searching for theater productions, especially if there is something that is especially suited for your band's image. For instance, if your band has imagery or a sound that is inspired by early 20th century French culture, you might turn to *Phantom of the Opera* for some ideas.

Take these ideas and sketch out your set design. What is essential? What elements would you like to have? Now, look up each of these items and consider the cost to build or buy, the logistics of incorporating them into your performance, the ease of setting up/tearing down, transporting them, and the effectiveness of those items. Create a budget and a plan for your set design, then work on bringing it to life (even if it is only one area at a time).

At the very least, every band should have a large, durable banner with their name/logo on it. They're fairly inexpensive, very visible, and easy to work with (especially if you hang it with large clips or grommets and rope).

Activity 2: Update What You Already Have

If you already have some elements of stage design - be it lighting equipment or visual pieces - it might need some update or work. Heavy usage of these items often beckon maintenance, especially with items that sit directly on the stage or that get moved often. Things get dirty, scuffed, and scratched. However, a little maintenance can go a long way to prevent failure on stage.

Some items might need to be replaced entirely. For example, if you have an old stage banner that features outdated artwork or is promoting a Myspace page that you no longer keep up, it's time to replace it. If you have any items that show a different band lineup than your current one, those things should be updated.

Take a look at what you have and see if any items need some attention to prolong their life, update their look, or need to be removed altogether.

Activity 3: Find Options When You're on a Limited Budget

There are plenty of options for set design, even when you are on a limited budget. Here are some ideas that you can explore/consider:

- **Slide Projector**: You can usually find a used slide projector at the local thrift store, Craigslist, Ebay, and many other places for less than $50. Then, have a custom slide created of your band logo to project above the band on stage (or at the merch table). You can even load a camera with some 35mm slide film and take a picture of your logo to project. You could also have an entire set of slides, projecting them over the band for an artsy look. Another option is using a transparency projector, though that is much larger to move around.

- **LED lights**: LED lights are fairly inexpensive and easy to work with. In fact, you can buy LED strips in bulk, then add special effects by connecting them to controllers and dimmers. In fact, you could sync flashing lights, color changes, and brightness directly to your music through MIDI. LED lights also provide a simple, inexpensive way to light up your amplifiers and drums as well.

- **Getting Artists:** You could get custom-created artwork by using Craigslist, asking friends, or even contacting local art schools about collaborating on a live music project. Often, aspiring artists are willing to give an incredible rate, especially if it means creating something for their working portfolio. You might even find some theater set designers willing to help as well!

- **Free or Clearance Items**: Keep a watch on the "free" section on Craigslist. There are often unique items that you could repurpose for the stage. For instance, I know of a drummer who picked up an old cabinet, cut it in half, and turned it into a custom drum riser. You might also talk to local theater companies, high school theaters, or colleges who are often discarding stage set items that you could use. After Halloween, you'll often find theatrical items such as strobe lights or fog machines on clearance for extremely discounted rates.

- **Repurposing**: If you are imaginative, just walk through a hardware store to get some ideas. They often have lighting, displays, tool chests, and other items that could be repurposed for the stage with just a few simple tools.

Your set design doesn't always have to be limited by your budget - often times, it's only limited by your imagination. If you look around, you can often find a solution for your needs.

7. Get More Out of the Show

What do you get from playing a single live show?

Most musicians would list one or more of the following:

- Money
- Publicity/press
- New fans
- Personal satisfaction/fun
- Deeper relationships
- Help a good cause
- Personal growth
- New skills/experience
- Networking
- Enhanced reputation

In other words, you can quite get a lot from one 30 minute set on stage! However, none of these things are simply given to you. They are all things that are earned and usually require a bit of hard work to get. For example, if you want to get paid well, you need to promote the show and bring a decent crowd. If you want to make new fans, you'll have to play well and find a way to earn their commitment to you, either in the form of merchandise sales and/or enthusiastically signing up for your mailing list.

So when you approach any upcoming show, you should thoughtfully consider your goals for it and what you can do to maximize the return on each of these areas. For some musicians, many of these come naturally - they set the mailing list out, they push their merchandise, they send a press release for each show, etc. For others, they observe other acts and try to emulate them. Then, there are those who just go from show to show without really thinking about how they can make the most out of each of these areas.

You can approach each of the goals above by thoughtfully adapting them to your music career. Here are some ideas on how you can get more from some of the goals listed above:

Money

Most of your money from a show will come from the venue and from merchandise sales.

If you want to play higher-paying shows, you'll need to: develop your reputation to get higher guarantees, play longer sets/cover sets for promoters who pay well for that type of act, or improve your draw so that payouts based on the door increase.

If you want to sell more merchandise, you'll need to: create well-designed products that appeal to your target audience, have an attractive, well-lit display in a prominent location at the show, have reasonable pricing (and good price margins), be able to accept credit cards and other payment options, and have someone actively working the merch table. For more information, see The Ultimate Guide to Band Merchandise, Section 1, Chapter 19.

Publicity/press

To get more press, you need to have something press worthy (Section 1, chapter 3). Having a publicist will definitely help. If you don't have one, you can begin developing relationships with journalists. Just frame up the show with a story that is of interest to the media source's audience. At the very minimum, you should submit your show for local calendar listings. After the show, if something of interest occurred, you should contact the local media with a story.

New fans

In all honesty, playing for people is not how you get new fans. While your performance might impress them, most of the crowds at local bars will forget about the 3-5 bands they watch at a show. In order to turn those crowds into fans, you'll need to develop a relationship with them - this is usually done by staying vigilant with your mailing list (Section 1, chapter 12).

Personal satisfaction/fun

When it comes to the live show, my band has holds a simple rule: never leave the stage with regrets. In other words, we put on the best performance possible at every show, no matter the size of the crowd, issues with the venue, or any personal issues. If you make it a goal to make every show one that you're proud of, you'll get much more out of the experience.

Deeper relationships

In order to develop deeper relationships (with the promoter, venue staff, existing fans, etc.), you have to be proactive about approaching each of these groups and understand their needs. For example, to build your relationships with fans, you could: recognize/thank them individually, send them a note after the show, invite them on stage, or find other unique ways to show your appreciation.

When you think about your live shows, you should also set some goals for the experience - and a plan for reaching those goals. A little mindfulness can go a long way.

Activity 1: Set Goals for Your Live Show or Tour

The best way to make sure you're getting everything possible from your live shows is to plan it. If you go from show to show hoping it will improve your career somehow but don't have any kind of target, you won't get anywhere. As Zig Ziglar says, "If you aim at nothing, you'll hit it every time."

Sit down with your band and talk about what you want to get out of each show. Prioritize that list: is it more important that you come out financially ahead after a tour or that you get new fans? What does each member of the band think is the ultimate priority? The results may surprise you - and ultimately, let each person know if their personal goals are in line with everyone else's. Apply the S.M.A.R.T.E.R Goals concept to your live shows (Section 1, chapter 9), then think carefully about what you can do to meet those goals.

Activity 2: Create Metrics or Ways of Measuring Your Success

In addition to having goals for your live performance, it's also good to have a tangible way of measuring your achievement of those goals. Besides playing well (at least in the mind of your band), how do you measure whether it's a successful show or not? If everyone in the venue loved you so much that they bought a CD, but there were only 4 people there, would you consider that a success?

Once you determine what you want to measure your shows by (money earned, fans gained, merchandise sold, publicity gained, etc.), you'll want to record it. Some musician tools such as ReverbNation will keep track of this for you. Alternatively, you can keep track of it on your own by creating a spreadsheet or database that tracks the results of each show. That way, you can quickly create a chart and see if there is steady improvement over time, and in what areas.

As you try new things to improve any areas that you're measuring, having actual numbers to compare with will let you know if those attempts are successful or not. For example, if you want to keep track of attendance over time, you can get a headcount for each show (most of the time, the door person will keep tabs of this for the house). If you want to experiment with different kinds of ads, press releases, or even compare your draw on different days of the week, you'll have hard numbers to compare and contrast your performance against.

Activity 3: Work on One of the Goals Differently

If you have a goals set for your live show/tour, try thinking about it in a completely different manner. For example, if your approach has always been to hang up flyers on certain streets, try a different part of town. If you have been using Facebook invites, try focusing on personal invitations or postcards instead.

Too often, we get comfortable with the tools and processes that we're used to. While there's something to be said for consistency and proven success, it's also important to be flexible and creative when it comes to approach your music career.

8. Learn How to Treat Touring Bands Properly

As a touring artist myself, I'm sometimes booked with local acts who are either new to the industry or unaware of common courtesy when it comes to working with an out of town band. There are certain unspoken rules that really come down to common sense and decency when you play with other bands. One hopes to treat others well so that in the karmic circle of touring, you'll have other acts treat you with the same respect in return. Plus, most musicians hold grudges for a long time…if you screw them over, you'll lose opportunities in the future yourself.

Here are some of the ways you can treat a touring band right:

- **Door Money:** If you're playing with a band that is going to be on the road for the next several weeks (or months), give your share to the out of town act, especially if you're opening for them. The only exception is if they have a large guarantee and will be set for their travels. But if they're struggling by playing small to mid-size rooms and are just trying to grow their fan base or they will be driving all night because they don't have place to stay, step it up and give them your share - or at the very least, a larger share. Not only will they be grateful, but they'll be more likely to help you get a show or some fans when you play in their town. You'll also make the venue happy because you'll ease their guilt if they aren't able to pay a hardworking touring band as much as they'd like. Of course, if they're total jerks and treat everyone poorly, all bets are off.

- **Shorten Your Set**: If you are opening for an out-of-town act, play a shorter set so that they get more stage time and won't be going on after midnight. You don't want to be the ones on the other side of the coin, playing thousands of miles from home at 1:30am because some lame local act played so long, that everyone left the club. In fact, you could simply ask which slot they'd prefer or work with the promoter to make sure they're taken care of.

- **Engage Your Fans**: Encourage your friends/fans to buy merchandise from the band on tour first, then to consider your own things after. Whenever I go to shows and see an artist promoting someone else, I buy something from both bands. It's the decent thing to do.

- **Headliner**: Unless they are an established national artist, most touring bands prefer a strong local to headline instead. If you know you can get a crowd to the show, don't be afraid to headline. It will make you look good anyway.

- **Share the Hospitality**: I remember once, on a very long tour, we got to the club late because of traffic (and drove over 14 hours straight to get there too). We were starving and exhausted. The club provided food but the other bands and their guests that they invited to the green room ate almost all of it so the five of us had to share the one remaining slice of pizza that was left. Consider the needs of the other act - save them something.

- **Use Your Brain…and Your Heart**: If you remember the golden rule (treat others how you want to be treated), it'll be likely that other bands will throw more shows your way. Your opportunities to tour with a band who has an established following in other markets will increase. You'll feel good for helping a starving artist. But if you are a greedy douche bag, no one will want to help you get you where you want to go.

- **A Place to Stay**: If you feel comfortable and are able to offer a place for the touring band to shower/sleep, it's always nice to extend the offer - especially if they don't know anyone else in town. Often, it'll give you a contact/place to stay in return when you go to their town.

These things aren't always intuitive, it takes time learn the nuances of working with other bands. Sometimes, it just takes a bad experience for you to learn how inconsiderate other acts can be. Either way, you don't want to be known as the jerk band that screws over touring acts. The better reputation that you hold, the better you'll be treated when you're on the road yourself.

Activity 1: Set Your Expectations and Initiate Contact With the Touring Band

Before you decide to hand your share of the door money to a touring band or change your performance slot, make sure that everyone in your band is on the same page in regards to how you want to handle helping bands on the road. Communicating these things in advance can prevent heated arguments later on.

Once you decide what you're able to offer the traveling band, contact them in advance. They'll appreciate the initiative and you can begin that working relationship much sooner. It'll also allow them to plan - and hopefully, give them an incentive to treat you better while there as well as motivate them to work harder in terms of promoting the show. You might even be able to set up a show exchange in advance as well, and ask for their help in booking a venue in their area.

By planning in advance, you could also do a bit of cross-promotion: video blogs talking about each other's bands, design promotional materials in advance, have a contest or friendly competition, etc. All of these things will benefit you much more than if you only just showed up at the venue on the same day to play.

Section 5: How to Tour Effectively

This section is dedicated to artists who make touring an essential part of their business model. Specifically, it discusses specific activities to make touring far more productive and effective. For many artists, touring is one of the most enjoyable aspects of being a musician. It provides a great opportunity to travel, make new fans in new markets, and often builds the kind of momentum needed to get publicity. However, bands can get so much more from the experience by utilizing the extra time available to be more productive.

Over the years, I've noticed that even tours with aggressive back-to-back schedules can have periods of downtime. Most artists should be able to find some time during long commutes or between shows to do any number of things: vehicle maintenance, marketing, preparation for other work, etc. It's also important to balance that with activities that keep the tour fun and rewarding as well.

The chapters in this section are my recommendations and suggestions for things that you can do easily while on tour. You might find yourself gravitating towards some of the activities more than others. Whatever you decide to do, it should align with your S.M.A.R.T.E.R Goals (section 1, chapter 9) so that everything is working towards a larger purpose.

Of course, I believe that you should be doing all of these things but that will ultimately be up to you and the members of your band, what your goals are for you touring, and how you want to approach your music career. Like all of the other sections in this book, I encourage you to use these suggestions as inspiration for creating your own ideas, activities, and habits.

1. Vehicle Maintenance

If you are going to be doing any kind of extended traveling, it's important to do some basic maintenance and preparation on the vehicle to prevent any unexpected breakdowns.

Some of the basic things that you should check on your vehicle and/or trailer include:

- **Tires:** Inspect all tires (including spare tires) to make sure that they are properly inflated and are not worn out or damaged. An easy way to check tire tread is to use a penny: simply place the coin into the tire tread with the head facing toward you and down. If the area above the head is visible, it's time to replace the tires. Remember, tire pressures change during cold weather so use the measurements inside the driver's door rather than the ratings on the tire during winter months. Keeping tires in top condition also helps increase fuel efficiency.

- **Fluids:** You should continuously check the oil, coolant, and transmission fluids. Keep a log of when you change fluids - regular oil changes are one of the most important things that you can do for your vehicle.

- **Brakes:** If you notice any vibrations, grinding, or pulling to one side when applying brakes, you should have them checked.

- **Battery:** Before taking a long trip, take the battery out and have it checked by any parts store. Batteries are usually good for 3-5 years...but they are easier to replace before you leave for tour rather than in the middle of one.

- **Belts/hoses:** Take a look at the belts and hoses under the hood for cracks, soft spots, or wear. Be sure to give extra attention to the hoses going into the radiator as well as the condition of the serpentine belt.

You should also have an emergency road kit with extra fuses, a flashlight, road flares, jumper cables, and spare bottles of fluids. I also recommend keeping a small tool kit as well, especially if you have someone traveling with you who knows a little about maintaining vehicles.

Before you leave for tour, you should do the following:

- **Get any scheduled maintenance done:** This includes everything from major repairs to a basic tune up.

- **Check the air filter**: The air filter is inexpensive and easy to change. They should be changed every 10,000 miles or so. Keeping a clean air filter also helps improve fuel economy.

- **Consider roadside assistance**: Whether you join AAA or get roadside assistance from another source, it's a good idea to have help readily available. If you're worried about the added expense, you can usually add roadside assistance to any cellphone plan for about $5 per month. At the end of the tour, simply remove it from your plan.

- **Check all of the above:** Before you head out, check the fluids, tire pressure, battery, etc.

- **Load your gear evenly:** Try to distribute the weight of your equipment evenly from side to side (whether it is in a trailer or inside a tour bus). It's best to keep the heaviest items over the axles, as opposed to the very front or rear.

A little preparation in advance can help prevent costly breakdowns on the road. If you don't have a regular mechanic or want to save some money on maintaining your tour vehicles, consider contacting your local community college with a certified auto repair program. They often provide the service with little or no charge for labor. However, they usually need more time to work on the vehicles, so be sure to communicate with the auto instructors in advance.

Activity 1: Assign Vehicle Maintenance Responsibilities

If you have a shared vehicle (tour bus, tour van, etc.), it's important to have someone accountable for keeping it well-maintained. That person should be keeping track of regular scheduled maintenance, oil changes, etc. If you share that responsibility, keep a log in the vehicle so that everyone can check up on what needs to be done. Also, keeping a mileage and repair log is useful when filing for taxes, since the IRS requires these types of records anyway.

On tour, it's important that basic safety and maintenance checks are conducted throughout the trip. Doing so allows you to help spot potential hazards in advance and address issues before you have lengthy stretches of travel without many repair shops en route. In many of the bands that I've been in, each person is responsible for a task (oil, tires, transmission fluid, etc.) and we check those items every day during regular stops (gas station or before leaving a city).

Activity 2: Do Safety Checks While on Tour

On tour, it's especially important to have a regular system of doing basic safety checks. This includes checking the oil (especially if you have an older vehicle), tire pressure, radiator fluid, and transmission fluid. If you're unsure how to do these things, there are great videos available on YouTube.

Some items, like checking the oil, should be done on a flat surface and before you begin a long drive. Others, like the transmission fluid, should be checked after the engine has been running for some time. If you create a regular pattern of checks in the morning (before the drive) and afternoon (after some distance), you should be good.

You might even have a clipboard, calendar reminder, Google spreadsheet, or whatever system you like to serve as a checklist. Either way, just make sure that you get it done.

Activity 3: Get a Tune-up Before the Next Tour

Before you hit the road, make sure you take your vehicle to a mechanic to do an overhaul. If you let them know you're going on a big trip, they'll be sure to take care of any major safety and performance issues so prevent any breakdowns and to improve fuel economy.

You can usually save money by working with a friend or going to a community college with a certified auto program. However, you could also consider talking to shops about a potential sponsorship, endorsement, or partnership deal as well. If you work with a regional chain, you might be able to have an even stronger safety net when it comes to tires, brakes, or other common repairs on the road.

2. Develop a Proper Driving Schedule

For over a decade, I toured in bands where we would rotate drivers based on who was the least tired, switch when someone volunteered, or we just had a vague notion of who had not taken the wheel in some time. It was the same pattern in nearly every act until one day, I thought of creating a simple, reliable system to put in place. I created a driving schedule.

In our band, we list out the names of everyone traveling in a specific order. Each person is responsible for three hours worth of driving. At the end of their shift, it just moves to the next person on the list. With six people in our bus, this often means that we only need to drive every other day. And because you know when your shift is coming up, you can take proactive actions to prepare for it - taking a nap, not drinking, etc.

Of course, if someone is too tired or otherwise unfit to drive, we place them into rotation elsewhere. No matter what though, a driving schedule ensures a fair amount of driving time for each band member, sets clear expectations, and can curtail ugly arguments about the unequal distribution of driving responsibilities.

Activity 1: Set Up You Driving Schedule

Get together with your bandmates and decide on a realistic schedule that you can follow. You can base it on length of time, distance, days of the week, or whatever you'd like. Just be sure that you have buy-in from all members of the group and that expectations are clearly expressed.

Here are some of the examples of rules we've set in my band:

- **3 hour shifts:** We always limit driving to 3 hours so that no one person gets worn out, especially before or after a show. If we are driving overnight, we'll usually reduce the requirement to 2 hour shifts.

- **Next driver up**: We always save the bed or most comfortable sleeping space for whoever is on deck to drive next. It's important that they're well-rested before they begin driving.

- **No drinking**: Whoever is assigned to drive isn't allowed to drink before their shift, even if it is at a show earlier in the evening.

- **Co-pilot**: During night driving, we always have at least one other person stay awake to provide some company for the driver. They help make sure the driver is taken care of, is alert, and helps direct or navigate the roads.

You'll probably have your own specific situations, conditions, or rules but this should give you a basic idea of how you can approach it.

3. Secure Your Gear

We all know stories about bands who get their gear ripped off during tour – people break into trailers, steal vans, or sometimes steal gear from the back of the venue. These are some of the ways you can protect your equipment on the road:

- **Add deterrents**: A wheel lock is an inexpensive deterrent that will make it harder for someone to break in or steal your vehicle. More advanced versions will have loud alarms and flashing lights as well. You might also consider investing in other options such as an ignition kill switch, GPS-tracking, or alarm as well.

  Another easy trick to protect your bus/van is to unhook the distributor cap at night. This prevents thieves from being able to drive off with the vehicle, since most people won't think of checking for this when it doesn't start.

- **Get better locks**: If you have a trailer or are using any kind of external lock, you better be using a "puck" style lock. It's much stronger and can't be cut off. You should also get a locking hitch and locking hitch pin as well.

- **Park smart**: When staying the night somewhere, back the vehicle up and park against walls so that it is harder to open large doors. If you have another car, have it block the main touring vehicle in. Use these natural barriers to protect your things.

- **Night guard**: In my band, if we are unsure about an area, 1-2 people will sleep in the vehicle overnight. In the past, I've also created a dummy using a sleeping bag and a mannequin head, to feign someone sleeping inside.

- **Cover the windows**: It seems simple, but if people can't see what's inside, they can't tell if expensive equipment is actually inside.

- **When in doubt, unload**: I can't tell you how many times we've unloaded gear into hotels and motel rooms, just to be safe. It's better than getting your stuff stolen!

- **Inventory and serial numbers**: Before you leave for tour, take inventory of your equipment and record the serial numbers (you can store them in Google Drive as a document). Take photos of the equipment as well. That way, if anything happens, you can create a police report right away.

Most of these are simple, inexpensive precautions that serve as deterrents to protect your tour vehicle and equipment.

Activity 1: Anti Theft Checklist

Get your band in the habit of checking all of your gear and taking precautionary measures prior to parking for the night. Use any or all of the tips in this chapter, including looking over all of your gear. Too often, bands only find out that something is missing or remember an unlocked door when it is too late.

Activity 2: Unload or Cover

If you're unsure about the area where you are staying but don't have any other options, consider unloading the equipment into the house/hotel where you are staying. Another option is covering the equipment with some old blankets (and of course, backing the vehicle against a wall so that things can't be removed form it). This is especially the case if you have things visible through the windows.

If you are touring with a trailer, that can be an open invitation for unwanted attention, so it is often even less secure. In this instances, it is better to be safe than sorry – just go ahead and unload.

4. Strengthen Your Vocals

It's important to continue building your vocal strength daily by keeping up with some of the exercises covered earlier (Section 3, chapter 11). The additional strain endured on tour, especially with nightly performances, requires even more diligence. Not only will basic exercises help protect your vocals, but they will strengthen and improve them as well.

For example, the practice of eating and drinking or abstaining from certain foods (The Singer's Diet) should be observed even more closely while on the road. Doing exercises to warm up and cool down before each show is also important to preserve vocals for the length of the tour. Most experts agree: the way to strengthening vocals isn't through singing; it's through specific activities designed to work the muscles of your vocal chords.

Activity 1: Vocal Exercise Set 1 - Breathing

Breathing properly is one of the most important parts of strengthening your voice. However, you can also learn how to use less air to improve the sound and be more efficient. By learning to control the vibration of your vocal chords, you will also enjoy an improved range as well.

Lip Trills

Lip trills are a very common exercise for vocalists. To perform them, gently blow air through closed but relaxing lips while singing an *ah* or *uh* vowel. Try to sustain notes for at least four counts. This will cause your lips to trill/vibrate. Try not to let your chest collapse while doing this exercise, let your lower body carry the work. This exercise helps build endurance and maintain cord closure.

Stirring Straw Exercise

Pick up some small stirring straws during any of your tour stops (available at any coffee shop, bar, or restaurant) for an easy exercise. Simply blow air through the straw while phonating/expressing simple scales up and down your range. The air resistance of the straw will press on your vocal chords to decrease puffiness.

The Squeaky Door

The squeaky door (also known as the creaky doors or creak) helps build coordination for cord closure. All you have to do is make a sound like a creaky door or rusty gate opening. Do a simple scale using this sound while using as little air as possible. The goals is to not let the sound get breathy.

Activity 2: Vocal Exercise Set 2 - Tongue Control

Research shows that many of the best exercises for your vocal chords are tongue related. One scientist believes that the strength of your voice is dependent on the hyo-glossus muscle in the tongue. These are simple tongue exercises designed to strengthen muscles for your voice.

Tongue Curls

First, completely relax your tongue - it should be completely flat in your mouth. Then curl your tongue inwards so that the two sides make a groove down the middle. Uncurl, then repeat. Repeat this for one minute.

Ngs

Make an *ng* sound, as in the end of the word *tongue*. Run through basic scales using the *ng* sound and pressing the tongue with the soft palate. Practicing this helps the transition between upper and lower registers easier, otherwise known as the chest and head voice.

Activity 3: Vocal Exercise Set 3 - Vocal Chord Control

Gee

This is an excellent exercise for singers who experience excessive tension. Using a deep, almost cartoon-like voice, say the word *gee* with a hard *g* sound, like in *goat*, *geek*, or *girl*. When you do so, you should feel your larynx drop. It also helps chord closure, allowing you to better access your upper register with stability. Developing these muscles help with healthy singing. Try singing scales up and down with a low, *gee*.

Coo

Sing vocal scales up and down specifically with the word *coo*, like a hooty owl sound. This helps muscles used in working high notes in your vocal range.

Goog

Once you've been fully warmed up and doing vocal exercises on a regular basis, you can try this more advanced exercise. Begin single scales up and down with the word *goog*, with a soft *g* and *oo* like in *good*. The hard *g* will help with cord closure and the *oo* will help stabilize the larynx. As you move higher up in the scale, be sure to retain proper pronunciation of the and the *oo*; widening the vowel can actually cause tension.

Vowel Widening

Using one sustained word to move from a closed vowel to a wider one will help train your balance of resonance. Hold a note while saying *ooh-oh-uh-ah* (your mouth should also widen with this as well), but keep the resonance at the same level.

5. Build Healthy Touring Habits

Touring artists often must endure some grueling work conditions. The long hours, fast food, sleepless nights, stress, and miles traveled on the road can take a serious toll on one's health. To ensure safety, awareness, and a condition to maintain top performance, it's important to take steps to protect physical, emotional, and mental health.

Here are some basic guidelines for staying healthy while on tour:

- **Stay hydrated**: Drink lots of water to stay hydrated and try to avoid alcohol, carbonated soda, or other sugary drinks.

- **Sleep as much as possible**: Touring requires a great deal of energy and often doesn't provide many opportunities for sleep. Despite the arduous schedule, it's important to get rest while you can, especially before taking a turn at driving. Don't underestimate the power of sleep.

- **Wash your hands often**: Keep a bottle of hand sanitizer or wet wipes on hand. Between the hand shaking and the general cleanliness of many venues, you will come into contact with many germs. Take care of yourself through this basic, but oft-ignored action.

- **Eat well**: Most tours are filled with fast food, pizza, and beer. Try to change things up by stopping by markets for fresh produce (it also saves money on food costs as well) and taking vitamin supplements. In general, avoid fried and high-fat foods, meals offered at gas stations, or processed foods. Check out *Eat This, not That* or other fast food guides to help you make better choices in restaurants.

- **First aid kit**: Keep a first aid kit with some basic medicine and nutritional supplements. You might consider herbal supplements as well. Allergies often kick up, so keep a ready supply of prescription medicine and over-the-counter remedies.

- **Exercise**: When possible, find time to do some exercise - taking a walk, using a gym at the hotel, etc. While performing on stage does provide a workout, the long periods of driving can create deteriorate your muscles.

- **Spiritual and Mental Health**: It's important to tend to your psychological needs. If you have religious needs, build in time for meditation, prayer, or other devotional practices. It's also important to break away from the monotony of touring: find time to explore each city, call loved ones at home, etc.

Taking care of yourself on tour will help keep you healthy and sane, ensuring that you are in the best condition possible for the demanding needs of the road.

Activity 1: Basic Stretches and Exercises

Here are some basic stretches and exercises that you can do from inside a bus, car, or van:

Spine Stretches

Hold onto the steering wheel with your hands at the 10 o'clock and 2 o'clock positions and round your back. By gently pulling on the steering while rounding your back, you can stretch the muscles between your shoulder blades and mid-back. Breathe, then release.

Body Roll

Begin a shoulder roll but continue the motion down your body, as if you were trying to touch your stomach . From there, continue with your hips, then roll on through in front of you. Finally, reverse the motion. Continue with five to tend sets back and forth in order to improve blood flow and reduce aches in your upper body.

Head and Neck Roll

Gently rotate your neck to begin blood flow. Begin by drawing small, imaginary circles with your chin. Gradually increase the size of the circles until you are at a comfortable range of motion (about twenty reps). Reverse the direction, starting small and working your way up again.

Spine Decompression

While sitting, bring your knees up to your chest and hug them. Take a deep breath, hold for a second, then exhale slowly. As you exhale, gently rock yourself back and forth in your seat. Repeat five times to help alleviate back pain and improve mobility.

During rest stops, you can do any number of stretches and exercises to improve overall fitness, including: push ups, burpees, jumping jacks, lunges, etc. Whenever you can, find ways to work your muscles to alleviate soreness and improve mobility.

Activity 2: Tour Grocery Shopping

One of the best ways to stay healthy and save money is to get the right kind of groceries and food on the road. You might not have a refrigerator or cooking appliances, but you can still have some tasty and healthy snack options available. Below are some examples of things you can buy, bring, or make while on the road.

Things to pack in the cooler

Pick up a travel cooler and fill it with ice. You can then pack it with things like Greek yogurt (much less sugar than conventional yogurt), bottled water, juice, fruit, low-fat cheeses, applesauce, and veggie snacks. You might even consider getting some hummus or peanut butter to eat with veggies or pita chips.

Nonperishable options

Healthy choices include nuts and seeds (in small portions), popcorn, and rice cakes. You can also try dried fruit or fruit leathers, beef jerky, and low-sugar energy bars. Another good option is trail mix - either bought in bulk at the grocery store (much less than buying packages of it at convenience stores), or making your own with granola, raw nuts and seeds, and dried fruit. Finally, you can easily keep peanut butter, jelly, and a loaf of bread at room temperature for simple meals to stave off hunger.

Best options at a convenience store

If you aren't able to go to a grocery store, you can usually still pick up some decent options at a convenience store. The best options include: whole grain cereal, peanuts in the shell, yogurt, 100% vegetable juice, single servings of baby carrots, skim-milk string cheese, bananas, trail mix, and fruit cups in light syrup.

Being mindful of nutrition will give you more energy for the tour and save you money. If you avoid fast food for your trip, you'll feel much better by the end of the tour (your gut will appreciate it as well). Plus, your vocals will stay stronger (See the Singer's Diet in Section 3, chapter 11).

6. Meet Up With Fans

If you have an established fan base, using offstage moments to connect with them can be a great way to build the relationship and create enthusiasm with your target audience. If you are relying on fans for a place to stay or help with promoting your show, this can also help show your appreciation.

Even if you are playing a new market where you don't have an established audience, you can still create unique experience by offering a webcast (such as Google Hangout) or even connecting with a specific interest-based group. For instance, if you have any kind of online or national community (religious group, hobby, sports, Yelp, etc.), you can organize or participate in an existing event. This can be another way to network, meet new friends, and let people know about your show.

Activity 1: Make it Social

When you have any kind of event, you should leverage social media to get some more publicity out of it. If you're launching a tour and doing a series of meet up's, consider using a specific hashtag to collect social media posts across Twitter, Instagram, Facebook, Tumblr, and Pinterest. You can also document it using video and posting a vlog recap later on. Whatever you do, just be sure to find ways to create some more excitement and a thoughtful way to share the event with others.

Some of the ways you can add an online element or create some momentum for the event include:

- Make it part of a crowdfunding campaign (perhaps an exclusive party can be part of a reward or it can be a fundraiser for your tour/album).
- Use Facebook invites, Eventbrite, or any other kind of online invite/reservation system.
- Create your own hashtag to encourage and collect social media posts, then publish the best posts using Storify (storify.com).
- Ask attendees to blog about the experience (you should also post a blog).
- Interview fans for your video blog.
- Host an online contest to win a prize or even the ability to get some exclusive hangout time with the band: private concert, backstage access, photo or video shoot, etc.
- Stream a show or meet up (try Ustream or Google Hangouts) with people "attending" and "participating" online.
- Work with a club, school, organization, other band, sponsor, or other entity to tap into their audience for a cross-promotional campaign.
- Issue a press release.

Most of the time, it just takes a thoughtful approach to get more out of these types of events. Spend some time brainstorming with bandmates, your management, and your most enthusiastic supporters to come up with the type of campaign most appropriate for your band and your fans.

Activity 2: Ninja concert

A ninja concert is a (seemingly) spontaneous show that can be held just about anywhere: think of it like the music version of a flash mob. It requires a little bit of planning, a little bit of help, and a lot of energy/promotion. Usually, a ninja concert is going to be much easier to pull off as an acoustic performance with no PA system or amplified instruments, unless you use ultraportable gear.

You can also take advantage of existing events, areas where busking is common, or simply create your own shows with your fans. Some ideas include:

- Open market (farmer's market, etc.)
- Parades
- Protests, marches, or other political events
- Public parks
- Outdoor festivals
- Amusement parks

In some places, a permit will be required so it's a good idea to check with the city or property management office first. If you plan on performing while something else is happening (such as an outdoor play), you might want to check with event organizers ahead of time so there isn't any conflict. Often, you can work together to create memorable events for the community

Activity 3: Dinner and a Show

You can create a special experience for your most dedicated fans: dinner and a show. You can even offer this experience through a contest, crowdfunding, or in exchange for a place to stay. If you and/or your bandmates know how to cook well, you can offer to make dinner. Or, you could always simply order a pizza. Some bands just skip the food altogether and simply just host a house party show.

In one of my previous bands, an entire nationwide tour was launched that focused almost entirely on fan-organized house parties. For another, we offered a private party and dinner cooked by band members as a Kickstarter backer reward. We also filmed the show and gave a DVD of the experience to the fan who paid for the party.

How you set this up is up to you and your band. Just don't rule out the incredible experience that you and your fans can enjoy.

7. Financial Overview

A financial overview is a process for examining the entirety of your band's financial situation.

Whether or not you file taxes for the income received from your music business (hopefully you do), you will still want an accurate record of the finances of your tour. Tracking income and expenditures will allow you to measure return on investment, plan the remainder of your trip, identify tax deductible expenses, and invest finances into other areas of the group.

Band money should be kept separately from personal money (especially important for taxes). Money from the music business should be kept in its own account, with receipts that can line up to your accounting.

You should be able to identify the sources of income, knowing how much money comes from:

- Live performances
- Merchandise sales
- Sponsorship money

- Donations and tips
- Online sales and royalty payments earned during tour
- Other money earned

You should also be able to identify where the money is being spent during the tour:

- Fuel and auto expenses
- Lodging
- Meals/food
- Supplies
- Parking and tolls
- Equipment
- Publicity/Advertising
- Other expenses

The receipts for these expenses should be grouped together by category. Not only will this help you identify where your cash outflows are going, but you'll be much more prepared when filing taxes for the tour.

At minimum, you should be following these guidelines:

- Decide on a tax structure for the band: sole proprietor, partnership, or company. Each have their advantages and disadvantages. Whatever you choose, follow the rules for that specific structure.
- Keep all your receipts. Making digital copies will help you greatly - whether you use a receipt scanner or take photos of them using your phone, it will make life much easier later when you need to find them, especially if you organize them into folders
- Only pay for things with an invoice or where a receipt can be furnished.
- If band members need to contribute money for something out

of their own pocket, keep a record of how much each person puts in and how much/when they are paid back.

- Pay special attention to items that are deductible for your tax structure with supporting evidence.
- It's best if you can get a Certified Public Accountant (CPA) to overlook your finances and assist with filing taxes. In the meantime, you can reduce the amount of work needed when filing taxes from your tour by staying on top of the finances now.

Activity 1: Collect and Organize Receipts

Gather all of the receipts from the expenses accrued during your tour. You can separate expenses into individual envelopes based on their respective category, scan them, or take photos using your phone and send them to an online storage system such as Evernote (www.evernote.com), Dropbox (www.dropbox.com), or Google Drive (drive.google.com).

Knowing how much you spend on fuel, lodging, meals, and other expenses helps you create more accurate budgets for future tours. You can even find out the average cost per day for touring (add up all expenses and divide by number of days) or even the cost per mile (add up all expenses and divide by total number of miles).

Activity 2: Keep a Running Till

Your band's cash box should be treated like a cash register: you should have a running till (a set amount of petty cash for change and expenses). Whatever amount you decide to keep on hand, you should keep it consistent at a set amount (and no more than $250). The cash box should be balanced on a regular basis so that it always has that set amount. Excess amounts should be deposited or secured on a regular basis during the tour.

If you are using an iPad to run credit card transactions, you can use the Square Register app (www.square.com) to record cash transactions, which will help maintain accuracy as well as record merchandise inventory levels.

Activity 3: Spreadsheets and Apps

If you are having trouble with maintaining consistent, transparent, and accurate financial records, you can download any number of tools to help you.

These are some suggestions:

- **BandLoot** (www.bandloot.com) is a free money management tool made for bands. It's an online tool where you can create an account, manage income/expenses from each band member, receive email notifications, and allow you to manage your overall cash together.

- **Quickbooks** (www.quickbooks.com) is one of the most popular accounting programs used. It can sync with your bank account, has some more advanced features geared specifically for business, and allows data pull with programs like TurboTax which can make filing much easier. It usually runs for about $50.

- **TurboCash** (www.turbocash.net) is a free, open source small business accounting package which has some features most bands won't even touch (such as stock control) but it does generate invoices, has a general ledger function, can produce balance sheets and income statements, and even multiple companies (if you have more than one band, this is quite handy).

- **GnuCash** (www.gnucash.org) is a free register program with some powerful features, including the ability to track supplies, invoicing and bill payment, and currency conversion. It is also able to generate reports so you can get statistics about where money is coming from or how it is being spent. You can download versions for PC, Mac, Linux, or Android.

Staying on top of your band's finances, especially when you are dealing with most of your transactions (during tour) will make life much easier during tax season. It's also a good way to track your income and expenses so you can do a better analysis of your financial situation when you need it most.

8. Build Important Relationships

During any tour, there are stretches of time that can be used to build important relationships that are being made along the way. These relationships can include venues, promoters, record shops, media outlets, potential sponsors/partners, other bands, new fans, people in the music industry, or other contacts. You can find time to develop these relationships during long drives, between soundchecks and show time, or whenever you can find at least fifteen minutes of downtime.

Just as you should find time to contact loved ones back at home when you're on the road, you should find some time to extend gratitude to those who have helped you, provide business-related updates to partners, and remind newly introduced contacts who you are. More than anything, it is about maintaining personal contact - something more than subscribing them to your band's mailing list without their explicit consent. In fact, don't sign them up for anything unless they ask or directly approve.

Activity 1: Handwritten Thank You Notes

If you want to leave an impression wherever you go, keep a box of thank you notes and a roll of stamps with you on tour.

Take the time to personalize and sign thank you notes to promoters, sound engineers who have done a great job, people who let you stay in their homes, radio station managers that have played your music, or anyone else that you met along the way who helped you in some manner. Mail the thank you card to the respective parties shortly after working with them.

Most of the time, the staff involved with putting on shows have a thankless job. They have to work long hours, deal with self-absorbed bands/musicians, are expected to keep the bar or venue where they work afloat, and are under a constant barrage of emails from people who want something from them. If you want to stand out from the crowd, show a little graciousness by sending a personal thank you card.

Activity 2: Following Up on Business Cards Collected

Here's a trick I've learned over the years when trading business cards with others: as soon as possible, write down any notes or details about the conversation that you had with the person on their card. It might be a simple fact about their kids, about what they are looking for, what you discussed, or even a hobby that you have in common. Whatever it is, it will help you jog your memory later on, especially as you collect more cards. Also, when you follow up with the person, you can use those notes to help trigger their memory as well. This is especially helpful if you are touring around music industry networking events or festivals where you will be meeting with lots of people.

Another step that you can take is creating a contact list, spreadsheet, or other document that has the contact information as well as additional notes: where/when you met, what their needs are, what they're interested in, a contact record of when you last shared

SIMON S. TAM

correspondence, and any other important information. From time to time, you should review that to help spur ideas for potential sponsors, promotional campaigns, or other endeavors.

Activity 3: Initiate a New Relationship with a Contact

If you have already been using your time to keep in touch with important contacts that you've made during the tour, as well as current partners already helping you on a regular basis, you could also take some time to research new potential contacts.

Earlier in the book, the topic of researching potential new sponsors is covered (section 1, chapter 5). Often, the momentum, excitement, and surrounding press around a tour can provide an impetus for communicating with potential sponsors, even if you haven't had success with working something out in the past. For example, you could offer to meet in person ("I'll be in your area on X date, would you be willing to quickly meet/allow me to drop off an album and some information, etc."). Sometimes, it can also be a way to secure press, especially if national news or other related media sources have covered a story about you recently.

Think about who you want to talk to, why the should want to meet with you, and begin reaching out to them. You never know what you can accomplish simply from an ask.

9. Local Media Blitz

A note about this chapter: If you have a publicist already contacting media outlets about your tour, be sure to talk to them before you reach out to any yourself. You want to coordinate efforts whenever possible to avoid confusing or annoying media contacts.

During your tour, you can often create opportunities to get some more promotion or buzz about your appearances. At the minimum, you should be working press releases, submitting event calendar listings, and looking for opportunities to get earned media (interviews, features, etc.). Most of these things should be done well in advance of the tour - four to six weeks for local or regional press, two to three months for national. However, as you get closer to your show, you can usually do a few other things to increase the local media buzz.

Activity 1: Ticket giveaway

Many radio stations, especially independent or college-owned channels, love giving away things to their listeners. You can often call the station manager of on-air personality and tell them that you'd like to give away a pair of tickets to your show in town. Often, they'll be excited to do so. Sometimes, they're even willing to play some of your music on air so be sure to have a source for them to pull radio-friendly content from right away if they don't already have your songs on hand.

For publicly funded stations that are hosting fundraising or membership drives, such as local National Public Radio affiliates or community radio stations, you could always offer music or tickets as rewards for listeners who call in and donate to their station. Each station handles these things differently. All it takes is a little research and a quick phone call or email.

Activity 2: Connecting with a larger national story

If you are already receiving some national press for your album or another story, it's usually much easier to get local media interested in you. For example, when I travel to other towns (even when I am not on tour), I'll often contact their local public broadcasting stations to see if they'd like to do an exclusive interview in connection to a larger story that I'm a part of.

If you are not receiving national press, you can still look for other opportunities to get some air time. If local talk shows are discussing a hot topic that you are knowledge or opinionated about, you can contact them about doing a short interview (or just calling in live when the show is on air). Then, you can find ways to connect it back with your band or let them know that you are performing in town. For example, if your band is so passionate about environmentalism that you've decided to tour entirely on bio-diesel, you might find appropriate topics about that being discussed on local radio talk shows, publications, or college papers. Simply look up local stations in the town you will be appearing in and see what kinds of on-air shows they have. If something looks appropriate, you can reach out to the production manager or station.

Activity 3: Blog Roll Call

Some cities have a popular blog or podcast that chronicles local shows, interesting articles, or other events happening specifically in the area. For example, in New York, *Brooklyn Vegan* (www.brooklynvegan.com) is one of the most popular resources for live music in the city. Find the popular blogs in a city and invite them to your show, give them free passes, offer a chance to do an exclusive interview, offer a giveaway for their audience, etc. Talk to your publicist, fans local to the area, or do a quick search online to find new resources to help promote your show.

10. Play More Shows

If one of your tour goals is to perform for as many people as possible, then you might want to examine other opportunities available to you outside of the traditional venue. Whether you are touring with a full band or you are going at it solo as a singer-songwriter, there are many platforms to share your live performance. If you have a scalable show that can adapt to different environments (such as being able to have an unplugged version of your show), you'll have even more events to choose from.

You won't always be able to choose where you play or who you play for, but if you look for opportunities related to your target audience, your chances of success will be much higher. For example, if you perform in a Christian rock band, you could contact youth groups, local churches, ministries, Christian-owned stores, etc. for other chances to play outside of your scheduled venue show. If your music has a strong literary theme, you could play in libraries, in bookstores, for book clubs, at author readings, and so on. Find ways to tie in your target audience whenever you make the pitch to places you want to play that caters to them.

Activity 1: Look for in-store opportunities

Performing in stores, restaurants, or other places can often be good business for both the acts as well as the establishment. You get another place to sell your music to new fans while they get entertainment and a chance to sell their products and services to your fans. If both people promote the show, it's even better.

In fact, at large festivals such as SXSW, it's quite common to see live music in nearly every kind of shop in the city. If you approach it from the right angle, you could often line up these kinds of opportunities on your own during these major events.

Here are some stores that you can approach:

- **Record shops**: Many independent record stores are open to in-store performances, signings, or other appearances, even if your album isn't being distributed there. Often, they'll just set you up with consignment so that they can process album sales while you are in the store.

  You can check with members of the Coalition of Independent Music Stores (CIMS), The Alliance of Independent Music Stores, shops that participate in Record Store Day, or just do a search in each of the cities where you are playing. If you have physical distribution, you can check with your distributor. Places that are already carrying your record will be much more inclined to have you coming in than cold contacts.

- **Niche retailers**: If you cater to a particular niche audience, you can contact stores related to those interests. Some ideas include skateboard shops, clothing stores, bookstores, hobby shops, or retailers with high foot traffic. In the past, Hot Topic used to allow touring acts to play acoustic sets in their stores. You might be able to contact the store manager of other stores that would provide a decent fit.

My band, The Slants, caters to a geek crowd. In previous tours, I've booked several afternoon appearances at comic book shops, anime stores, museums, game stores, and other similar venues. They often created more interest in the shows later in the evening, helped us sell more merchandise, and let us play for all-age crowds even if we were only playing 21+ venues in town.

- **Restaurants, wineries, breweries, and coffee shops**: Many restaurants and beverage retailers (other than bars, of course) have great walk-in traffic that will allow you to reach a new crowd or pick up some extra cash mid-tour. In fact, establishments that have performers on a regular basis will have a sound system, will usually pay well, will feed you, and are used to helping promote the show as well. However, be prepared to also play for diners who could care less that you are there. Before booking a restaurant or coffee shop, you could check out reviews online to see what patrons say about the live music experience there.

There are many places who are interested in having entertainment but don't know how to approach setting up or running a show. If you travel with a portable P.A system, can demonstrate a good value for them, and can find something suitable for your music, you can create more opportunities for yourself than only playing venues during your tour.

Activity 2: Busking

Busking is the art of performing in public spaces in exchange for tips. In some cities, this is more common than others. In fact, some cities have regular areas for musicians to perform - some even allow for low-volume amplification. However, some cities are also now requiring performs to seek a license or permit as well. It's good to do some research on the areas where you'll be playing.

For many cities, you'll find websites that list information about busking in their area - what locations are popular, what is required, or view footage of other musicians who busk in the area. If there are known buskers in the area, you can usually just ask them for some tips.

Here are some general guidelines that you'll want to keep in mind:

- If you do perform in a popular area, don't set up too closely to other people busking.
- Don't be too loud - you don't want to annoy people.
- Prepare 1-2 hours' worth of material,
- Find a way to make your act stand out, be worth watching.
- Engage with the audience - talk to them, entertain them, smile at them.
- Have signage pointing to your website, your show, etc.
- Make it easy for people to donate - open guitar case, large hat, large bucket, etc.
- Find ways to tie in social media.

Busking certainly isn't for everyone but it's certainly worth trying. If you decide to engage in it, keep track of how much you earn, changes to your website traffic or social media, and other metrics as you would after playing a show to se if it is really worth your time. Most of all, have fun!

Activity 3: Open mic night

If you have a day off during your tour (or trouble filling in the tour calendar), you might consider getting involved with a local open mic night.

Open mic nights are usually free and open for anyone in the audience to participate (though there's usually a time to sign up for slots). Generally, they allow performers a limited time slot so that everyone can perform. However, if you notify the event in advance, you can often swing more time in as a touring act (or perform a set before/after the event). Also, you might even talk to event organizers about hosting, being the backing band like live karaoke (having participants submits songs in advance), or getting a few extra performances in.

While an open mic night generally doesn't pay (it's usually for tips only), it does provide a way to meet local artists, perform for a friendly crowd, and a chance to sell some merchandise!

Activity 4: Check the classifieds

If you still have a few gaps on tour and want to look for all possible appearances, try searching the classifieds in a particular region. Sometimes, you can find opportunities listed on Craigslist - especially if you use the search function in the community, events, and gigs categories. Try using these search terms like "band," "bands," "live music," "artists," "musicians," "performers," etc.

Often, you'll find any number of listings that might be a good fit: private parties, weddings, grand opening events, film cameos, and more. It's always worth taking a look and seeing what is available.

11. Work on Your Mailing List

Hopefully, you already have an established newsletter that is going out on a consistent schedule. If you haven't already, go over the section on *Use an Email List Effectively* (Section 1, Chapter 12) to learn some best practices when working with a mailing list. For each show, you should also already be prominently displaying a mailing list sign-up and encouraging people to fill it out. Now that people are signing up each night on tour, you should be following up.

First, some email management programs allow you to create an automatic message to be sent to fans when they first sign up for your mailing list from your website. If you turn this option on, you can deliver some fan rewards, such as some free mp3 downloads, desktop backgrounds, or exclusive content. If you enter contacts in manually (usually from a mailing list sheet), make sure that each new contact still gets these rewards.

Second, you should send as many personal messages as possible to new fans who sign up. If you or someone in your band remembers who the person is and some other details or exchange shared from the show, it will show thoughtfulness in a way that an automated message can't express.

Finally, you should use your mailing list to help communicate with fans who are going to be in the areas where you are playing on tour. Sort your contacts by zip code or city so that you can send messages to specific audiences rather than spamming your entire mailing list with a shows that may or may not even be near them.

Activity 1: Entering in New Contacts and the First Message

A general rule of thumb when it comes to contacts who sign your email list: the sooner that you get them in, the better. It's best to enter new fans into your database and contact them within 24 hours. If you are consistently on top of this task, it isn't too bad.

When you email the new fan, you should try and include some kind of personal message. At minimum, let them know what they can expect from the email list - what kinds of content they will receive, how often, etc. It's a simple task that goes a long way.

Activity 2: Targeted Emails to Promote Shows

Hopefully, you have an email management system that can sort out contacts by their location. Programs such as FanBridge automatically ask for zip codes when people sign up on the email list online. You should try the same thing by including that when printing out mailing list signup sheets for your band.

About two to three weeks out from every show, you should send a targeted email to contacts who are within range of your show (no more than 60 miles). Let them know that you are playing their town specifically - don't waste their time by including your entire tour route.

During the week of the show, send a personalized reminder, inviting each fan to your appearances in the area. You could even offer a free pair of passes or guest list spots to the first person who RSVP's as well.

Targeted emails make sure that your messages are going to the most relevant audience. That way, your fans won't perceive it as spam. If you're using your entire list for every show that you have, people will get tired of it really quickly – especially if they don't live anywhere near those shows.

Section 6: Other Voices in the Industry

It's always good to get a second opinion. Or a third. Or dozens of others. No career path is the same for all aspiring artists, some have different experiences.

When I set out writing this book, I wanted to also consult the opinions of others in the industry – some resonate the messages contained in earlier chapters, some have a different perspective altogether. This section contains contributions from booking agents, independent artists, A&R reps, entertainment attorneys, and more. Each has their own take on what musicians ought to tackle on a daily basis. This section is a little bit of a music industry potpourri, containing wisdom from many different facets of the musician's career.

Read. Learn. Take action. Grow.

1. Five Things Every Musician Should Be Doing

By: Joseph Becker

What is the most important thing that a musician should do? Well, I believe that there are five that you should consider:

1. Register All of Your Works With the U.S Copyright Office.

When you create a song or a sound recording (that is original and somehow written down, recorded, or as the law requires, 'fixed in a tangible medium of expression',) you also create--and own—its copyright. This gives you special rights towards the work that no one else has. But your job does not end there. You should register such copyrights with the United States Copyright Office.

Registration of a copyright in your name acts as evidence and a public record that the work belonged to you on a certain date. But that is only the beginning. Registration also offers a slew of other benefits that make the $35 dollar price tag on the application a sin to consider as an obstacle, especially considering the fact that you can (in many cases) throw your entire catalog of songs (or sound recordings) onto one application. If your artistic works are (and will be) the goods you'll be earning your livelihood on, then merely registering them as yours is the most basic and important thing you can do. Submitting a copyright application is something you can do without an attorney if you've done the research, but this is not advised.

2. Know Exactly Who Owns What.

Generally, the author (or creator) of a song or sound recording is the one who owns its copyright. But identifying the author(s) of a song is not always so clear. Say you wrote the lyrics and some of the melody, but your pianist helped with the melody, your drummer changed the rhythm, and your producer switched everything around while laying down the tracks. Who owns the song? Who owns the sound recording? How much of the pie does each author get? (You may want the owner (or one of the owners) to be a company that you create for such a purpose.)

There are rules for this, but they are not always clear. For this reason and others, you must set out such matters in a Band Agreement and/or some other agreement (such as an Operating Agreement for your LLC, etc.) You'll also want to determine which band members can use the band (or company) name (in the event of a breakup), sign or write checks on the group's behalf, and how a member can quit, buy-out another, or invite other people into the group.

3. Hire An Attorney To (At Least) Look Over ANY Contracts You Enter Into.

This is especially true for any contracts in which you are selling, licensing, or otherwise dealing with the ownership rights of your sole livelihood: your songs or sound recordings. Fraud exists--and I've seen it. I've seen people sell songs they don't own and enter into one-sided contracts with unfair terms regarding the term, price, rights sold, or venue. There are countless pitfalls here that only a seasoned attorney can spot. Look out for your rights! Even if you have an attorney merely 'look things over', this is one place you should invest in being more safe than sorry.

4. Choose A Band Name No One Else Is Using.

Why? Besides diluting your name with the public, choosing a band or artist name that someone else in the music (or similar) industry is using can present tremendous issues for you in the future, including the danger that someone else can stop your from using your name (that you may at that point have spent thousands of dollars and hours building) at all.

5. Network! Hustle! Get OUT There!

If you think making good music is enough for success, you're sadly mistaken. The story of a hidden Youtube video becoming a hit is far, wide, and exaggerated, if true at all. I am amazed how many musicians I speak to (and personally know) who do not take part in LinkedIn conversations (let alone even have a page), network with other musicians, music supervisors (who, by the way, often listen to the opinions of musicians they've placed before as well as other sources), managers, and their audience. So jump on Twitter, LinkedIn, Facebook, and all those other great sites, and reach out!

At the same time, educate yourself about the business. Though it is not your full time job to master the industry it really pays off to spend some of your free time reading about this. After all, these songs are your babies. Get to know their legal status well, and before long, they may go out and make you proud (and wealthy at that).

Joseph Becker recently worked as in-house counsel and head of licensing at Tuff City Records, where he negotiated and drafted various licensing arrangements with major companies including HBO, MTV/Vh1, CBS/Paramount, and Warner Brothers. Now he is been representing clients on his own. Information is available at www.jrbeckerlaw.com.

2. Busking with the Best

An interview with Natalia 'Saw Lady' Paruz

Natalia 'Saw Lady®' Paruz has played the musical saw anywhere from the NYC subway to Carnegie Hall, Madison Square Garden and Lincoln Center. From live performances with orchestras such as the Israel Philharmonic, Westchester Philharmonic, Royal Air Moroccan Symphony, Riverside Orchestra, Amor Artis Orchestra, Manhattan Chamber Orchestra etc., to televised performances on the Discovery Channel (Oddities), FOX (Good Day New York), ABC (Good Morning America), NBC (New York Live), MTV (Andy Milonakis Show), VH1 (Behind the Music), History Channel (Tool Box), etc., to film soundtracks of movies such as Another Earth, Dummy, American Carny, I Sell the Dead, etc. and recordings for Capitol Records, Universal Records and Atlantic Records - Natalia is single handedly reviving the almost lost art form of playing music on a carpenter's handsaw.

The following is an interview with her regarding the art of busking.

How can artists stand out when busking from other performers? What will make them memorable for people passing by?

Needless to say one has to be proficient in one's playing technique. The street doesn't lie - if you have not mastered your instrument, the street barometer will throw it in your face. But assuming you can really play: some buskers use visual gimmicks such as wearing a mask, a costume, an elegant suit. If you do that, it is good to stick with the same visual gimmick, so it becomes your "brand", your recognizable mark. Some buskers go overboard with flashing lights (battery operated) on their instrument, clothes or where they stand.

I find that the best way to get people to remember you is by interaction. Don't bury your face in your instrument, ignoring the audience. Instead - look people in the eye as they pass by you, and project a friendly, welcoming persona, inviting them to interact with you. Have fun and participate people in the fun. Through your sound and demeanor turn a dirty, smelly street corner into a place as welcoming to people as a cozy living room.

There is an unspoken set of rules among street performers - respecting space, time, etc. If someone is on tour or new to the area, what can they do to help learn the busking environment of a new city?

Whenever I get to a new city, the first thing I do is scout out the local busking scene. If nobody plays at a particular area - it probably means that area gives buskers a hard time... Today I prepare ahead of time by searching the Internet for busking rules in the city I am going to, and I also seek out local buskers there and e-mail them to ask for advice about busking in their town. I receive many such requests from buskers coming to NYC and I am always happy to share my knowledge with them. There's a sort of "global brotherhood of buskers" - reach out to local buskers and join the family.

How have you been able leverage playing public spaces to fuel your career?

My father jokes that the subway is my office, because that is where I do all my business. It's true - playing in a public space is like a constant audition - you never know who might be passing by. I got so many gigs out of playing in the subway - TV commercials, orchestra gigs, not to mention corporate & private parties galore. Also - playing in a public space is a wonderful way to spread word of your music and promote any album or upcoming gig you might have. Hand out flyers while you play, have business cards available, hang a poster near you with your social media info, and have a clip-board where people can sign up for your mailing list.

Another thing that often happens to me when I busk is that photographers and painters reach out to me, wanting to capture my image. This is a great way to get cool artwork for your next album.

Any other advice that you'd give aspiring artists?

One nice thing about playing in a public space is that your target audience will find you. It's different from playing a club with a built in crowd. A big city is a diverse arena for an artist to perform in and it's fascinating to see who gets what you are doing.

It takes guts to perform on the street. It also takes a positive attitude. While busking, if you concentrate your thoughts on what you can GIVE, rather than on what you can GET - most likely the street will be kind to you.

For more information on Paruz' music, visit www.sawlady.com

3. Three Things Bands Should Never Ignore (But Often Do)

by Chris 'Seth' Jackson

Simon asked me to write 3-5 paragraphs about specific "hacks" for the music biz that I could give you. Honestly, my brain broke down in overload because there's way too much to fit into such a small amount of space! So, instead, I'm going to focus on a few things that bands either miss out on or, maybe, just didn't know.

1. The Cycle of Booking Persistence

Many a musician has gotten frustrated by not getting a reply back when booking a show. Often, they never try again. This is a horrible mistake. Instead, here's a framework for booking that always gets me fully booked for as many shows as I want.

You send your booking email. If they reply back and give you the show, awesome! Job done. Most times, you don't hear back. So, wait exactly 2 weeks and send the booking email again. Repeat this every two weeks until they reply back and give you a show date. Sometimes, you get a flat out "no". At this point, wait 1 to 2 months and send another booking email. Go back to your 2 week cycle if you don't hear a response. Keep repeating until you get a show date.

Does that last one seem annoying or feel like spam? Maybe. However, from what I've seen of clubs, bookers come and go on a regular basis. Some clubs have a new booker every month. If the "no" is justified because your band is too small to play there or your genre doesn't fit, then use your better judgment about continually trying to play there. But, most of the time, persistence wins out.

As for bookers not replying to you, that just happens. A club can get bombarded with a hundred (or more) requests a week from bands trying to book there. One booker simply cannot reply to every email they get. Or, the email just gets lost. That's why you need to keep sending an email repeatedly.

2. Get Paid For Your Set Lists

Most musicians are unaware that they are owed money for their original music played at every show...if they have their music registered properly. That's right. Every time you play your music live, you are owed money for your performance.

The first step is to register your music with a Performance Rights Organization (PRO). In the US, this is usually ASCAP or BMI. These organizations' sole purpose is to collect royalties on behalf of the copyright holders on works performed publicly. Most music venues are required to pay fees to these PROs in order to have live music. In turn, this means that you are owed a portion of that money when you play their live.

So, register your music with a PRO. Then, contact that PRO to get your local representative where you can send your set lists to after performing. Finally, after every performance, submit your set lists. Warning: Make sure the venue you are playing at has paid their fees first. If you are playing an "underground" venue, then you probably don't want them to be on a PROs radar.

3. Always Have Merch

Not having merchandise for sale at your shows is the number one way to lose money. Though this sounds basic, most musicians I see don't have their merch stand set up for their shows. Or, if they do, the stand looks pathetic. Here are some tips for your merch that should get the cash rolling in:

- Have a folding table. Never be without a table just because of that weird club. Invest in a cheapo folding table. (Check your thrift shops for deals!)
- Have plenty of lights. Venues are dark, so an unlit merch booth is an invisible merch booth. No one will notice it. Get track lighting to wrap around the booth. Buy a few battery powered led lights to scatter around and highlight items. (You should also get a power strip and a 100' extension cord since power outlets are hard to find.)
- Have a "display". You can zip-tie some wire shelves together and make a folding, wire display for your shirts and swag. Just visit your local hardware store or Home Depot. If you get really long shelves, the display can stand on it's own without a table (but is harder to carry from show to show).
- Regularly update your merch. Your fans will want new stuff from you. If you keep having the same merch show after show, you won't make any new sales from them. Your super fans will want to buy everything from you. Give them that chance! Every few months, update your shirts, get new items (key chains, beer koozies, bottle openers, etc.), and add "limited edition" items with a bigger price tag.

Seth Jackson is the founder and owner of HowToRunABand.com and runs the podcast Work Hard, Rock Harder. Every week, he hosts a Google Hangout to answer music business questions for artists.

4. Creating an EPK That Works

An Interview with Simon Perry

Simon Perry is SVP Creative, Head of A&R at ReverbNation, a company that provides tools for nearly 3.5 million music industry professionals - artists, managers, labels, venues, festivals/events, and more. Their site receives over 30 million visits per month.

The following is an interview with him regarding EPK best practices.

What are the most important qualities of an effective EPK and how can artists develop some best practices to increase shows, partnerships, or other opportunities?

A press kit is essential for serious artists that want to play live, get heard and get noticed. Ours (ReverbNation Press Kits or RPKs) allow artists to present a professional snapshot that talent seekers can size up and react to quickly. They're built directly from ReverbNation profiles so it's essential that the profile is populated in a thoughtful manner. That means three things:

- **Music**. Don't post too much. Three, even two great songs is much better than 8 or 10 that someone has to sort through.

- **Photos**. Put up a few photos that say something about the creative angle of the band. And make sure it's a good quality photo — if it looks like your mum took it, forget it.

- **Bios**. Keep it short. Everyone loved music since they were a toddler. Skip the early life details unless it's really catchy or particular to where you are now. Tell us what's unique about you.

We've been looking closely at all the new music coming into ReverbNation every day. Since the start of the year we've looked at and listened to more than 100,000 artists' and their music. And I can tell you definitively that it's not about being good or bad these days. It's the difference between good and great that really stands out. There are a lot of good artists out there. You have to work really hard to stand out and demonstrate if you're more than just good.

How can artists use EPK service sites like ReverbNation to build stronger relationships with other acts for touring, collaborative projects, or other endeavors?

A complete press kit is a good representation of who you are right now and tells other musicians at least part of the picture. I would recommend that artists interested in collaboration also create one of our new Musician Pages. These pages allow for historical information and individual representation for musicians that are in a group. For example, The Beatles would have a ReverbNation profile and a press kit. But Paul would have a Musician Page too. This network of musicians is proving to be a great way for artists to meet and exchange ideas.

What do the top artists on ReverbNation have in common? What about profiles that don't perform well?

Great music. There's no way round that simple truth. An artist that's worked hard on their music will understand more about how they want to present themselves. Writing a great bio, taking great photos or creating a killer video stems naturally from that artistic journey of discovery. But it all starts with the music. The music naturally informs the way you position all your other assets.

What is one thing that every artist can do right now to improve their EPK?

Make your bio shorter. Don't start at the beginning when you're telling your music story. If you formed your band in college mention that but skip high school music accomplishments. Share something creative and unique to you or your group; why you got together plus maybe three or four things that you've achieved since that moment.

What's not interesting, if you're at the beginning of your career or as yet undiscovered, is insight into the creative process. If you were famous it might be. But if you're a new act, allow us to discover the music for ourselves - don't lead us by the nose.

In short, use your bio to tell us a few things that hook us til the music can speak for itself.

Simon Perry is a hit writer/producer from Oxford, England. He has worked with many name artists, including Echo & The Bunnymen, Westlife, Sandi Thom, and Anthony Costa. He also wrote and co-produced the multi-million selling album Me for the Chinese Idol winner, Chris Lee. Simon co-founded and served as President of Archangel Media, a Film & TV venture in LA.

5. Three Ways to Incorporate a Video Strategy into Your Social Media Marketing

By Kim Schultz

Video is definitely a hot, emerging social media trend for 2014. There are so many free and accessible tools available online to deepen engagement with your fans. Get out there and start experimenting with the many ways to help promote your music and build more meaningful, authentic relationships with fans.

Give your fans something special and unique, something they won't find on your Facebook page or YouTube account. Fans will appreciate receiving exclusive content, intended just for them.

Here are some quick social media tools and tips you can use to increase engagement and strengthen your online community:

1. Instagram Direct:

This new Instagram feature allows you to send a 15 second video or photo in a private group message. This is a great way to provide fans and followers with exclusive video clips and behind the scenes footage. Here are a few ways that you can use this tool:

- Send a sneak peek of a new song or music video to fans and followers
- Follow and engage with music publications and editors your music aligns with. Use Instagram Direct to showcase to the media a brand new song or music video
- Send a video message with a free download to your top influencers and fans
- Tip: Make sure videos still look professional and are not too 'choppy.'

2. Google Hangouts:

With Google+ Hangouts, your Page can start a video chat with up to nine people. This is a great opportunity to connect with your audience. You can:

- Promote a live Google Hangout to discuss an upcoming record release
- Invite engineers and audiophiles to join a conversation about recording techniques
- Use Instagram Direct to select a few loyal fans to participate!
- Do a monthly Hangout and select new topics for each one
- Tip: Don't forget to create a hashtag exclusive to your Hangout events! Encourage fans to share and participate in the conversation online.

3. Live Streaming

The Grateful Dead pioneered a "freemium" business model, allowing concert goers to record and trade concert tapes, building a powerful word-of-mouth fan network powered by free music. You can learn from their example by incorporating a few of their techniques into your band's business model. For example, you can try:

- Embrace free live streaming. Why limit your show and reach locally? Go for national, even international reach!
- Live stream your concerts for free using YouTube Live, Usteam, Livestreamand Stageit
- Plan ahead. Contact music venues to see if they have live streaming capabilities

- Promote your show on platforms like IROCKE (www.irocke.com)
- Encourage fan participation during a live stream. Have fans tweet in what songs to play or questions they have for the band.

Kim Schultz is a California based marketing consultant who's combined her love for music, hospitality and social media to create memorable and impactful digital marketing campaigns for music brands (Bob Weir, TRI Studios), celebrities and hospitality clients.

6. Your People Skills Determine Your Success

By Lee Silber

Quick, name a Rolling Stones song. It's not that hard, right? Now, name a Mick Jagger solo song. Not so easy, eh? You see, even one of the greatest front man of all time benefits from being in a band and partnering with others—like Keith Richards. Even Don Henley of the Eagles said, "Mick Jagger can't even make a successful solo album, and the Stones are the biggest rock group that ever was."

Most musicians can keep a beat and hit the right notes, but the ones who make it are able to not only get along with others, but make others better because of their partnerships with them. People skills are one of the most important skills (outside of our musical chops) that can make or break us in the music business.

Those old sayings like, "It's who you know," and "Nobody makes it alone," are true—especially in the music business. It's all about relationships (healthy, positive, and long lasting ones, that is.) It is who we know that determines how high we can go with our careers, it's also about who knows us and what they know about us (our reputation). People want to partner with and promote those they know and like.

So who are the most well-liked and respected rockers of our time and what do they all do that we aren't? It's a long list (both in numbers and number of things they do to have others wanting to help them reach their goals.) Let's just pick one and see what we can learn. Dave Grohl, founder and leader of the Foo Fighters knows what it's like to be in a dysfunctional group (Think: Nirvana) as well as how to function in a group of guys that truly seem to get along (his current band.)

It seems like everywhere you turn Grohl is jamming with other major musicians, having the biggest of the big names appear in his "Sound City" documentary (Paul McCartney comes to mind), and his band has remained intact (for the most part) for years. What is the one thing he does that sets him apart?

- **Grohl keeps his ego in check and shows respect for other musicians**. Could he play all the drum parts for Foo Fighters? Absolutely. Does he? No. He lets Taylor Hawkins bash away while he plays guitar and sings. In interviews he is constantly praising the level of play by his bandmate . . . and friend. Give honest and sincere praise as often as possible and respect people for what they do and how they do it—even if they do it differently than us.

- **He does the right thing by others**. People don't care how much we know or how good we are until they know how much we care about them by how good we treat them. Doing the right thing is hard, but in the end it makes life a lot easier. We eliminate guilt, worry, and fear that comes from trying to live a lie. We also have a lot less enemies and more friends. When we help others get what they want and give them what they need, they will help us get what we want and need.

- **Dave Grohl is known for being down to earth** and the kind of guy you would want to hang out with—even if he weren't a Grammy Award-winning artist. Dave Grohl said, "My songwriting is like extending a hand to the listener." Be better at remembering names, birthdays, and details about the people you meet and work with and remember, it's not

363

about us, it's about them.

A friend of mine met Queen guitar-great Brian May when he stayed in the hotel where he works as a bellman. They talked for a short while when the guitarist checked in on his first stay, but my buddy never got a chance to say goodbye. The next year May stayed at the same hotel and not only did he remember my friend's name, he recalled what they had talked about a year before and his wife's name as well.

If we can be better at remembering names and pay more attention to others, they will become fans for life.

LEE SILBER is not only the best selling author of 19 books he is also a drummer and bassist with his own band and is known for going the extra mile for other musicians. To learn more about Lee go to: www.leesilber.com.

7. How to Impress an A&R Rep

By Ray Daniels

The one thing that musicians should be doing is living everyday like it is an audition. Michael Jackson was the greatest because he lived MUSIC that's why when he danced and sang, you felt it. You cannot be great until you have nothing else to be. When it's your life, everything comes your way. The energy you give will come back to you.

Study! It's like school but it should be easy for you because if you are a true artist, you should love what you do. Study the greats! Musicians tend to compare themselves to their peers when they should really compare themselves to the greats. Anybody can be the best in their neighborhood, but living up the standards of being the best in the world will completely change how the game is approached.

The thing about A&R's is that we are always looking for great talent. My advice to each artist would be to focus on being the best. It is a cat and mouse game, much like when a man is chasing a woman. A beautiful woman doesn't chase a man, because if she did, it would make him question her beauty. A beautiful woman makes herself beautiful and allows the man to chase her.

Greatness is undeniable and it is never silent. If any artist is working on his/her craft and becoming great, the word will get out about them. Artists should dedicate their time to perfecting their craft and building their fan base. The A&R's will come calling because the word will get out.

Labels are looking for game-changing artists. When I say game-changing, I mean the artists who know who they are and know who their fan base is. The artist's job is to serve their audience and know how to speak to them. If they understand and know how to grow that audience, this translates to a good investment for a label.

Bruno Mars is a great example of this. Bruno Mars is a student of great songs. He studied songwriters like Babyface, Stevie Wonder and Michael Jackson. Bruno Mars was an Elvis impersonator from the time he was a toddler. He studied the greats and found his own identity. He knows how to deliver music. Bruno knows how to write classic songs that are simplified for his audience. He doesn't complicate the message and he doesn't emulate other artists or trends. His musicianship, individuality and creativity are well beyond most artists of his time.

So study the great, find out what makes them unique, and learn from their undying passion. Focus more on developing your craft. Let it speak for itself so that it attracts A&R reps and labels – you don't need to be chasing them down, let them do the chasing. That's how you can make a lasting impression!

Ray Daniels is a leader in the new school of entertainment executives; an embodiment of the music industry's newfound culture. As VP of A&R for Epic Records under the leadership of L.A Reid and CEO of his own conglomerate RAYDAR Entertainment; Daniels is undeniably one of the most accomplished executives in today's business of music. Under his management songwriting team Planet XI has written some of the biggest records in the last decade with #1 records for Rihanna (Pour It Up), Miley Cyrus (Don't Stop), Chris Brown, Justin Bieber, and many more.

8. The Kind of Artists Managers Are Looking For

By Michael Stover

Finding good, hard-working representation is not an easy task. The music business has a reputation of being full of "sharks" that are just looking to earn a paycheck off the backs of artists who have stars in their eyes. Fortunately, we are not all like that. If you are an artist, please do your research when you are seeking out a manager, label or PR firm. You want to make sure that you are hiring someone that has a good reputation for furthering their artists' careers and for making good on their promises. You want to sure that they are going to fit YOUR needs, as well. Don't be afraid to ask the hard questions that pertain to you, as an artist:

1. What have they done for their artists in the past?
2. Do they have a good reputation? (Google Search is a wonderful tool!)
3. How long have they been in business?
4. What is their professional background?
5. What can they do for you, that you can't do for yourself?
6. What does it cost?

I also have a checklist of things that I ask myself, before considering whether or not to work with an artist:

1. Does the artist have a commercial, radio friendly sound? I am such a big proponent of radio, as part of an artist's promotional campaign. Dollar for dollar, you will get the most bang for your buck by going to radio with your music. So, when I'm checking outa new artist, I always ask myself, "can I hear this on the radio?" If I don't hear a big radio hit, I will probably pass on an artist.

2. Does the artist play live? One of the most important things for a musician, is the ability to play live. Touring, whether regional or national, is where musicians have the chance to sell their music and connect with fans, both established and new. While online sales and downloads have decreased over the years, sales at live events continues to be the way that artists can supplement their income and support their craft. Plus, it's one thing to deliver in the studio…but I want to see you do it live. Touring also helps to build credibility within the industry. It's one thing to be the biggest band in your hometown, it's quite another to be able to take that reputation with you on the road, and have it return in tact.

3. Does the artist have their own website? Something as simple as this, can make or break it for me. If the artist doesn't have a website, yet they want management, it shows me that they really have no idea of how things work in today's music business. It shows me that they lack a certain level of Do It Yourself commitment. An artist needs to be doing all they can to help further their own careers and get to a certain level, before anyone else will get on board with them. So, if you have a website, with all of your music, videos, photos, social media links, purchase links, etc., you are already ahead of a lot of artists out there, who use Facebook or Reverbnation as their website. Don't make me look all over the internet for your music. If you have a dedicated website with everything on it, then you are on your way…

4. Does the artist have the drive and desire to make it to the next level? This also seems like a given, but it's not. There are many artists that enjoy playing music and they say they want to do what it takes, but when push comes to shove, they don't have the drive. The music business is one of the hardest industries to forge a living from, and you have to give it all to succeed. Just saying you want it is not nearly enough. You've got to bleed and sweat it! I need to see real dedication to achieving goals.

But, I also need to know that the artist is willing to listen to advice and have the ability to let go of total control of their careers. That can be difficult pill to swallow for some artists.

5. Does the artist have a budget to work with? Artists should have a means of income to pay for their music business, until the business become viable to pay for itself. Just like any other business. There's a reason behind the statement, "Don't quit your day job." An artist should never quit their day job to work on their music career, until they are making more money at the music, than they are at the day job. Plenty of big stars had steady jobs before their ship came in. If an artist thinks he or she is above working a day job, they are not ready for management, or a serious career…unless they are independently wealthy or have investors.

Chances are that if they don't show a means of giving investors a return on their money, they aren't going to attract investors. Everything costs money in this business, from recordings to publicity and promotions, to radio promotions, to photography, videography, manufacturing of CDs, press kits, website design, and down the line. So, not having a source of income to pay for these things takes me back to my last question: Do they have the drive to do what it takes to make it?

Don't count on a record company to come along and "discover" you. It rarely happens like that…at least until you've gotten to a certain level on your own.

6. Does the artist give back? Believe it or not, this goes a long way in my decision. When I work with an artist, I want to know that they are just as good of a person, as they are an artist. It's just my preference. I have always worked with a sense of doing the right thing and doing things the ethical, honest way. So, I believe that charitable work falls in the same category. Show me an artist that goes out of his way to do things for others, and I'll show you a very successful artist. Those communities will want to stand up and support the artist. They will reciprocate!

369

I am very blessed to work with all of my artists, who work with many causes that are close to their hearts. That's just the type of artist I like to surround myself with.

Just remember, that there are 6 million artists in the world, and they are all vying for the same attention and the same dollar from a weary consumer, with shrinking disposable income. While you should follow your dreams and shoot for the stars, you should do everything you can to position yourself for success. Set yourself apart from the masses. Good representation can help you do that…but you need to take the first steps and make yourself an appealing investment of time and money. Good luck!

Michael Stover is a music manager, publicist and record label owner, with more than 25 years in all facets of the business. His artists have earned #1 airplay singles on nationally recognized charts, received press coverage in top publications and have performed on major concert bills, alongside the biggest names in their genres. More information is available at mtsmanagementgroup.com

9. A Day in the Life of an Independent Artist

An Interview with Gayle Skidmore

A born songwriter, Gayle Skidmore has written over 2000 songs since she began songwriting at the age of 8. She was named Best Singer-Songwriter in the 2013 San Diego Music Awards and her song "Paper Box" was recently featured on HBO's "Looking."

The following is an interview with her about creating music for a living:

Many artists have this romanticized notion of doing music for a living - but the reality is that it needs to be treated like a job. What are some of the things that you do day to day in order to sustain your career?

It is important to keep in contact with your business associates and to continually reach out to the people in your circles that believe in what you are doing. Many artists try to take on everything on their own instead of building a team around themselves. I have always found that treating my career as a group effort has been much more successful than going it alone. Something that I strive to do daily is to delegate some of my tasks and responsibilities to capable people in my circles who can give them more attention than I can.

Being an independent artist often means doing the job of about twenty people or more, so delegation and distribution of the immense workload is key to one's success.

Walk us through a "typical" work day or week. What kinds of things do you focus on? How much time are you spending on the business vs. the music?

I am constantly waging war with my artist's brain. I am naturally flighty and prone to daydreaming, so making lists is crucial to my weekly success. Oftentimes I will remember a task that I haven't finished at around three in the morning, and then will work frantically to finish it, much as I am doing with this interview now.

There really isn't a "typical" day or week for me. Every musician has their own rhythm of creativity, and it's really important as an artist to pay attention to your artistic promptings. I find that it becomes very difficult to buckle down and focus on the less creative aspects of the business if I haven't taken the time to create for at least a good portion of my week. I have definitely established patterns over the years, but between touring, recording, writing, practicing, composing, rehearsing with the band, working online, booking tours, doing interviews, photo shoots, tv spots, etc., there is always something new and exciting to get done.

The only established pattern is that I have a never-ending amount of emails to write, blogs and websites to update, and statuses to post. It is difficult for me to estimate the exact proportions of time spent on music versus business, and the two are so interchangeable at times that it confuses me all the more. What I am sure of is that I eat, sleep and dream music and business. When one is driven to succeed, one must pour themselves completely into their goal.

What kind of training would you recommend to aspiring artists?

It seems to me that people have very different paths to success as artists, though there are common threads. It's hard to give advice to someone whose career I'm unfamiliar with, or recommend training to people whose skill sets I can't name. So, I will discuss less specific but, I believe, important elements of what I have learned from my years as an artist.

Some artists have a break early on in their careers, while others plod along for years without recognition. Often, there is really no rhyme or reason to it. The key is to be passionate about what you do and to be diligent in honing the skills that you have been given. It's important to know what you are willing to give up and what you aren't willing to give up for your art, and just how much of yourself you want to put out there... and WHY.

I recently had a chance to sit down with Asthmatic Kitty artist Linda Perhacs, who, after 44 years, is finally releasing her second album. For years she has been creating music without sharing it with the world, and finally, due largely to my good friend Fernando Perdomo, she has recorded an amazing album and is getting a ton of attention. It was a very enlightening conversation, and what I took from it was a reminder that it is crucial to know who you are as an artist.

Find your voice, and surround yourself with people who have a similar vision. The industry is a strange beast. What makes you an artist is not whether or not you are recognized by the music industry, but what you give of yourself in creating your art.

You may not be a savvy businessperson, but they key to being an artist is to create art. It's pretty straightforward. If your goal is to be a star and what you crave is fame, then there are those who can give you great advice and an outline of tasks for you to check off. If you would like to be an artist, then start creating! Linda Perhacs did not cease to be an artist during her years of silence, and I did not get the sense that she felt that that time was wasted.

As someone who has struggled for years and self-released 13 albums in a fraction of the time that Linda Perhacs was waiting to release her already highly acclaimed album, I can say confidently that my time has not been wasted either. Even if I don't reach her 'level' or I decide to take a day job, I know that I have created music that is from the best that is in me, that is sincere, and that has lasting value because it contains my soul.

What is one thing that every indie artist should be doing on a consistent basis?

Every indie artist should take time to rest. There is a lot of pressure on independent artists to be constantly doing something to further their career. There have been numerous times throughout my career when I have kept running on basically zero sleep, coffee, whisky, and late night Mexican food. I have felt that I can't go to sleep because I haven't conquered the world yet. I have neglected my physical health because I needed to be the last person to leave my show, even though I needed to get up in three hours to drive to the next town on my tour route.

While I do believe that it is important to be very dedicated to my work, I have come to realize that I can't continue to pursue my music career, to write well or play well if I haven't taken care of myself. As artists, we are generally more sensitive to the world around us, and therefore we need to take breaks from it here and there to recharge. We give of ourselves from our very cores, and we need to have something there to draw from. Artists: take a nap! I mean it.

A born songwriter, Gayle Skidmore has written over 2000 songs since she began songwriting at the age of 8. Named Best Singer-Songwriter in the 2013 San Diego Music Awards, Gayle continually processes her adventures, experiences, thoughts and emotions through music; writing, playing and singing from the depths of her soul. Her song "Paper Box" was recently featured on HBO's new show "Looking." **Gayle Skidmore's music can be found at gayleskidmore.com.**

10. Things Every Artist Should Be Looking Out For When it Comes to Contracts

By Brandon Leopoldus

There are a number of things musicians should look for in any sort of business agreements. When it comes to agreements discussing an artist's performance, there are five specific areas artists need to make sure are covered in detail in the agreement:

1. Payment

Artists who are getting paid for their work are professionals, and they need to treat their musical performances as a business. Some information regarding payment artists should have locked down in writing before agreeing to play include: when do I get paid? How will I be paid? Is the money guaranteed? Is there anything that can decrease the amount of money I receive? Are the riders included in the payment?

2. Schedule

Hammering out the schedule for the day of the concert can eliminate much of the headache when that day arrives. Musicians need to know the time they can load in equipment, hold sound check, prepare in the dressing room, take the stage, and the end time. However, other musicians (whether openers or headliners) can cause

375

this schedule to change. Musicians who get the schedule in writing and signed off by all the parties typically have much less stress the day of their performance and can focus on their music.

3. Promotions

Musicians should understand how they will be promoted, the target audience, and who will be handling promotions. No musician wants to play to an empty house, to a hostile audience, or to be portrayed inaccurately. Even if these items are not an issue, musicians need to understand if there is a requirement, and what is required and expected by the artist to promote the concert through social media or by any other means. Details such as promotions should be understood to eliminate any problems during the course of the agreement.

4. Insurance

Insurance is a safety net for anyone involved in music. For concerts musicians should be covered on a variety of fronts. Musicians should have coverage for their equipment, their health, any claims made by audience members, the venue, and cancellation. An agreement to perform should cover which party, or parties, are responsible for obtaining insurance and what the insurance policy needs to cover. The best-case scenario is you never use the insurance, but in the worst case scenario insurance can be a lifesaver.

5. Cancellation

Concerts get cancelled. It happens. Musicians get sick, venues close, things happen. One area not often covered in one-concert contracts is what happens when a show gets cancelled. Who is responsible for the costs? Will the concert be rescheduled? What is the artist required to do in the event of a cancellation? Is insurance available? No party will likely enter into an agreement to put on a concert with the intention of canceling, but this is a contingency that should be addressed.

On Licensing Agreements:

These types of agreements are sought after by artists because typically their work will be exposed to a larger audience. However, this does not always mean it is a good thing for the artist. An artist needs to make sure the terms of such an agreement are acceptable, and also understand the ramifications of the agreement.

When it comes to agreements discussing an artist's performance, there are several specific areas artists need to make sure are covered in detail in the agreement:

1. What is being licensed?

In a licensing agreement, the exact item or items should be spelled out so there is no question about the material being licensed. If an entire album is being licensed, then the album name, release date, and each song on the album should be listed. The more information about the specific items being licensed the better because there is no question later on about if the content being distributed has been done with authority.

2. Term

Just like with any agreement, the length of the term is a critical element of the agreement. Without a set period of time (e.g. two years, until a certain date, for a certain show, etc.) the party which is licensing the content can make a strong argument that the content is being licensed in perpetuity. However, if a term is for a set period of time, this allows an artist to license it to another party afterward, or renegotiate the terms of the license once the term is complete.

3. Exclusivity An exclusive license is one in which the artist promises to license the content only to the other party during the stated term. These licenses can be lucrative for an artist because the party licensing the content is insured that no other party or competitor will be able to use the content. If the license is non-exclusive, the artist can license to a number of different parties, but each of these other licenses is likely to be less valuable than an exclusive license.

4. Payment Terms

One critical term of a licensing deal many artists know to look for, but do not always understand is how payment is calculated and when payment will be made. In many distribution agreements, the artist receives different percentages for the different types of methods the licensed content is sold. For example, digital downloads will pay the artist a different percentage than a sale of a compact disc.

It is important for an artist to know the differences in these percentages as well as what venue streams the artist will generate the most money. Typical distribution deals cover every aspect of the artist from digital downloads, to physical sales, merchandise, and live performance. If one of these 360 deals is reached, an artist should negotiate the percentages in favor of the avenue which is believe to make the artist the most money.

Just as important as the percentages, is the payment timetable. Some artists will receive an advance, but often the advance will be considered a loan rather than a bonus. Other agreements will not provide an advance, but will stick to a straight percentage payment. If this is the case, the artist needs to know when to expect to see the funds, and the method by how the amount was reached. Artists should know the date, time, method, and details of how the amount was reached. Understanding these terms will allow an artist and the artist's team to spot problems immediately if payment is not received as promised in the agreement.

Brandon Leopoldus is a Los Angeles based attorney with a variety of entertainment clients. His music clientele includes independent bands, venues, concert production companies, and instructors.

11. Establishing Your Band's Home Base

by Terry Currier

A lot of musicians think that just having great music is the key to being successful in the music industry, but in order to get that success, they really have to be strategic about it. That means consistent hard work, like any other job, and looking for every opportunity possible in your area.

Often, this means finding the right people in town to connect with. Of course, there's no guarantee that something will happen, but there are many outlets: public radio, local papers, independent organizations, local blogs, and other outlets that people forget about. While each one has a small audience, each one is important for creating that story in their hometown. We can't just focus on the mainstream radio stations – most of those won't even play new artists anyway.

Really, artists should look at the hometown as the center of their music business circle, as home base. It's important to establish a solid base and do the best job possible at getting their music exposed in the area. Then, they can slowly expand, letting the circle spiral outward and extending into other nearby markets. Over time, the circle gets bigger and bigger. And with it, a bigger audience to play for, more contacts to work with, and more stages to play.

Sometimes it might feel like a slot machine, but it's important to take risks and find the right people. It's important to find a champion for your music. Bands are not necessarily marketing geniuses or booking agents, and they might not have the ability to do everything that is needed in the band. The skills are needed though, which means it's important to surround oneself with the right kind of people, in order to get to that next level. This sometimes just means starting out small – starting within the circle, like having an enthusiastic fan help in the beginning. Then, as that circle grows, perhaps the band can pick up someone else to help with their music.

Management companies and booking agencies ultimately will pick up artists that bring in money – they need to earn a living and can't always afford to take risks on new artists who don't have that home base built.

We'd like to think that the great music will always rise to the top, but that isn't necessarily the case. It's hard work, great music, and a little luck. The more hard work that you put in and the more avenues that you take to exposure your music, the more luck you'll find that you have. Getting a good manager and a booking agent is one of the toughest things to get, but it's also one of the most important members of your team.

This business is all about relationships. Sometimes, it's more about who you know rather than what you know. I've helped many bands who have walked through my store's doors by giving them the first show or a place to hold their CD release party. If they have a lot of potential, are hardworking, and have a good attitude, I'll often introduce them to club owners or promoters that I know in town. So sometimes, that entrance to the music industry will be in your own home town.

A lot of bands get away from their home base because they want to be on the same level of national acts, including having their album in record stores all over the country. They think that if they get a national distributor, they'll sell a bunch of records…but that isn't the case. Most distributors won't want to work with a band unless there is a major story or selling point to the band. Like managers or booking agents, distributors need someone that can help bring in a sustainable income. To do this, bands need to have that foundation.

The best thing that an artist can do is to go out in their "circle" or home base meet everyone that they can: promoters, bloggers, radio stations. They should especially meet all of the record stores in their area and get their record store on consignment so that it's in the bin. They should talk to the employees, give a free in-store copy. They might even be able to get a free spot on a listening station for a few months. Build those relationships so that you'll have another mouthpiece for your music.

Finally, it's important to work with other artists in the community. They can be some of your biggest advocates, a source for shows or industry connections. If one of those artists that you work closely with become successful, they might help you in the future by offering a tour slot.

Don't look at it as a competitive thing, look at it as a community. If you go in with the right attitude, many more opportunities are going to come your way.

Terry Currier is the founder/owner of Music Millennium, one of the most influential independent record stores in the country, and president of the Oregon Music Hall of Fame. He has over 40 years of experience in the music industry as a record label owner, promoter, distributor, and record store owner.

12. The Strength of Many Little Customers

by Derek Sivers

Many small entrepreneurs think, "If we can just land Apple, Google, or the government as a client, we'll be all set!" Software companies often do this. They hope to make some technology that a huge company will want to build into every product or install at every employee's desk.

But this approach has many problems:
• You have to custom-tailor your product to please a very few specific people.
• Those people might change their minds or leave the company.
• Whom are you really working for? Are you self-employed or is this client your boss?
• If you do land the big client, that organization will practically own you.
• By trying so hard to please the big client, you will lose touch with what the rest of the world wants.

Instead, imagine that you have designed your business to have NO big clients, just lots of little clients.

• You don't need to change what you do to please one

382

client; you need to please only the majority (or yourself).
• If one client needs to leave, it's OK; you can sincerely wish her well.
• Because no one client can demand that you do what he says, you are your own boss (as long as you keep your clients happy in general).
• You hear hundreds of people's opinions and stay in touch with what the majority of people want.

So much of the music business is actually the star business—people hoping to catch the coattails of a huge mega-star. But I wanted nothing to do with that, for these same reasons.

When you build your business on serving thousands of customers, not dozens, you don't have to worry about any one customer leaving or making special demands. If most of your customers love what you do, but one doesn't, you can just say goodbye and wish him the best, with no hard feelings.

You know you can't please everyone, right?

But notice that most businesses are trying to be everything to everybody. And they wonder why they can't get people's attention!

You need to confidently exclude people, and proudly say what you're not. By doing so, you will win the hearts of the people you want.

Hotel Café, a folk- and rock-music venue in Los Angeles, is a no-talking club. Big signs say, "No talking during performances!" Performers are encouraged to stop the show if someone is talking, and let the person know that he can go to any other club in town to talk over the music. This is the one place in LA where you can sit and really listen to the music; this, of course, makes it the most popular music venue in town.

When CD Baby got popular, I'd get calls from record labels wanting to feature their newest, hottest acts on our site. I'd say, "Nope. They're not allowed here." The record label guys would say, "Huh? What do you mean not allowed? You're a record store! We're a record label." I'd say, "You can sell anywhere else. This is a place for independents only: musicians who chose not to sign their rights over to a corporation. To make sure these musicians get the maximum exposure they deserve, no major label acts are allowed."

It's a big world. You can loudly leave out 99 percent of it. Have the confidence to know that when your target 1 percent hears you excluding the other 99 percent, the people in that 1 percent will come to you because you've shown how much you value them.

Derek Sivers is best known as the founder of CD Baby and popular TED speaker. CD Baby was the largest seller of independent music on the web, with over $100M in sales for over 150,000 musician clients. In 2008, Derek sold CD Baby to focus on his new ventures to benefit musicians. His current projects and writings are all at http://sivers.org

Appendix A: Interband Agreement

The following is an example of an interband agreement that I created for my personal band (with the legal names omitted). Each band might be structured differently or have their own particular needs. Feel free to make adjustments that make the most sense for your band, then have your attorney look it over.

A few other tips/things to keep in mind:

- Think of this in terms of best case scenario/worst case scenario. If you make a lot of money, how would you want that distributed? If lose a lot of money or need to do a lot of work, how will that be divided?
- Who "owns" the band name? If the band members part ways, who gets to keep using the name?
- How will you divide up credit for songs and artwork? What about shared property like a band bus or PA system?

Once you have an attorney approve the agreement and get everyone to sign it, print out copies for each person to keep for their records.

BAND MEMBER AGREEMENT

Agreement By and Between:
[list band members' legal names here]

We hereby agree to the following:

1. BAND. This contract sets forth the terms of which the individuals set forth above participate in the musical group _____[band name here_____ (the "Band"). The legal entity through which the Band does business is _____. The "original members" of the Group are _____[list band members here].

2. NAME AND LIKENESS: The name of the Band is "_____" In the event of a split between the original members, the name _____ and its derivatives (including but not limited to logos) may continue to be used only by a group comprised of _____ and at least one other of the original members.

3. INTELLECTUAL PROPERTY: All written music, recordings, and artwork created during the term of this Agreement by any member, belong solely to the band and may not be used by a Band member at any time without prior written permission of the Band. The individual Band members retain their songwriting rights as agreed to in writing or outlined by industry standards. _____ shall act as the music publisher for all music recorded or performed by the Band.

3. COMPENSATION: The profits made from the Band are to be split evenly between the then current members. This does not include profits due to individuals from non-group revenue streams such as songwriting, publishing, etc., which shall not be considered Band income. Compensation will be paid to band members when agreed by a majority vote, with the manager breaking all deadlocks. As a general guideline, the band will try to follow these standards when

determining appropriate compensation:

(i) All expenses will be paid first, including, but not limited to Publicity, Advertising, Management, Travel, Vehicle Maintenance, Lodging, Etc.

(ii) The money will be put into a general fund under _____for normal operating expenses as well as a reserve to cover up to six months of said expenses.

(iii) If no outstanding debt exists, 70% will be divided evenly between the members, 30% will be kept by _____ as a general band fund.

(iv) Band members may also vote (by majority) to distribute funds differently if the situation is more appropriate. Use of general band funds will be agreed upon by Band members and management.

4. CONTROL: Except where specifically noted otherwise in this Agreement, any Band business decision will be made by group vote with member having an equal vote and the majority rules. The group manager will break all deadlocks. Band members have no authority to enter into any agreements with any persons on behalf of the Band. Under no circumstances are Band members allowed to talk to club owners, record labels, radio stations, etc. in relation to any Band commitment. Band members should direct all such inquires to management.

5. BAND MEMBER RESPONSIBILITIES: All members shall have the following responsibilities. Failure to perform these responsibilities shall constitute a material breach of this agreement.

(i) Show up for practices and performances, prepared with equipment and skill required to perform; and

(ii) Maintain all equipment in good working condition, and upgrade appropriately when the revenue is available. Band members are responsible for the upkeep and reoccurring (or replacement) expenses of their allotted equipment. Band equipment is considered allotted to a member when it is used by such member exclusively. Members may request that upkeep or replacement be covered by the band fund. In such instances, the decision will be made by majority vote, with the manager breaking all deadlocks; and

(iii) No excessive drinking or smoking on stage, members shall always maintain good showmanship/performance quality as determined by management and agreed upon by all members; and

(iv) Follow all reasonable instructions of the artist/management team; and

(v) Ensure that member conducts him/herself in an appropriate manner in all professional situations.

(vi) Work the merchandise table or other appearances (interviews, panels, workshops, etc.) at times by the designated by manager. Band members shall actively promote and sell all products by the Band.

(vii) Give scheduling priority to Band appearances including shows, interviews, or other requests. If the member is unable to accommodate the appearance, member must provide at least 30 days prior written notice to Band.

6. TERMINATION: Band members may be terminated only after a unanimous decision by all remaining members (excluding the member in question). Members may terminate their membership in the Band at any time. Terminated members are still entitled to their rights and income relating to such member's authorship of musical compositions. Terminated member shall have no rights (including copyrights and rights to income) relating to any master recordings, including record royalties, nor to any other income other than income relating to such member's authorship of musical compositions. Percentages for musical composition such payments will be either agreed in advance by the parties, or determined by industry standards as outlined by ASCAP guidelines. Upon termination, the terminated member shall have no rights to any other Band intangible assets or intellectual property.

7. DISTRIBUTION OF HARD ASSETS. If a member terminates his/her membership, he or she surrenders all rights in the Band's hard assets

(e.g. equipment, instruments, cash). If a member is terminated, he or she is entitled to his or her percentage of the current value of the hard assets that were purchased during his or her term as a member of the Band, as agreed upon by the remaining members of the Band. These hard assets include but are not limited to sound equipment, instruments, and cash, but not debt, unless the member incurred an unreasonable amount or abused his/her shared rights as a member of the Band. The current value of these hard assets will be paid out by the Band to the ex-member in lump sum at the time of firing, unless paying in lump sum would put the Band in financial distress, in which case the Band will pay out the current value of the tangible assets over the course of a reasonable period of time with interest on the unpaid balance included. This "reasonable period" will be determined at the time of the firing by balancing the needs of the terminated member with the requirement that the Band not fall into financial distress at any period in time due to the schedule of the payouts. Notwithstanding the forgoing, all equipment previously owned by Band member is solely the property of the Band member. All equipment purchased by Band Member is solely the property of Band Member. Any equipment purchased by The Band is solely the property of _____unless an agreement is made between all members. All merchandise (Apparel, Albums, Promotional Items, etc) is solely the property of _____ and may not be taken by Band member for any reason without permission.

8. HIRING: New Band members may be added only after a unanimous decision by the then current members. New Band members will not be considered original member. Their rights in and benefits from the Band will be decided at the time of their admission and such new member shall be required to enter into a written band member agreement prior to admission.

9. FINANCIAL CONTRIBUTIONS: Financial contributions to the Band will be required of then-current members only after a unanimous vote is reached on the specific amount.

10. INCURRING EXPENSES: Band financial spending must be approved by a group vote, with each member having an equal vote and the majority rules. Exceptions to this rule include expenses incurred by the manager as outlined by the band-manager agreement. The group manager will break deadlocks.

11. AMENDING THE BAND MEMBER AGREEMENT: The terms of this Agreement may be amended only by a Band member vote, with each original member having an equal vote and the majority rules. The group manager will break deadlocks.

12. DEATH OR DISABILITY: In the event that a Band member dies, he or she will be treated as if he or she terminated their membership. In the event that a member becomes disabled (physically, mentally, or otherwise) and is therefore unable to fulfill their role in the group, the other Band members can vote on course of action.

13. LEGAL. This Agreement is the entire agreement of the parties in relation to the subject matter hereof and my only be modified in writing as set forth herein. The Agreement shall be governed in all respects by the laws of the State of Oregon as they apply to agreements entered into and to be performed entirely within Oregon between Oregon residents, without regard to conflict of law provisions. Exclusive venue for any claim or dispute relating to this Agreement shall be the courts located in [county/city/state]

AGREED TO AND SIGNED:

[Band member names, signature lines, date]

Appendix B. Booking Email Template

If you really want to make an impact on a venue, you should do your homework first. Make an effort to find out their booking requirements, get the name of the talent buyer, network with other bands who have played there before. As mentioned a few times in the book, you should really spend time working on your band's pitch.

That being said, I've included a general guideline/outline on writing a booking email as well as some examples.

Subject: Booking [name of act] at [name of venue] for Friday, August 1

Hi [name of talent buyer],

My name is [your name] and I'm interested in booking [name of act] at [name of venue] for Friday, August 1.

[Insert two-three sentence pitch for your music/act here. Focus on why you are unique, big accomplishments, and why they should book you. Don't list band members or extraneous details].

[Insert press mention, review, or other "wow" factor here].
To watch a video, click here [insert url]. To listen to the music, [click

here].

Do you have availability on this date?

Regards,
[Your name, contact info, and any other relevant links]

Here are some examples of actual booking emails from actual clients that I've written and used.

Example 1: TOMMY ALTO

Hi,

I'm interested in booking TOMMY ALTO at your venue for Tuesday, August 5.

TOMMY ALTO is an up-and-coming band that hails from Vancouver, CA. Their latest release, "Oceans \\ Carolina," was met with strong radio play across North America and Europe, speaking at #20 on Earshot. Their sound is reminiscent of Vampire Weekend, Minus theBear, and Fun.

"Fellas raise your fists in the air and ladies uncross your legs, Tommy Alto is what Red Bull drinks to get energy." (*Vancouver's Hottest Music*)

"Tommy Alto is changing the landscape of Indie music with their well-crafted, insightful lyrics and high-octane musical performance." (*Peace Arch News*)

Links:
Website: www.tommyalto.com
Band Camp (audio): http://tommyalto.bandcamp.com
Facebook: www.facebook.com/TommyAlto

They're getting great radio spin and have a Western region following from previous touring efforts.

Do you have any availability?

Regards,
Simon
Simon@laststopbooking.com

Example 2: The Slants

Hi,

This is Simon from Last Stop Booking. I'm interested in booking The Slants for your venue on 08/26.

Portland's The Slants are the only all-Asian American dance rock band in the world. They offer up catchy dance beats, strong hooks, and a bombastic live show that is "not to be missed" (The Westword) They've been featured on NPR's "All Things Considered," IFC, TV/Comast Xfinity, and over 1500 radio stations, tv shows, magazines, and websites.

The Slants have toured/provided support for The Decemberists, Girl Talk, Men Without Hats, Vampire Weekend, Apl.De.Ap (Black Eyed Peas), and many more. The band has a strong touring history (14 North American tours). Press will be by In Music We Trust PR.

This is for Monday, August 26. Do you have any available slots (headlining or support)?

Regards,
Simon Tam
(503) 754-8703
Last Stop Booking Agency/The Slants
www.theslants.com
www.youtube.com/slantsvideos
EPK: sonicbids.com/theslants

Example 3: Priory

Hi,

I'm interested in booking electro/indie rock band, Priory, for your venue on Thursday, February 10th.

Priory is the new darling of Expunged Records. Featuring an all-star indie line up of former members and associates of Horse Feathers, Blind Pilot, The Shins, and Jay Clark/Pretty Girls Make Graves, Priory has exploded on the scene in Portland, OR and has been packing out mid-sized rooms across the Northwest.

The band will be on tour in support of their new release, produced by Skyler Norwood (Talk Demonic, Viva Voce, Blind Pilot) with a full-blown publicity campaign. Already securing heavy FM radio rotation across multiple markets and armed with seasoned touring veterans, Priory is in position to have a great draw for your venue.

For more information:
www.priorymusic.com
www.myspace.com/priorymusic

Again, this is for 02/10. Please let me know if you have any opening slots.

Regards,
Simon Tam
Simon@laststopbooking.com

Appendix C: Sponsorship Email Template

Email Template for the Touring Band: The Generic Ask

This is a general template that I shared on my music industry blog (www.laststopbooking.com) that artists could adapt to begin communication with potential sponsors. In fact, this is nearly the same email that I have used to successfully connect with thirteen of the current sponsors for my band, The Slants. Simply fill in your information and send (be sure to get a direct contact if possible). Send this one message at a time and make sure you cater each message to the company you're pitching.

Dear [contact name],

My name is [your name] and I manage the band [band name]. We are [elevator pitch here]. I am contacting you today because I would like to schedule a time where we can talk about doing some cross promotion through a partnership.

Since [start date, we have toured the country [x] times, released [x] albums, and have been featured in press such as [x,y,z]. We typically book venues in the [x] capacity range with a draw of [x]. Through the years, we've collected over [x] contacts on our mailing list and social media websites combined. With our [upcoming tour schedule or new album], we can give you company great promotion through efforts such as [your best co-branded marketing campaign idea here].

We are looking to build a long-term relationship that will benefit all parties involved. With other partners such as [sponsors/endorsements], we can provide great referrals regarding the return on investment you will receive from working with [band name].

[List website + Social Media Sites or EPK here]

I look forward to your prompt response and would love to discuss details further by email or phone. What other information can I provide to further this discussion?

Sincerely,
[your name]
[your phone]
[your email]

Email Template for the Touring Band: Specific Campaign

If you have a specific ask, such as a tour that you are trying to support, this would be a better fit because it is more direct and can be catered specifically towards the sponsor:

Dear [contact name],

My name is [your name] and I manage the band [band name]. We are [elevator pitch here]. I am contacting you today because I would like to schedule a time where we can talk about doing some cross promotion through a partnership.

Our band has been especially successful working with this a target audience of [insert niche market here] and we perform for [x number] fans every year throughout [target area]. I know you've been looking to grow your business in this area and I'd like to talk about specific ways to reach this audience for you. One idea is [best specific partnership idea here].

We've worked with companies such as [x,y,z] and have a track record of success. If you're able to provide just 15 minutes of your time, I'd love the opportunity to go over this idea in more detail. When would be a good time to schedule a call or meeting?

Sincerely,
[your name]
[band/your contact information/websites]

Appendix D: Sample Manager Contract

Whether you have a band member, friend or parent of the band, business partner, or an actual manager, it's important to have an agreement in place over the terms and nature of that relationship. It's also important to have an attorney look over the agreement as well (generally this would cost 1-2 billable hours).

This is an example of a manager contract that I've used in one of my past. Feel free to copy, edit, adapt, or use at your leisure.

CONTRACT FOR MANAGEMENT SERVICES

[Manager Name] and [Artist Name]

SECTION I

1] This Master Agreement ("Agreement") is made by and between _____ ("Manager"), with its principle location at [insert physical/mailing address here] and [Artist Name] ("Artist") in whole or in part. The terms and conditions contained in the Agreement exclusively govern the management and/or counsel of the Artist and any other related activity.

2] This Agreement shall be amended only by mutual agreement of the parties. Any such amendment shall be signed by the respective parties.

If any term of this Agreement conflicts with any term relating to the purchase of the Artist contained in any issued or other agreement and/or performance contract, this Agreement shall take precedence.

SECTION II- TERM OF THE AGREEMENT

This Agreement shall commence on [insert date] and ends one (1) years later (Initial Period") .This contract may be re-negotiated at the end of the term of the Agreement.

This Agreement shall also be in effect if one of the following conditions exist; 1) Artist changes its name from [Artist Name]   and 2) Individual members are replaced, deleted or added

SECTION III - MANAGEMENT RESPONSIBILITIES

Manager accepts said employment and agrees subject to The Artist's availability and cooperation:

To advise and counsel band name or artist with respect to decisions concerning employment, publicity, selection of literary, artistic and musical material, wardrobe, public relations and advertising, selection of theatrical and booking agencies and/or Artist's agents and all other matters pertaining to my professional activities and career in the entertainment, amusement, music, recording and literary fields.

To advise and counsel The Artist with relation to adoption of the proper format for presentation of my talents and in the determination of proper style, mood and setting in keeping with band name or artist's talents and best interests.

To advise and counsel The Artist with regard to general practices in the entertainment, amusement, music, recordings and literary fields, and with respect to compensation and terms of contracts thereto.

To use reasonable efforts to promote and enhance the band's professional reputation and standing.
To be available to The Artist for consultation and rendition of services to The Artist at all reasonable times.

To advise and counsel The Artist on the selection and final use or contractual agreement with any theatrical and booking agencies.
Management will be responsible for the overall management of the Artist to include but not limited to:
1] Career Development
2] Management of Artist business affairs
3] Money management by account
4] Recording Contracts
5] Merchandise Management
6] Location of a Tour Manager
7] Overall professionalism of Artist
8] Publicity and Promotion

Management will not forecast and/or guarantee success within the entertainment industry, but will represent and manage the affairs of Artist to the best of management's ability. Manager will act on the best interest for the potential future success of the Artist at all times. Manager will at all times counsel and propose all business opportunities to client. All major business decisions will be jointly agreed upon by both Manager and Artist. Manager will maintain all records, ledgers, inventories and accounts for the Artist. These records, ledgers, inventories, and accounts will be available for Artist audit at all times. Manager will publish periodic reports as to the activity of management and status of all accounts and business activity.

All business decisions will be approved with the Artist prior to completion or commitment on any business arrangement or contract with a third party. Management may or may not be present at all performances or Artist related functions, but will make best efforts to insure proper management representation as required and determined by management at all times at each function and/or engagement. These employees of Manager, shall act in the best interest of the Artist and any other management guidelines established by management or that particular Artist. Manager will not be the sole financial source to the artist. If Manager finances anything on behalf of the artist, a timely repayment schedule will be scheduled in advance.

In a band voting situation related the to the business of the band, the Manager has the right to one vote and ability to break all deadlocks. If the band chooses to revoke the manager's decision or position, manager may not exercise both votes in those circumstances.

SECTION IV - ARTIST RESPONSIBILITY
General
Artist shall abide by all guidelines and bylaws established by Manager at all times.

All the terms and conditions of this Agreement shall apply to all subsequent agreements and/or contracts. Artist shall not enter into any contract, or agreement without counsel from Manager. If Artist chooses, after counsel, to enter into any contract or agreement, Manager will not be responsible for the outcome of such agreements). Artist can not enter into any other management Agreement without the completed termination of this Agreement. All business leads and/or proposals made to Artist by third parties shall be referred to Manager at all times. Manager will then propose said lead to the Artist for counsel and review. Artist shall on a period basis review all business accounts and activities with Manager. A sign off of joint approval shall take place at such time that all accounts balance and meet the approval of both the Artist and Manager. Artist agrees to reimburse Manager for any and all reasonable expenses which Artist Management Services may incur on the Artist's behalf or account, including but not limited to those in connection with postal correspondence, long distance telephone calls, faxes, publicity material, tapes, posters, press kits, merchandising, ads and travel expenses. Reimbursement of expenses as aforesaid shall be due within thirty (30) days after the receipt of an invoice of itemized statements setting forth the nature and amount of each such expense.

The Artist will not be responsible for any administrative costs of Artist Management Services including but not limited to rent, overhead, utilities and salaries of any employees of Artist Management Services. Artist agrees that at all times to devote themself/themselves to the furtherance of the Artists career and to do all the things necessary and desirable to promote the Artists career and earnings there from. Artist will not enter into any agreements or commitments which shall in any manner interfere with the Managers ability to carry out the terms and conditions of this Agreement.

Agency Representation
Artist shall at all times engage and utilize proper talent agencies and theatrical agents to obtain engagements and employment. Artist understands that Manager is not a licensed booking agency and is not in the business of procuring employment or engagements. Although, Manager shall advise the Artist concerning prospective employment or engagements. Management is not obligated to seek employment not do any acts or things done by talent agencies unless mutually agreed to by both the Artist and Manager. Manager will do booking arrangements for their acts in lieu of obtaining professional talent or booking agencies.

Consultation
Artist shall refer to Artist Management Services all verbal or written leads, communications, or requests for the rendition of Artist's services. Artist shall consult with Management concerning each and every engagement, performance, booking or contract offered and the Artist shall consult with Manager regarding each engagement,

performance, booking or contract that the Artist accepts.

SECTION V - CONFIDENTIALITY

Manager and Artist shall at all times keep the terms and conditions of this and any subsequent Agreements confidential. None of the terms and conditions and/or documents associated with Artist and Manager shall be reproduced or distributed without both the Manager and Artist approval. All financial data associated with both the Manager and Artist shall not be released or discussed without proper approval by either the Artist or Manager. This information will be released to "need to know" individuals only. "Need to know" is defined as individuals who directly affect the overall financial and legal success of the Artist. Examples would include, Artists attorney, potential investors etc.

SECTION VI - PAYMENT TO MANAGER

Manager will also receive payment for other related activities and accounts per the percentages below:

15% percent of gross revenue of everything except non covered items. Non Covered Items: Second jobs (outside of the entertainment industry) Gifts and awards
Payment shall be on a monthly basis or after anytime the band exceeds revenues of $1,000 in one week.

If Artist gross revenue exceeds two hundred thousand dollars, the manager may receive an additional 5% of gross income, for a total of 20%.

Payment to Manager shall be in check, money order or certified moneys drawn from Artists escrow accounts with the prior notification and approval by Artist. All payments to Manager shall be audited as part of the account audit process.

SECTION VII - ADDITIONAL COUNSEL AND MANAGEMENT

At some time, it will become necessary to employ legal counsel and/or financial advisors for the Artist. The selection process will be done jointly by both the Manager and Artist. The legal and financial counsel shall become an integral part of the overall management team for the Artist. All business and financial decisions shall then be jointly approved and made. This is mandatory when Artist acquires a recording contract. The Artist shall represent and warrant that the Artist has been advised of their right to seek legal counsel of the Artists own choosing in connection with the negotiation and execution of this contract.

SECTION VIII - TERMINATION FOR CAUSE
The occurrence of any of the following constitutes a breach and is cause for Managers and Artists termination of this Agreement
a] Artist and/or Manager does not meet the terms and conditions of the Agreement.
b] Artist and/or Manager acts in any illegal or engages in any illegal activity.
Manager and Artist must cure any of the above breaches and notify Manager or Artist of such cure within thirty (30) calendar days from receipt of a notice to cure from either the Manager or Artist. If Manager or Artist fails to so cure, either party may terminate this Agreement upon written notice from the terminating party. Upon termination of this Agreement for any reason, all Artist and/or Manager funds will be transferred back to the proper party, net of any funds owed each other. This Agreement will not be considered until both parties have been properly compensated per the terms and conditions of this Agreement. All property of the other party must also be returned immediately upon termination.

SECTION IX - TERMINATION FOR CONVENIENCE
Manager or Artist, at his/her discretion may terminate this Agreement for convenience ninety (90) calendar days after giving the other party written notice. Upon receipt of such written notice to terminate, the Manager or Artist must then meet with the other party to clear and

complete all transactions and obligations under this Agreement. The Artists obligations in the event of termination will be to compensate Manager for all moneys owed to Manager within fifteen (15) calendar days from the date of termination.

SECTION X - NOTICES

Any notices given under this Agreement shall be written or telegraphic. Written notice shall be sent Registered Certified mail, postage prepaid, return receipt requested. Any telegraphic notices shall be deemed given upon receipt, provided that such notice is followed in three (3) days with a written notice. All notices shall be effective when the first notice is received. All notices under this Agreement shall be sent to the following addresses: [name & address]

SECTION XI - SURVIVAL

The provisions of this Agreement dealing with Payment, Confidentiality, Perpetuity, General Provisions (subsection C) shall survive termination of this Agreement.

SECTION XII - AUTHORITY / POWER OF ATTORNEY

Manager, on the Artist's behalf, do the following: approve and permit any and all publicity and advertising: approve and permit the use of Artist name, photograph, likeness, voice, sound effect, caricature, literary, artistic and musical materials for purposes of advertising and publicity in the promotion and advertising of any and all products and services: execute for the Artist in the Artist's name and/or on the Artists behalf, any and all agreements, documents, and contracts for Artist services, talents and/or artistic, literary and musical materials, provided that the Artist is unavailable to do the same on the Artist's own behalf, Artist has been apprised of the material terms thereof and the Artist has granted Manager the authority to execute such agreements in each specific instance.

SECTION XIII - INDEMNIFICATION OF THE PARTIES

Manager shall at all times, defend, indemnify and hold the Artist, the Artist's respective agents, employees, representatives, affiliated entities, successors, heirs and designees or legatees, harmless from and against any and all claims, damages, liabilities, costs and expenses, including, without limitation, reasonable legal expenses and attorney's fees, arising out of any breach by the Manager of any warranty, representation or agreement made by Manager hereunder or otherwise arising out of Manager's services on the Artists behalf as a result of this Agreement. The Artist shall at all times defend, indemnify and hold Manager, manager's respective agents, employees, representatives, affiliated entities, successors, heirs and designees or legatees, harmless from and against any and all claims, damages, liabilities, costs and expenses, including, without limitation, reasonable legal expenses and attorney's fees, arising out of any breach by the Manager of any warranty, representation or agreement made by the Artist hereunder.

SECTION XIII - GENERAL PROVISIONS

Only the authorized representatives of the parties may amend or waive provisions of this Agreement, and must be agreed to in writing. If either party fails to enforce any term of this Agreement, failure to enforce on those occasions shall not prevent enforcement on any other occasion. All rights and remedies conferred by this Agreement, by any other instrument, or by law are cumulative and may be exercised singularly or concurrently. If any provisions of this Agreement are held invalid by any law or regulation of any government or by any court, such invalidity shall not effect the enforceability of other provisions herein. This Agreement issued hereunder shall be governed by and interpreted in accordance with the laws of the Commonwealth of [insert city, state here].

Manager shall not assign Manager's rights under this Agreement without the Artist's express written approval exercisable in the Artist's sole and absolute discretion (unless such assignment is to a company at which Manager shall during the term hereof continue to act as the Artist's personal manager on a day to day basis). Upon termination of this Agreement for any reason, both the Artist and Manager either in whole or in part shall not disclose the reasons for termination or act in any manner either written or verbally that could jeopardize the future business success of the other party. If Artist or Manager is in breach on this provision, the other party could be liable for punitive damages as determined in a court of law. Specialized provisions requested by artists:

_____

_____

_____

_____

IN WITNESS, the parties have executed this Agreement effective the commencement of the contract period.

Band Name: _____

Manager/Management Service Name: _____

_____ date_____

Band Member

_____ date_____

Band Member

_____ date_____

Band Member

_____ date_____

Band Member

_____date_____

[Manager]

ABOUT THE AUTHOR

Simon Tam is an award-winning musician, author, entrepreneur, and social justice activist.

Simon is best known as the founder and bassist of The Slants, the world's first and only all-Asian American dance rock band. His approach to activism through the arts has been highlighted in thousands of media features across 82 countries, including: BBC World News, NPR, TIME Magazine, MTV, CBS, and the Wall Street Journal.

Since 2000, he has been a performer, presenter, and keynote at events and organizations such as TED, SXSW, Comic-Con, The Department of Defense, Stanford University, Rotary International, and over 1,200 others across North America, Europe, and Asia.

Simon also serves multiple non-profit organizations as a board member, leader, and volunteer. His marketing projects and volunteerism has earned several innovation and service awards.